ETHNICITY AND INTERNATIONAL LAW

Ethnicity and International Law presents a historical account of the impact of ethnicity on the making of international law. The development of international law since the nineteenth century is characterised by the inherent tension between the liberal and conservative traditions of dealing with what might be termed the 'problem' of ethnicity. The present-day hesitancy of liberal international law to engage with ethnicity in ethnic conflicts and ethnic minorities has its roots in these conflicting philosophical traditions. In international legal studies, both the relevance of ethnicity and the traditions of understanding it lie in this fact.

MOHAMMAD SHAHABUDDIN is a lecturer in law at Keele University, where his research focuses on the postcolonial critique of the concept of ethnicity and its role in the making of international law.

ETHNICITY AND INTERNATIONAL LAW

Histories, Politics and Practices

MOHAMMAD SHAHABUDDIN
Lecturer in Law, Keele University

CAMBRIDGE
UNIVERSITY PRESS

CAMBRIDGE
UNIVERSITY PRESS

University Printing House, Cambridge CB2 8BS, United Kingdom

Cambridge University Press is part of the University of Cambridge.

It furthers the University's mission by disseminating knowledge in the pursuit of education, learning, and research at the highest international levels of excellence.

www.cambridge.org
Information on this title: www.cambridge.org/9781107096790

First published 2016

A catalogue record for this publication is available from the British Library.

Library of Congress Cataloguing in Publication data
Shahabuddin, Mohammad, author.
Ethnicity and international law : histories, politics and practices / Mohammad Shahabuddin.
New York : Cambridge University Press, 2016.
LCCN 2016004588 | ISBN 9781107096790 (hardback)
LCSH: Ethnic groups – Civil rights. | Minorities – Legal status, laws, etc. | International law – History. | Ethnic relations – History. | Ethnic conflict.
LCC K3242 .S49 2016 | DDC 342.08/73–dc23
LC record available at http://lccn.loc.gov/2016004588

ISBN 978-1-107-09679-0 Hardback

For My Family

CONTENTS

FOREWORD

What we might term 'ethnic conflict' has been an enduring feature of human history. International law has responded to this phenomenon through a variety of means, and the 'rights of minorities' is a topic that has featured prominently in the discipline since perhaps the beginnings of modern sovereignty in the Peace of Westphalia. Scholars have written extensively on the issue and the related questions of self-determination, secession, autonomy, and now, the topic of remedial secession. It is in this context that Dr. Shahabuddin presents his own work on this classic theme. Remarkably, he succeeds in this book in presenting a fresh perspective on a problem that has been the subject of so much writing. This he achieves principally by reversing the traditional analytic framework which presents all the legal challenges associated with the management of ethnic conflict as a derivative, a by-product, of international law; Dr. Shahabuddin also argues – with a persuasiveness derived from deep research into history, political theory, and the history of international law – that ethnic conflict has shaped international law and, indeed, sovereignty itself as law attempts to account for its political and sociological origins. The 'self–other' distinction that is at the heart of ethnic conflict assumes a number of other forms and roles in international affairs, and these affect each other in complex ways.

The provocative argument Dr. Shahabuddin makes is that we might see international legal responses as playing out an ongoing and apparently insuperable tension between what he terms 'liberal' and 'conservative' views of ethnicity. Liberalism sees ethnicity as peripheral and undesirable and primitive, a feature of politics that must be discouraged and suppressed; the conservative approach rather sees ethnicity as a fundamental aspect of political identity and the nation that must be integrated into any political arrangement. Dr. Shahabuddin covers new and interesting ground in tracing the evolution of these traditions and, in particular, the relationship between their formation and the colonial policies of Germany and France. The book is notable for presenting a rich account of the attempts of international law to deal with the challenge of the 'self' and 'other' through different phases and episodes in history and for offering a new genealogy of this theme, one that includes that colonial encounter as well as the more traditional story of the minority treaty system.

The questions raised by Dr. Shahabuddin's work are profound. The liberal approach may be inadequate as it continuously compromises to accommodate ethnic identities that it would rather not recognise, and yet, it is easy to imagine how the adoption of a 'conservative' approach to statehood could result in the subordination of minorities, inequalities, ethnic cleansing, and worse. His historical approach suggests we are condemned to repeating, albeit in some new guise, the same essential dynamic. If this is the case, his work could suggest two very different responses. If the project is to somehow resolve this tension, then we must develop another politics of 'self' and 'other' in order to erode the dichotomy at the heart of the problem? We might inquire into how other historical and political traditions approach the question of pluralism and the complexities of identity. Perhaps, however, this dichotomy is inescapable and inevitable because it is itself a product of modern sovereignty when applied to plural societies – in which case what is required is a radical re-thinking of sovereignty itself? Alternatively, we see the tension between the two traditions as productive, creating new ways of dealing with a complex and endlessly mutating phenomenon. After all, globalisation, rather than eroding these dichotomies, seems to have reproduced, transformed, and exacerbated them. Minorities are changing in their political and social character, and ethnic identifications persist. Some diaspora communities living in liberal democracies seem to be vehemently intent on asserting ethnic identities in the homelands they have left. Liberal democracies themselves are now struggling to maintain their identity and renunciation of ethnic politics as they are transformed by migration and refugees.

Dr. Shahabuddin has written a fine work that sheds important light on an issue that continues, despite its ancient lineage, to challenge the ambitions of contemporary international law.

Antony Anghie
Salt Lake City, November 2015

ACKNOWLEDGEMENTS

This book originated as a doctoral thesis completed at the School of Oriental and African Studies (SOAS), University of London. I am thankful to Matthew Craven for all the engaging debates and discussions during supervision meetings and, more importantly, for incessantly provoking me to ask better questions. I also thank my thesis examiners – Antony Anghie and David Kennedy – for offering valuable advice on converting the thesis into a book. I must specially register my sincerest gratitude to Antony not only for writing the Foreword to this book but also for his kind mentoring and moral support over many years and in so many different ways, which facilitated my intellectual transformation. I am indebted to him for his generosity.

Completing this colossal task has been made possible by the help and support of Sundhya Pahuja, who took the trouble of reading the manuscript and provided valuable comments. I also thank Patrick Thornberry and Catriona Drew for reading draft chapters and helping me present arguments more coherently.

I am grateful to a number of friends for their important contributions at various stages of the publication of this book. Of them, Jean D'Aspremont, Luis Eslava, Michael Fakhri, Charlotte Peevers, and Jothi Rajah deserve special mention. I take this opportunity to thank the Third World Approaches to International Law (TWAIL) and Harvard Law School's Institute for Global Law and Policy (IGLP) network of scholars; engagements with them have enriched my scholarship in significant ways.

I am grateful to Ichiro Araki and Hyuck-soo Yoo for inviting me to Yokohama National University for a year and thereby enabling me to resume writing this book after a long pause. It would be less than fair if I did not also thank my colleagues at Jahangirnagar University and Keele University for their encouragement and support.

Parts of this book have been presented in various conferences and previously published, albeit in different forms, in journals and edited volumes. I am grateful to the publishers, numerous conference participants, and my readers for their constructive feedback.

Special thanks to Elizabeth Spicer and Richard Woodham at Cambridge University Press for their support in publishing this book. I am also thankful to Allison Turner for her help with editing. I thank Integra for completing the painstaking task of copy-editing and typesetting.

Writing this book was made possible by the sacrifice of Aznin and our two sons – Ehan and Eshan. I respectfully recall their patience when I had to work long hours in my office, sometimes even on weekends. My mother and other family members from Dhaka also expressed their excitement about the work. I appreciate each of them. And finally, memories of my father, who would have been so happy to see this work published, have always been an important source of inspiration for writing this book.

ABBREVIATIONS

CDDH	Steering Committee for Human Rights, Council of Europe
CERD	International Convention on the Elimination of All Forms of Racial Discrimination
COE	Council of Europe
CSCE	Conference on the Security and Co-operation in Europe
ECE	East and Central European
ECHR	European Convention on Human Rights
ECtHR	European Court of Human Rights
ECOSOC	Economic and Social Council
EU	European Union
FCNM	Framework Convention on National Minorities
FRUS	Foreign Relations of the United States
HCNM	High Commissioner on National Minorities
HR	Human Rights
HRC	Human Rights Committee
ICCPR	International Covenant on Civil and Political Rights
ICESCR	International Covenant on Economic, Social and Cultural Rights
ICJ	International Court of Justice
IMF	International Monetary Fund
NATO	North Atlantic Treaty Organisation
NGO	Non-Governmental Organisation
OSCE	Organisation for Security and Co-operation in Europe
PCIJ	Permanent Court of International Justice
SDP	Social Democratic Party
SFRY	Socialist Federal Republic of Yugoslavia
UDHR	Universal Declaration of Human Rights
UN	United Nations
UNDM	United Nations Declaration on the Rights of Persons Belonging to National or Ethnic, Religious and Linguistic Minorities
UNDP	United Nations Development Programme
UNESCO	United Nations Educational, Scientific and Cultural Organisation
WGM	Working Group on Minorities, United Nations

TABLE OF CASES

Introduction

The management of ethnic conflict has been crucial to the maintenance of international order – whether in the period of the League of Nations, when a minority treaty system was created in an attempt to resolve the problem of nationalism, or the time following the fall of the Soviet Union, when ethnic groups once again asserted their right to self-determination. More recently, the success of grand projects of 'nation building' that have been undertaken in countries such as Iraq and Afghanistan has depended crucially on the management of ethnicity – in this instance, religious differences. The propensity of nationalist claims and their accompanying tensions and conflicts to threaten global order is amply demonstrated by the complex chain of events originating in Balkan nationalism, which led to World War I. Despite this fact, no histories of international law explore the relationship between ethnicity and its significance for the development of the discipline. Rather, ethnic conflict and the legal response to it – which invariably entail creating a human rights regime designed to protect minority rights – are seen as a specialised area of international law. This book, then, undertakes the task of writing a history of international law that recognises and engages with the central issue of ethnicity and its impact on the making of international law.

One of the peculiarities of the post–Cold War moment of international law in relation to ethnicity remains in the fact that the collapse of the Soviet Empire is, on the one hand, celebrated as the triumph of liberalism, the End of History, and the harbinger of liberal-democratic progress and peace and, on the other hand, identified as the trigger for the eruption of violent 'ethnic' conflicts even in Europe. These developments brought the issue of ethnicity – a primitive notion in liberal understanding – to the forefront. Ethnic conflicts of various scales and intensities in Armenia, Bosnia, Bulgaria, Croatia, Hungary, Romania, Russia, Serbia, Slovakia, Turkey, Ukraine, and so on have also posed a threat to European stability. Even in a number of Western democracies, such as Belgium, Canada, Spain, and the United Kingdom, minority groups kept challenging the existing state structures in one form or the other. Similarly, ethnic violence has been a defining feature of a number of Third World countries as a result of nation-building projects following decolonisation.

Despite this, liberal international lawyers failed to properly consider the normative significance of ethnicity and instead pursued the moral end of a post-ethnic world order that complied with the liberal individualist premise of international law. The liberal understanding of ethnicity is as something primitive and backward. At the same time, the relevance of ethnicity remained alive in the conservative tradition (within political philosophy that was translated into international law); indeed, ethnicity is perceived as the central element of political organisation of nation-states. Liberal international lawyers, driven by pragmatic needs, often seek to reconcile these conflicting traditions of understanding ethnicity. As a result, at the normative level, ethnicity remains a peripheral issue in international legal discourse and appears relevant only as a pejorative descriptive criterion, as in 'ethnic conflicts' and 'ethnic minorities'.

Ethnicity and International Law is an effort to reverse this understanding of the relationship between ethnicity and international law by tracing the central role that ethnicity plays in the historical development of international law. The central argument of the book is that the present-day hesitancy of liberal international law to engage with ethnicity in ethnic conflicts and ethnic minorities has its root in the way international law developed along the lines of the nineteenth century's liberal and conservative traditions of understanding the salience of ethnicity in political-identity formation. The development of international law since the nineteenth century is characterised by the inherent tension of the juxtaposition of these philosophical traditions of dealing with what might be termed the 'problem of ethnicity'. And the liberal ambivalence towards ethnic conflicts and ethnic minorities will continue, given that the hegemonic cultural connotation of liberalism leaves international law with rather few means to meaningfully engage with ethnicity within a normative framework, as opposed to the make-shift pragmatic arrangements which are currently in place. In international legal studies, the relevance of ethnicity, as well as the traditions of understanding it – the subject of my scrutiny in this book – lies in this fact.

Taking a historical approach, this book demonstrates the critical role played by ethnicity in nineteenth-century international laws about colonialism, the interwar minority protection regime, and the current discourse on minority protection and ethnic conflicts. Although all thinking about ethnicity is characterised by the dichotomy of 'self' and 'other', when this dichotomy is seen through the prism of the liberal and conservative traditions, quite a different narrative of it appears in relation to these moments of international legal history. In this connection, this book also examines what happened to ethnicity when liberal individualism emerged as the dominant vocabulary of international law and how such individualism in international law interacted with the conservative notion of ethnicity in ethnic conflicts. In this sense, this book reveals the role of ethnicity in international legal history; this is a history of international law seen through these two nineteenth-century traditions.

The first chapter provides the general framework of the ethnic dichotomy of 'self' and 'other' that is to be found in both the liberal and conservative traditions but with very different implications. Here I first explain various discourses on ethnicity and define it for the purpose of this book. This is followed by an etymological exposition, through which I demonstrate two things: how the notion of ethnicity travelled through time and, with the emergence of nationalism as a political language, came to depict the 'self-image' of a nation in the Romantic literature of the nineteenth century and how, in contrast, the liberal image of the national 'self' constantly attempted to depict ethnicity as something undesirable in a liberal culture and hence denied that ethnicity had any relevance to its making. In other words, while ethnicity is to be the central focus of the nation-building process in the conservative tradition by way of excluding non-ethnics, the individualist as well as the universalist end of the liberal nation dictates the marginalisation of ethnicity by way of assimilation into the liberal high culture. Next, I explain how both the liberal and conservative Romantic nationalist agendas sought 'scientific' justification in another dominant nineteenth-century doctrine, social Darwinism, for their respective projects of assimilation and exclusion. Having set the socio-political context, I then offer an in-depth analysis tracing the ethnic underpinning of nineteenth-century international law along the lines of these two traditions, a phenomenon that has remained omnipresent in the development of international law since then.

The modern versions of ethnic conflict are intimately related to the rise of nationalism in the eighteenth and nineteenth centuries. Nationalism developed a very clear sense of 'self' and 'other'. The liberal and conservative philosophical traditions in the nineteenth century took very different approaches to conceptualising and managing the relationship between 'self' and 'other'. My argument, then, is that these two traditions have had an enduring significance for the creation of international legal regimes devoted to managing ethnic tension.

Chapter 2 examines the colonial policies of nineteenth-century France and Germany to explore how their respective liberal and conservative treatments of ethnicity in relation to the construction of the national 'self' distinctively informed their understanding of colonialism as well as their execution of colonial policies. Though based on two particular state philosophies and practices, this account presents the contrast between the liberal and conservative notions of colonialism and native relations and exposes how such interactions with the colonial 'other' were reflected back in the dynamic process of the construction of the 'self' in the metropolis. While providing this narrative, I also demonstrate how nineteenth-century international lawyers' perceptions of the state – the legal form of the national 'self' – in the liberal and conservative traditions were essentially reflected in their justifications for colonialism as well as the atrocities associated with it.

The relationship between nineteenth-century colonial practices and the legal approaches to managing twentieth-century ethnic conflicts has not been adequately recognised in the existing legal literature. My argument is that the two traditions of nineteenth-century nationalism and thinking about ethnicity need to be properly understood in order to appreciate subsequent developments.

Chapter 3 uses the example of the interwar minority protection regime to demonstrate how interwar international law relied on an ethnic discourse with three different layers that were expressed through the liberal and conservative traditions. First, the interwar minority protection system was the outcome of a compromise between the conservative notion of self-determination on the basis of ethnic identity and the liberal denial of that. Secondly, a dichotomy between the liberal West and the conservative Eastern 'other' was evident in the imposition of special minority protection obligations on Eastern and Central European (ECE) states, whereas minorities within Western Europe remained outside any international protection. And finally, the inherent drawbacks of the system that became evident in its operation demonstrated another layer of the 'self–other' discourse. In this layer, the agenda of mutual exclusion of the ethnic 'other' was brutally pursued, bypassing the international system, in the process of constructing an ethnic self-image along conservative lines in both Germany and Poland.

The last two chapters explain what happened to ethnicity with the emergence of liberalism as the dominant vocabulary of international law in the aftermath of World War II. While the minority protection regime under the League was of a hybrid nature – incorporating both collective and individual rights – in the post–World War II moment the idea of replacing the minority protection system with a human rights regime exclusively centred on the universal protection of individual rights took hold. In this regard, Chapter 4 deals with three different aspects of the liberal hesitancy at the conservative notion of ethnicity in relation to minority protection. First, when a minority is juxtaposed with the majority within a given polity, the minority is defined as an ethnic phenomenon and therefore perceived as the primitive 'other'. On the other hand, given that in the liberal understanding ethnicity not only turns the minority into the victim of oppression by the majority but also undermines the individual rights of the minority group members, the liberal way of minority protection logically leads to the suppression of ethnicity through the individualist principles of equality and non-discrimination. In other words, the liberal individualist response to minority *protection* endeavours to remove this conservative notion of 'ethnicity' from 'minority'. Thirdly, in the post–Cold War European context, the dichotomy of the liberal West and the conservative Eastern 'other' again explains why the differentiated minority protection mechanism within Europe is very much in line with the interwar minority protection regime.

The fifth and final chapter of the book argues that international lawyers' treatment of ethnicity along the lines of the liberal and conservative traditions informs their respective responses to ethnic conflicts. It also demonstrates how international lawyers rely on a reconciliatory approach to these philosophical traditions in order to work out pragmatic solutions to ethnic conflicts yet deny the relevance of ethnicity within the normative liberal architecture of international law. This, in turn, shows that even in the era of normative primacy of liberalism, the liberal world view falls short in the face of violent conflicts defined by the protagonists themselves or by outsiders, or both, along ethnic lines. My argument, then, is that the success of any international legal engagement with ethnic minorities and ethnic conflicts largely depends on the means and extent of the reconciliation between these two traditions. In this connection, this chapter also discusses what normative issues this reconciliatory approach will have to overcome in the process.

In this sense, this is a book on the historical relationship between ethnicity and international law within the framework of the 'self' and 'other' and as defined by the liberal and conservative traditions in each epoch of international law's development. In other words, this book can be perceived as an ethnicity-informed alternative politico-legal history of modern international law with reference to key events of each epoch. Although the relationship between international law and history may be understood in terms of the 'history of international law' (a narrative of its origins, development, progress, or renewal), 'history in international law' (the role that historical events or personae play in discussions and arguments about law), or 'international law in history' (the way international law and its proponents are involved in creating history), it turns out that in practice it is difficult to maintain such a categorisation of this relationship, for 'each type of engagement with history and international law will interweave various different types of historical narrative'.[1] Yet, this categorisation remains useful to point 'to the typically multi-layered nature of international lawyers' engagement with the past'.[2] In discussing international legal history in relation to ethnicity, my approach in this book has been to deal with both the history of international law and history in international law, especially the roles that individuals have played in shaping this discipline.

Given that the idea of ethnicity is not itself a legal concept but rather a notion that shapes international law in a wide range of ways, from the outset my narrative of international law's engagement with the key events develops within the relevant socio-political contexts of various events and texts that I examine. In this sense, my approach to history in this book accommodates certain elements of the Cambridge School of intellectual historiography, which emphasises the role of historical texts as political interventions in the particular socio-political contexts in which they were produced and warns against the use of past texts to make sense of present concepts, debates, and discourses – in short, against anachronism or 'presentism'.[3] Nevertheless, my approach to history can be equally condemned as being anachronistic, in that my narrative of the historical engagement between ethnicity and international law is largely genealogical: although I pay due attention to relevant socio-political contexts of the texts that I discuss in the book, far from confining them merely to those

[1] Matt Craven, 'Introduction: International Law and Its Histories' in *Time, History and International Law*, ed. Matthew Craven, Malgosia Fitzmaurice, and Maria Vogiatzi (Leiden: Martinus Nijhoff, 2007), 7.

[2] Craven, 'Introduction', 8.

[3] See, for example, Quentin Skinner, 'Meaning and Understanding in the History of Ideas', *History and Theory* 8 (1969), 3–53. For a general discussion, see Q. Skinner, *Visions of Politics*, Volume I: *Regarding Method* (Cambridge: Cambridge University Press, 2002).

specific contexts, I rather consider the way they have played a crucial role across time and space. As a matter of fact, so far as the political promise of critical international legal scholarship is concerned, international legal history within this genre is inherently genealogical in its approach, for, in the words of Orford: 'To refuse to think about the ways in which a concept or text from the remote past might be recovered to do new work in the present is to refuse an overt engagement with contemporary politics.'[4]

Besides international legal history, this book can also be described as a work on the international law of minority protection. In Chapters 3 and 4, I use the theoretical framework described in the first two chapters to underscore how minorities are first perceived as the conservative 'other' in relation to the liberal West and, then, how the liberal project of minority protection uses an individualist approach of suppressing ethnic conservativeness – an approach that results in the diffusion of ethnic groups into a collection of individuals. And the final chapter, in this connection, explains the fallacy of such a project of suppressing ethnicity in relation to ethnic conflicts, wherein mere individualism leaves rather few options for international law to deal with ethnicity in ethnic conflicts.

This book, however, has been developed in the shadow of the discourse on self-determination – a concept that I perceive through my theoretical framework as an expression of the continuity of the ethnic dichotomy of 'self' and 'other' within the liberal and conservative traditions. On the one hand, the conservative notion of ethnicity defines the self-image of a nation that exercises an external right of self-determination, that is, sovereign equality, territorial integrity, and so on, as a state. Simultaneously, on the other hand, ethnicity not only identifies the 'other' – minorities, for example – within the ethnic nation-state but also provides that 'other' with the potential for nationalist claims in conservative terms. In this continuity, the internal 'other' then constructs the ethnic self-image to claim a homogeneous political unit of its own. Conversely, liberal self-determination counts on a concept of the state that accommodates the liberal nation as a territorial expression. In conformity with the principles of Enlightenment, here self-determination in the internal context means the rights of individual citizens to participate in governance, while in the external context it allows the state a set of privileges to be enjoyed along with other members of the international community. An understanding of national self-determination is, therefore, informed by the views one takes about the self-image of

[4] Anne Orford, 'On International Legal Method', *London Review of International Law* 1 (2013), 166–197.

a nation.[5] It is, thus, not unexpected that in this book several references have been made to the right to self-determination, albeit without getting into any detailed discussion of the concept, while discussing minority rights as a compromise between the liberal and conservative versions of self-determination. Similarly, many of the ideas that this book deals with have implications for the rights of indigenous peoples. However, given that indigenous peoples fall under a very different legal regime and that discourses on their special rights evolved in a distinct way, my discussion of minority rights does not engage directly with this, otherwise significant, field of study.

My approach to international law in terms of its relationship with ethnicity is informed by the postcolonial scholarship in the field of international law. Especially, major recent works on the colonial character of international law, for example, by Antony Anghie,[6] Matthew Craven,[7] Karen Knop,[8] Martti Koskenniemi,[9] Sundhya Pahuja,[10] and Ralph Wilde,[11] set the premise

[5] Koskenniemi sees the incompatibility of these two notions of self-determination in relation to the legitimacy of states: while the liberal notion of self-determination, 'classic' to use his term, recognises only states as the legitimate holders of various goods of collective personhood, the Romantic notion values statehood to the extent that it represents the communal identification of the nation within it. See Martti Koskenniemi, 'National Self-determination Today: Problems of Legal Theory and Practice', *International and Comparative Law Quarterly* 43, no. 1 (1994), 250. See also *Aaland Islands Case*, Report of the International Commission of Jurists, *League of Nations Official Journal*, Special Supplement No. 3 (1920); *Aaland Islands Case*, Report of the Commission of Rapporteurs (1921), League of Nations Council Doc. B7 [C] 21/68/106; Conference on Yugoslavia Arbitration Commission, Opinion No. 1, *European Journal of International Law* 3 (1992), 182–183; Opinion No. 2 (1992), 183–184; Opinion No. 3 (1992), 184–185.

[6] Antony Anghie, *Imperialism, Sovereignty and the Making of International Law* (Cambridge: Cambridge University Press, 2005). Cf. James Thuo Gathii, 'International Law and Eurocentricity', *European Journal of International Law* 9 (1998), 184–211; J. Gathii, 'Imperialism, Colonialism, and International Law', *Buffalo Law Review* 54, no. 4 (2007), 1013–1066.

[7] Matthew Craven, *Decolonization of International Law* (Oxford: Oxford University Press, 2007).

[8] Karen Knop, *Diversity and Self-Determination in International Law* (Cambridge: Cambridge University Press, 2002).

[9] Martti Koskenniemi, *Gentle Civilizer of Nations: The Rise and Fall of International Law 1870–1960* (Cambridge: Cambridge University Press, 2002).

[10] Sundhya Pahuja, *Decolonising International Law: Development, Economic Growth, and the Politics of Universality* (Cambridge: Cambridge University Press, 2011).

[11] Ralph Wilde, *International Territorial Administration – How Trusteeship and the Civilizing Mission Never Went Away* (Oxford: Oxford University Press, 2008). See also R. Wilde, 'From Danzig to East Timor and Beyond: The Role of International Territorial Administration', *American Journal of International Law* 95, no. 3 (2001), 583–606; R. Wilde, 'Representing International Territorial Administration: A Critique of Some Approaches', *European Journal of International Law* 15, no. 1 (2004), 71–96.

for my project to understand international law in a new light, in this case through its relationship with ethnicity. As a result, despite being influenced by Anghie and Koskenniemi, my narrative of nineteenth-century colonialism deviates from theirs to the extent that it is seen through the framework of the treatment of ethnicity in the liberal and conservative traditions. This narrative goes beyond the monolithic idea of Europe and its colonial project. Rather, it demonstrates how the assimilationist thrust of liberal international lawyers as expressed in the notion of a 'civilising mission' was much different from the exclusionist project of German colonialism as endorsed by the international lawyers in the conservative Romantic camp. Similarly, while providing a narrative of the interwar international law of minority protection, I relied to some extent on the works of Nathaniel Berman on the interwar-modernist experimentation with nationalism but at the same time endeavoured to grasp much deeper complexities that the contrasting liberal and conservative traditions of perceiving ethnicity had produced at three different levels.

In offering my narrative, I have adopted David Kennedy's approach of historicising law: an approach of standing back at times and systematically exploring how various actors with various priorities played their part in the international plane and, at the same time, engaged with each other in a complex way. An essential character of such an intellectual cartography is its focus on the wide range of consequences – both desired and undesired – which emanated from this complex interaction of actors and their priorities for certain norms.[12] One can, therefore, trace the influence of Kennedy's powerful methodology while reading this book, in that without siding with any particular school of thought, I attempted to unpack ethnicity and various other notions, going beyond their conventional meanings, and then grasp the complex ways in which international lawyers engaged with these notions and the outcomes such interactions have engendered.

However, to meet the doctrinal thrust of this book, I concerned myself less with 'primary' knowledge construction than with the analysis of discourses. Whenever I had to tackle literatures of relatively wide

[12] Some of his representative works include David Kennedy, 'International Human Rights Movement: Part of the Problem?', *Harvard Human Rights Journal* 14 (2002), 101–126; D. Kennedy, *Dark Sides of Virtue: Reassessing International Humanitarianism* (to Princeton, New Jersey: Princeton University Press, 2004); D. Kennedy, *Of War and Law* (Princeton, New Jersey: Princeton University Press, 2006); D. Kennedy, 'One, Two, Three, Many Legal Orders: Legal Pluralism and the Cosmopolitan Dream', *New York University Review of Law and Social Change* 3 (2007), 441–459; D. Kennedy, 'The Mystery of Global Governance', *Ohio Northern University Law Review* 34 (2008), 827–860.

breadth, I tried to identify the major representative discourses so that the width and depth of my analysis remain in harmony. The same is true for the architecture of the book as a whole: it portrays a huge landscape but at the same time sticks to the in-depth analysis of the notion of ethnicity that, running beneath the surface, links the major building blocks of international legal history.

1

Ethnicity in the discourse on the 'self' and the 'other'

Liberal and conservative traditions and their implications

Introduction

In the introduction to an edited volume published in 1975, referring to 'ethnicity', editors Nathan Glazer and Daniel Moynihan claimed that it was a new term.[1] Likewise, Richard Thompson in *Theories of Ethnicity* claimed that the almost universal acknowledgement of the ethnic factor was a recent phenomenon and that its historical genesis was quite easily traced.[2] He found ethnicity largely absent in academic discourse in the 1950s and 1960s. In the context of the US, he argued, three concurrent events of the 1960s – the Civil Rights Movement, the Vietnamese War, and a period of impressive economic prosperity – combined in a way that shook the optimism and naïveté of American society about the malleability of ethnicity.[3] As a consequence, concern with ethnic and racial issues enthusiastically re-emerged at that time to the extent that in 1977, 'one commentator even noted that ethnicity is the social sciences' newest growth industry'.[4] However, as we shall see later in this book, far from being novel, 'ethnicity' as a notion has been playing a long-standing political role in the historical development of international law.

[1] Nathan Glazer and Daniel P. Moynihan (eds.), *Ethnicity* (Cambridge, Massachusetts: Harvard University Press, 1975), 1. Apparently, their claim relied on a number of facts that they referred to: the term 'ethnicity' understood as the character or quality of an ethnic group did not appear in the 1933 edition of the *Oxford English Dictionary*; it was only in the 1972 *Supplement* to this dictionary that this word appeared, where the first usage recorded was that of David Reisman in 1953. Although *Webster's Third New International* (1961) included the term, neither the Random House *Dictionary of the English Language* (1966) nor the *American Heritage Dictionary of the English Language* (1969) included it. However, four years later in the 1973 edition of the *American Heritage Dictionary*, the term 'ethnicity' was included.

[2] Richard H. Thompson, *Theories of Ethnicity – A Critical Appraisal* (London: Greenwood Press, 1989), 1.

[3] For details, see Thompson, *Theories of Ethnicity*, 1–2. [4] *Ibid.*, 3.

Our story of ethnicity in relation to international law begins here. In this chapter, I offer an account of how the ethnic dichotomy of 'self' and 'other' was expressed through a number of nineteenth-century ideas – nationalism, social Darwinism, and the state. This ethnic dichotomy developed within two powerful and mutually competing philosophical streams: Romanticism and the liberal response to Romanticism, which I loosely call here 'liberalism', characterised by individual freedom and equality among individuals. The interplay of these nineteenth-century thoughts had huge repercussions for the then international law, which itself was a product of that very moment. My narrative here links these nineteenth-century ideas seen through the paradigm of ethnicity to develop an analytical framework for the rest of this book.

Although the nineteenth century remains the focus of our discussion on ethnicity in this chapter, the concept of ethnicity as 'otherness' dates back to antiquity. However, before getting into this particular meaning, ethnicity as 'otherness', I first provide an account of various discourses on 'ethnicity' and the meaning of this concept for the purpose of this book. This is then followed by an etymological exposition of how the notion of ethnicity as 'otherness' travelled through time and came to depict the 'self-image' of a nation in the Romantic literature of the nineteenth century. The following section then explains how, in contrast, the liberal image of the national 'self' referred to ethnicity only in an instrumental sense – as a matter of convenient governance. The accounts of these two philosophical traditions regarding the contrasting role of ethnicity in the political organisation of nation-states are followed by an explanation of how both the liberal and Romantic nationalist agendas sought 'scientific' justification in another dominant nineteenth-century notion – social Darwinism. Having set the socio-political context, in the final section I offer an in-depth analysis of how the ethnic dichotomy of 'self' and 'other' in the liberal and conservative traditions informed the construction of nineteenth-century international law.

What does 'ethnicity' mean?

Major discourses on ethnicity can be broadly categorised into three major streams – those that relate to the constitutive elements of ethnicity, those that relate to the process of the construction of these elements, and finally, those that relate to the role of ethnicity in the political organisation of the nation-state.[5] First, the idea of ethnicity in relation to its constitutive elements so closely relates to 'race' and 'culture' that this complex notion appears even more complicated, given the significant proximity of these two concepts with ethnicity, not only in terms of their overlapping characteristics but also in terms of their general image. In his oft-cited study on minorities, Francesco Capotorti, the then UN special rapporteur of the Sub-Commission on Prevention of Discrimination and Protection of Minorities, maintained that ethnicity came to replace the notion of race only after World War II. It was at its third session in 1950 that the sub-commission, while considering a draft resolution on the definition of minorities, decided to replace the word 'racial' with 'ethnic' in all references to minority groups described by their ethnic origin.[6] This change took place, as Capotorti notes, largely due to the efforts of some member states to extend the rubric of 'minority' from a mere biological notion of race to a more inclusive notion of ethnicity that also considers cultural characteristics. These member states also argued that racial groupings entailed a false premise, in that they were not 'based upon scientific facts and tended to become more indistinct as a result of evolutionary processes, intermarriage, and changes in ideas or beliefs'.[7]

In an effort to distinguish ethnicity from race, Richard Burkey argues that while race, in most common usage, refers to 'aggregates of people based upon physical differences, particularly skin colour', '[e]thnic groups may be defined as peoples who conceive of themselves as one kind by virtue of their common ancestry (real or imagined) who are united by emotional bonds, a common culture and by concern with preservation of their group'.[8]

5 This categorisation is, however, arbitrary, in that the discourse on the contents of ethnicity is closely related to the discourse on the artificiality of these contents. Again, the discourse on the role of ethnicity in the political organisation of nation-states is, in a sense, a variant of the discourse on how ethnic elements are constructed and then directed towards attaining certain political goals.

6 See Francesco Capotorti, *Study on the Rights of Persons Belonging to Ethnic, Religious or Linguistic Minorities* (1977), UN Doc. E/CN4/Sub. 2/384/Rev1, 34.

7 *Ibid.* However, prior to this change, the Genocide Convention of 1949 had also used the term 'ethnicity' to refer to cultural, physical, and historical characteristics of a group as opposed to mere physical existence but simultaneously to exclude these features from its legal protection, in that the convention was primarily designed to protect the physical existence of certain groups. See Article 2 of the Convention. In this way, the Genocide Convention leaves the issues of cultural genocide unaddressed. See Joseph L. Kunz, 'The Present Status of the International Law for the Protection of Minorities', *American Journal of International Law* 48 (1954), 282.

8 Richard M. Burkey, 'Discrimination and Racial Relations' in *Report on the International Research Conference on Race Relations* (Colorado, 7–9 June 1970), 62.

Similarly, Richard Schermerhorn defines an ethnic group 'as a collectivity within a larger society having real or putative common ancestry, memories of a shared historical past, and a cultural focus on one or more symbolic elements defined as the epitome of their people-hood'.[9] Likewise, although Paul Brass admits that defining an ethnic group on the basis of objective features is problematic, in that it is usually extremely difficult to determine the boundaries of ethnic categories in this way, one of his definitional criteria of an ethnic group is having at least one distinguishing cultural feature that clearly separates one group of people from another, whether that be language, territory, religion, colour, diet, or dress.[10]

More recently, Barbara Harff and Ted Gurr, too, define ethnic groups in non-biological terms and as '"psychological communities" whose members share a persisting sense of common interest and identity that is based on some combination of shared historical experience and valued cultural traits – beliefs, language, ways of life, a common homeland'.[11] Another widely used textbook defines an ethnic group as

> a large or small group of people, in either traditional or advanced societies, who are united by a common inherited culture (including language, music, food, dress, and custom and practices), racial similarity, common religion, and belief in common history and ancestry and who exhibit a strong psychological sentiment of belonging to the group.[12]

Thus, ethnicity, as the character-making element of ethnic groups, is perceived broadly: going far beyond mere biological features, it incorporates a wide range of cultural attributes including language and religion.

In the context of Article 27 of the International Covenant on Civil and Political Rights (ICCPR, 1996), Capotorti argues that 'the substitution of

[9] Richard Schermerhorn, 'Ethnicity and Minority Groups' in *Ethnicity*, ed. John Hutchinson and Anthony D. Smith (Oxford: Oxford University Press, 1996), 17.

[10] Brass holds the view that there are three ways of defining ethnic groups: in terms of objective attributes, with reference to subjective feelings, and in relation to behaviour. While the problem with an objective definition of ethnic groups remains delimiting the boundary of distinctiveness, he believes that the difficulty with 'subjective' definitions is that they make it impossible to answer the basic question of how a group of people arrives at subjective self-consciousness in the first place. On the other hand, the 'behavioural' definitions, which are really a form of objective definition, merely suggest that there are cultural differences between ethnic groups but that the critical distinctions reveal themselves only in interaction with other groups. See Paul Brass, 'Ethnic Groups and Ethnic Identity Formation' in *Ethnicity*, ed. Hutchinson and Smith, 85.

[11] Barbara Harff and Ted R. Gurr, *Ethnic Conflict in World Politics* (Boulder, Colorado: Westview Press, 2004), 3.

[12] Ray C. Taras and Rajat Ganguly, *Understanding Ethnic Conflict – International Dimension* (New York: Longman, 2006), 1.

the term "ethnic minorities" for the term "racial minorities" and the omission of any reference to "national" minorities would seem to reflect a wish to use the broadest expression and to imply that racial and national minorities should therefore be regarded as included in the category of ethnic minorities'.[13] For the purpose of this book also, so far as the constitutive elements are concerned, I use ethnicity in the broadest possible sense to include attributes such as colour, descent, origin, religion, language, nationality, shared common ancestry, and history, among others. This understanding of ethnicity is deliberately wide and accommodative and is intended to avoid further confusion relating to the term. Of course, it is true that not all the religious or linguistic categories can be logically or practically brought under the rubric of ethnicity. This operational definition of ethnicity is, therefore, purpose built for this book and has no claim of generality.

Yet, it would be otherwise misleading *ipso facto* to attribute this wide cultural meaning to ethnicity. Primordialism, one of the major schools of thought on ethnicity, in its classical sense conceives of ethnicity as descriptive of those 'biologically given' features that the members of a social group share among themselves. The notion that ethnicity is a 'natural' primordial tie is premised on the assumption that a group identity is an indispensable aspect of one's personal identity.[14] One proponent of this thought, sociologist Edward Shils, for example, takes the view that social life revolves mainly around various kinds of 'primary group' relationships. Thus, he claims that the attachment that one feels to another member of one's kinship group is not just a function of social interaction; rather, '[i]t is because a certain ineffable significance is attributed to the tie of blood'.[15] Shils continues, '[t]he need for connections or relationships of a primordial character will be endemic in human existence as long as biological existence has a value to the individual organism'.[16]

Pierre van den Berghe identifies the vulnerability of this biological understanding of primordialism that asserts that ethnic sentiment is fundamental without explaining why this is so and provides us with an

[13] Capotorti Report, 35. [14] Thompson, *Theories of Ethnicity*, 55.

[15] Edward Shils, 'Primordial, Personal, Sacred, and Civil Ties', *British Journal of Sociology* 8 (1957), 142.

[16] Edward Shils, 'Colour, the Universal Intellectual Community, and the Afro-Asian Intellectual', *Daedalus* 96, no. 2 (Colour and Race) (1967), 282. See also John Hope Franklin (ed.), *Colour and Race* (Boston, Massachusetts: Houghton Mifflin Co., 1968), 8.

alternative socio-biological theory of primordialism. Drawing on Darwin, he argues that all social organisms are biologically programmed to be nepotistic to others in proportion to their real or perceived degree of common ancestry; altruistic investment in unrelated organisms is biologically wasted and therefore could not evolve. With this nepotism, social organisms maximise their inclusive fitness.[17] More than most other organisms, humans recognise and make fine gradations of kinship and respond to them accordingly.[18] Nonetheless, with the widening of ethnic boundaries, van den Berghe continues, the bonds of kinship were correspondingly diluted and sometimes became fictive. As a result, ethnicity became increasingly manipulated and perverted to other ends, including domination and exploitation.

> The urge, however, to continue to define a collectivity larger than the immediate circle of kinsmen on the basis of biological descent continues to be present even in the most industrialised mass societies of today. A wide variety of ethnic markers are used to define such collectivities of descent, but their choice is not capricious. Those markers will be stressed that are, in fact, objectively reliable predictors of common descent, given the environment in which the discriminating group finds itself.[19]

Thus, the use of these readily identifiable, unfalsifiable markers of probable common ancestry in forming a group arguably helps the discriminating group by significantly reducing the transaction costs for monitoring group membership.[20]

It is worth noting here that even sharp biological differences in the form of race have socio-political underpinnings. Paul Gilroy, for example, suggests that such differences do not 'bear with them a unique or constant order of determinate effects which applies regardless of the conditions in which they have to exist'.[21] Without dismantling the relevance of biology as a factor in the formation and reproduction of race, he asserts that race has to be socially and politically constructed by elaborate ideological work to secure and maintain the different forms of 'racialisation'.[22] Gilroy refers to how the naming of 'races' in Britain during the 1980s shifted from political definitions of 'black' based on

[17] Pierre L. van den Berghe, *The Ethnic Phenomenon* (New York: Elsevier, 1981), 11.
[18] *Ibid.* [19] *Ibid.*
[20] Cf. Francesco Caselli and Wilbur J. Coleman II, 'On the Theory of Ethnic Conflict', *Journal of the European Economic Association* 11, no. 1 (2013).
[21] Paul Gilroy, *There Ain't No Black in the Union Jack* (London: Unwin Hyman, 1987), 38.
[22] *Ibid.*

the possibility of Afro-Asian unity towards more restricted alternative formulations that have confined that concept of blackness to people of African descent. This shift, he argues, 'had its origins in an understanding of "race" which stresses the obstacles to political accommodation erected between groups by culture and ethnicity'.[23] It is thus begging the question to conceive of ethnicity as merely a biological or natural phenomenon – this approach cannot explain how new ethnic groups emerge from populations formerly identified as distinct from each other.

As a result, whereas the discourse on ethnicity in terms of its contents closely relates to race and culture in the broadest sense, there exists a parallel discourse on ethnicity that mainly draws on the process of its construction. This discourse on ethnicity follows three different streams: modified- or neo-primordialism, instrumentalism, and elite-constructivism. While primordialism in its classic version considers ethnicity as a 'given' or 'natural' phenomenon and understands ethnic groups in the biological sense, similar to races, later developments in primordialism explain ethnicity as a socio-culturally constructed primordial attachment developed in a historical process. Scholars within this modified primordial school emphasise the significance of cultural traits that ethnic group members share with each other in the process of ethnic group formation without any claim for the authenticity of these traits.

For example, anthropologist Clifford Geertz terms ascriptive features as 'assumed given', in contrast to 'given', for culture is inevitably involved in such matters of social existence. Although Geertz identifies immediate contiguity and kin connection as the icons of primordial attachment, he recognises that such ascriptive given-ness stems from being born into a particular religious community, speaking a particular language or even a dialect of a language, and following particular social practices.[24] Thus, he defines ethnicity as 'a primordial sentiment not because ethnicity is a natural, biologically based identity, but because ethnicity is a historically important cultural identity that, in certain parts of the world, has become particularly crucial or salient politically'.[25] For Geertz, in other words, ethnicity is important only insofar as it contributes to, or forms a focus for, cultural identity.

Locating the issue of primordialism within the socio-political context, Geertz takes the view that the people, especially in new states, are

[23] *Ibid.*, 39.
[24] Clifford Geertz, *Old Societies and New States* (New York: Free Press, 1963), 108–113.
[25] Thompson, *Theories of Ethnicity*, 53.

animated by two powerful motives simultaneously: one is the desire for their identity to be publicly acknowledged as having import, and the other is the need for economic well-being. Although these demands are related, they stem from different sources and respond to different pressures.

> Multiethnic, usually multilinguistic, and sometimes multiracial, the populations of the new states tend to regard the immediate, concrete, and to them inherently meaningful sorting implicit in such 'natural' diversity as the substantial content of their individuality. To subordinate these specific and familiar identifications in favour of a generalised commitment to an overarching and somewhat alien civil order is to risk a loss of definition as an autonomous person, either through absorption into a culturally undifferentiated mass or, what is even worse, through a domination by some other rival ethnic, racial, or linguistic community that is able to imbue that order with the temper of its own personality.[26]

Under such circumstances, primordial sentiments serve to define socio-political movements along ethnic lines.[27] Thus, Geertz conceives of ethnicity as a socially and historically constructed 'primordial tie', in that an individual is included in a particular ethnic group not merely because of 'personal affection, practical necessity, common interest, or incurred obligation, but at least in great part by virtue of some unaccountable absolute import attributed to the very tie itself'.[28]

Jack Eller and Michael Coughlan argue that ethnicity is an emotional issue, making it distinct from strictly material or instrumental issues, and that since this emotion has a clear and analysable sociology, it is not primordial.[29] In an effort to refine the idea of primordialism and refute Eller and Coughlan's claim, Steven Grosby contends that primordialism is not merely an emotion outside the fact that such emotions are aroused by the cognition of an object; in this case, it is the cognition of the property of kinship.[30] Although primordialism asserts that human beings classify themselves and others in accordance with primordial criteria, Grosby maintains that it does not say that the referents of the criteria necessarily exist in the form in which those who refer to them believe.

[26] Clifford Geertz, *The Interpretation of Cultures* (New York: Basic Books, 1973), 258–259.

[27] Thompson, *Theories of Ethnicity*, 62. [28] Geertz, *The Interpretation of Cultures*, 111.

[29] Jack Eller and Michael R. Coughlan, 'The Poverty of Primordialism: The Demystification of Ethnic Attachment', *Ethnic and Racial Studies* 16, no. 2 (1993), 187–192, 199–201.

[30] Steven Grosby, 'The Verdict of History: The Inexpungeable Tie of Primordiality – A Response to Eller and Coughlan', *Ethnic and Racial Studies* 17, no. 1 (1994), 167. Cf. Fredrik Barth (ed.), *Ethnic Groups and Boundaries: The Social Organisation of Culture Difference* (Prospect Heights, Illinois: Waveland Press, 1998).

Primordialism, according to Grosby, elucidates that human beings differentiate between the 'self' and the 'other' in accordance with such ascriptive criteria, and on the basis of such notions of 'us' and 'them', they form groups, membership in which influences the conduct of their members.[31]

Primordial attachments, understood in this constructive sense, are an integral part of the formation of ethnic groups. What makes an ethnic group distinct from other social groups is its formative criteria – the 'given' or 'assumed given' or socio-historically constructed features. The belief that these features exist, though they may or may not, claims for individual's loyalty to and sacrifice for the ethnic group. However, primordial attachments are not always fixed; the degree of the attachment is subject to context, time, and an individual's orientations. In this sense, the importance of ethnicity is not a matter of its truth function but of its social meaning. To put it another way, it is the ontology rather than the epistemology of ethnicity that is of central importance.

In contrast to primordialists, instrumentalists typically presume that human beings are rational individuals who act primarily to optimise their economic profit in a given situation. They thus conceive of ethnic groups as a collection of profit-maximising individuals who cooperate or contend over scarce economic resources. For example, Michael Banton's rational choice theory presupposes that individuals are rational human beings who act so as to maximise net advantage in a given situation. Banton's theory depicts ethnicity as an inclusive process wherein individuals utilise physical and cultural differences in order to create groups and categories.[32] When such groups interact, Banton argues, the form and intensity of competition affect their boundaries; individual competition tends to dissolve the boundaries that define the groups, whereas competing as groups reinforces those boundaries. Here again, 'individuals are pictured as optimising: they select the alternatives which give them the greatest benefits relative to costs'.[33] In his theoretical framework, Banton recognises that rational choice theory is rooted in 'methodological individualism', which views humans primarily as individual cost-benefit maximisers (as opposed to social beings), making rational choices from among alternatives that society provides.[34] Therefore, by considering human beings to be free from any emotive aspects of social

31 Grosby, 'The Verdict of History', 168.

32 Michael Banton, *Racial and Ethnic Competition* (Cambridge: Cambridge University Press, 1983), 104.

33 *Ibid.* 34 Thompson, *Theories of Ethnicity*, 8.

life, Banton completely discards the salience of the primordial affiliation in the formation of ethnic groups.

While Banton stresses the choices that individuals make, Michael Hechter, in his version of rational choice theory, asserts that in making such choices, individuals, as rational human beings, have a common preference for wealth, honour, and power, because attaining these goods often makes it easier for individuals to attain other goals. These common preferences provoke everyone in the group to act similarly, and the idiosyncratic preferences that may result in some singular actions cancel one another out.[35] According to this reasoning, individuals will fulfil their corporate obligations only when they receive a net benefit by doing so or a negative sanction for not doing so. Therefore, 'the more costly it is for people to choose a traditional course of action to achieve a given benefit, the more likely it is that they will consider an innovative alternative to reach the same end'.[36] It thus follows that members of any ethnic group will join a collective action only when they are convinced that by doing so they will secure individual economic benefit. In this context, ethnic 'groups' – 'organisations' in Hechter's term – play a vital role, first, by creating various incentives for the individual to decide to participate in ethnic collective action and, secondly, by controlling the information on the basis of which individuals conduct their rational cost-benefit analysis.[37] Hechter, therefore, argues that the likelihood of ethnic collective action varies with its organisational strength.[38]

An obvious question arises from this claim: why would rational profit-seeking individuals form a group (or coalition) along ethnic lines in the first place? Hechter is of the opinion that individuals make preferences for ethnic affiliation due to their learning processes beginning from their childhood.[39] Taking the example of the Amish community, he stresses that the parents keep their children away from the outside world not because of a desire to secure the parents' salvation in a religious sense but simply because the parents' livelihoods cannot be sustained should this community cease to exist. Similarly, Gypsy parents inculcate negative ideas in their children regarding the outside world, for Gypsy children contribute to household income, which would be diminished by their assimilation into the mainstream society.[40] Thus, Hechter concludes that preferences tend to be formed and moulded in solidary communities;

[35] Michael Hechter, 'A Rational Choice Approach to Race and Ethnic Relations' in *Ethnicity*, ed. Hutchinson and Smith, 90.

[36] *Ibid.*, 91. [37] *Ibid.*, 93–94. [38] *Ibid.*, 92. [39] *Ibid.*, 95. [40] *Ibid.*, 96–97.

alternatively, community solidarity is sustained by dependence and by a monitoring mechanism operated in conformity with rational choice principles.[41]

In contrast, the constructivist approach to the construction of the constitutive elements of ethnicity perceives ethnicity as an artificial construction of elites, in that various political elites invent ethnic groups by mobilising social groups along artificial ethnic lines to secure their own material interests.[42] Advocates of this position argue that rather than being historically rooted, most contemporary ethnic communities are of relatively recent origin and have been artificially constructed to serve practical and changing needs.[43] While primordialism in the constructivist sense perceives ethnicity as a socially and historically constructed primordial tie, elite-constructivism conceives of ethnicity as a mere tool for constructing group identity in the face of economic or political competition. Again, while instrumentalism considers ethnicity as the tool of self-interest-motivated members' sophisticated and material calculation, elite-constructivism perceives ethnicity as an instrument used by political entrepreneurs to mobilise masses along ethnic lines so as to materialise their own ambitions.

[41] *Ibid.*, 97–98. Two interesting observations follow Hechter's argument: first, Hechter's solidary communities are not monolithic so far as the motivation to sustain the community is concerned. While parents arguably inculcate certain beliefs in their children to ensure parents' economic well-being, their children act according to this belief which they believe to be true. At a micro level, this belief system results in moulding an individual's preference for forming a coalition along ethnic lines. And this is precisely what primordialism, understood as a socio-historical construct (as opposed to its biological version), tends to offer. Thus, ethnic attachment, in the primordial term, provides Hechter's rational choice theory with a necessary gap-filling device. Secondly, Hechter's argument does not explain why rational individuals first formed such ethnic communities for attaining their material goals. No doubt, incentives, monitoring, and allocation are indispensable concepts for maintaining group affiliation and for an understanding of collective ethnic action, but without considering primordial attachments, it is not yet clear why rational individuals would form ethnic groups. This is the key question that the instrumentalists often avoid; instead, perceiving the ethnic group as it is, they rather attempt to demonstrate the use of ethnicity for instrumental purposes, such as a cost-minimising tool used by rational individuals for the efficient functioning of a monitoring and allocation mechanism within a group.

[42] See, for example, Berch Berberoglu, *Nationalism and Ethnic Conflict: Class, State, and Nation in the Age of Globalisation* (Lanham, Maryland: Rowman and Littlefield, 2004); Amy Chua, *World on Fire: How Exporting Free Market Democracy Breeds Ethnic Hatred and Global Instability* (New York: Doubleday, 2003). Cf. Donald Horowitz, *Ethnic Groups in Conflict*, 2nd edn (Berkeley: University of California Press, 2000); Harff and Gurr, *Ethnic Conflict in World Politics*.

[43] Milton J. Esman, *An Introduction to Ethnic Conflict* (Cambridge: Polity Press, 2004), 34.

Despite the relevance of these two categories of discourse on ethnicity (*viz.* the constitutive elements and the process of the construction of these elements) for this work, they remain very different from the third major discourse on ethnicity that is set as the foundation of this book. This relates to the role of ethnicity in the political organisation of nation-states. Here I use ethnicity within the dichotomy of 'self' and 'other', expressed through two philosophical traditions of the nineteenth century, and explain how this notion of ethnicity plays a significant role in international legal responses to a number of key issues. I turn to this particular understanding of ethnicity in the following section.

Ethnicity: from 'otherness' to the conservative image of the 'self'

The term 'ethnicity' derives from the Greek word *ethnos*.[44] In ancient Greek, while *genos* was generally used by Greeks for Greeks themselves in a restricted kinship sense, *ethnos* was the term for the non-Greek 'others'.[45] For example, Plato believed that all Greeks, being a single people, were closely associated and natural friends. Therefore, even if they get involved in a fight among themselves, they should not treat each other harshly or take fellow Greeks as slaves.[46] But as for the *ethnos*, who were considered 'natural enemies', he thought no such restriction was necessary in dealing with them. Having established a regime of free enquiry conducive to intellectual pursuits, Plato claimed, the Greeks justified their superiority over the Egyptians and the Phoenicians, who only knew despotism and tyranny. 'Such a distinction between Greeks and non-Greeks', Bhikhu Parekh notes, 'implied that relations among the former were governed by different principles from those regulating their relations with non-Greeks'.[47]

Likewise, Homer used the word *ethnos* to describe large, undifferentiated groups of either animals or warriors.[48] Tonkin et al. trace similar uses of *ethnos* in other Greek classics too: Aeschylus uses *ethnos* to describe the Furies (*Eumenides* 366) and also the Persians (*Persai* 43,

[44] Elizabeth Tonkin, Maryon McDonald and Malcolm Chapman, *History and Ethnicity* (London: Routledge, 1989), 11.

[45] For the etymology of 'ethnicity', I largely depended on Tonkin, McDonald, and Chapman, *History and Ethnicity*, 12–20.

[46] Richard Tuck, *The Rights of War and Peace* (Oxford: Oxford University Press, 1999), 53.

[47] Bhikhu Parekh, *Rethinking Multiculturalism: Cultural Diversity and Political Theory* (London: Macmillan, 2000), 20.

[48] Tonkin, McDonald and Chapman, *History and Ethnicity*, 12.

56; also *Herodotus* 1.101); Sophocles uses it for wild animals (*Philoctetes* 1147; *Antigone* 344); Pindar employs the term to describe groups of like people, but 'again people whose location or conduct put them in some way outside the sphere of Greek social normality', e.g., the husband-killing women of Lemnos (*Pythian Odes* 4.448); Aristotle uses it for foreign or barbarous nations, as opposed to 'Hellenes' (*Politics*, 1324.b.10).[49] Tonkin et al., thus, assert that

> [a]spects of naturality, of non-legitimate social organisation, of disorganisation, and of animality, are strong in *ethnos* [. . .]. It is characteristic of this area of vocabulary, perhaps in all languages, that any term for 'people' in a general sense, has the potential for being taken up into a duality of 'us' and 'them', and from early use this has been the fate of *ethnos*.[50]

In later uses, in New Testament Greek, Tonkin et al. continue, *ethnos* appears as a religious indicator to refer to those who are neither Christians nor Jews. At this stage, the derived adjective *ethnikos* is very nearly synonymous with *barbaros* – those who spoke unintelligible languages and wanted for civilisation, who were beyond the bounds of meaning, order, and decency.[51] Because throughout the Middle Ages it was Church Latin that dominated literacy in Europe, the term *gentile* – a grouping for religious 'otherness' – succeeded *ethnos*.[52] In public Roman law, *jus gentium* represented a body of rules for Romans in maintaining relations with foreigners, while *jus civile* governed interactions between citizens. The term 'law of nations', the synonym for the present-day phrase 'international law', is the literal translation of the Latin term *jus gentium* into English.[53] Although *jus gentium* used to deal with individuals – as opposed to nation-states, which are the subjects of the law of nations[54] – the phenomenon of managing the 'other' is quite evident in both cases.

So far as the meaning of *ethnos* in relation to modern Greek is concerned, the social anthropologist Roger Just claims that the term *ethnos* as used for 'non-structured', 'tribal', peripheral peoples in classical Greek has, in some sense, been transmitted unchanged (except phonetically) from classical antiquity into modern Greek.[55] Yet, Tonkin et al. identify an inversion in the meaning of *ethnos* in the Greek context, which occurred

49 *Ibid.* 50 *Ibid.* 51 *Ibid.*, 13. 52 *Ibid.*

53 Arthur Nussbaum, *A Concise History of the Law of Nations* (New York: Macmillan, 1947), 19.

54 *Ibid.*

55 Roger Just, 'Some Problems for Mediterranean Anthropology', *Journal of the Anthropology Society of Oxford* 6, no. 3 (1978), 72.

during the Ottoman period. According to them, this inversion took place in this way: in the Byzantine and Mediaeval period, the term continued to be used for 'gentiles'. Within the Ottoman Empire, however, the Orthodox Christians themselves were the most prominent among various religious 'others', termed 'millets' by the Empire. It is probable that *ethnos* was the term used to translate the Turkish term *millet*, as it applied to the Orthodox Christians. The Greeks may, then, have been referring to themselves as the *ethnos* (that is, the Orthodox *millet*) from the fifteenth century onwards.[56]

This inversion of the reference from the 'other' to the 'self' is traced in English as well. The term 'ethnic' has long been used in English in its Greek New Testament sense as an unusual intellectual synonym for 'gentile', denoting 'pagan' or 'non-Christian', and it retained this sense until well into the nineteenth century.[57] But from about the mid-nineteenth century, scholarship has made of *ethnos* a word meaning something like a 'group of people of shared characteristics'.[58] In the Romantic literature, as we shall see soon, the notion of 'otherness' in *ethnos* shifted to the image of the 'self', expressed through the dominant political philosophy of the nineteenth century – 'nation'.[59]

Impetus for the relevance of biological features in the understanding of a nation came with the emergence of social Darwinism in the latter part of the nineteenth century.[60] However, before the scientific justification for racial superiority of a nation emerged, what dominated the quest for constructing the self-image in the nineteenth century was 'culture'. This quest appears, in Ernest Gellner's account, largely as the Romantic response to the Enlightenment. The Enlightenment was premised on the 'individualistic, universalistic and egalitarian' ethic as opposed to the 'oppression, dogmatisation, superstition and inequality

[56] Tonkin, McDonald, and Chapman, *History and Ethnicity*, 13. [57] *Ibid.*, 14. [58] *Ibid.*

[59] As the etymology of the term demonstrates, 'nation' is used to refer to shared biological characteristics. Deriving from the past participle of the verb *nasci*, meaning to be born, the Latin noun *nationem* connotes breed or race. See Walker Connor, 'A Nation Is a Nation, Is a State, Is an Ethnic Group, Is a . . .' in *Nationalism*, ed. John Hutchinson and Anthony D. Smith (Oxford: Oxford University Press, 1994), 38. At some mediaeval universities, a student's *nationem* designated the sector of the country from which he came. However, when introduced into the English language in the late thirteenth century, nation had its primary connotation of a blood-related group (*ibid.*). In this sequence, it is also argued that in the nineteenth century, as in the Middle Ages, nations were conceived of as units of common biological descent as well as of common culture. See Susan Raynolds, 'Regional Sentiments and Medieval Communities' in *Nationalism*, ed. Hutchinson and Smith, 139.

[60] We shall return to this aspect of an understanding of the nation in the following section.

of the agrarian age'.[61] Both the formulations of the Enlightenment philosophy – on the one hand, Hume's sensualistic philosophy that human morality is founded on humane sentiment, the capability for and sympathy to pain and pleasure of both the 'self' and the 'other', and on the other hand, the Kantian rationalistic philosophy that the source of human identity and morality is located in shared reason – advocated universalism devoid of links with either cultural or political boundaries.[62] Conversely, Romanticism praised a sense of specificity in the feeling and culture. The contrast is thus evident: where 'reason' is universal in its prescriptions, 'emotions are linked to specific communities, to "cultures", which are, precisely, associations engendered and sustained by the shared sentiment, shared by the members, and *not* shared by outsiders, by non-members'.[63] It follows, therefore, that the 'self' is defined as a locally and culturally specific homogeneous unit vis-à-vis the 'other' to accommodate this emotion. In this version, a nation is then the product of the process of creating the culturally specific 'self' in relation to the 'other'.

The need for, and the process of, creating a unified common culture shared only by a specified population gained momentum as a consequence of a number of crucial events of the nineteenth century. Gellner identifies industrialisation as the prime force in this social transformation.[64] The industrial revolution, facilitated by massive scientific innovations, caused immense social mobility that ultimately broke down the hierarchical structure of the agrarian age, laying the foundation for creating cultural homogeneity.[65] At the same time, Gellner continues, mobile pools of men who shared the same culture under the same political authority became very preoccupied with 'roots'; Romanticism, communalism, populism, vitalism, and biologism all combined to endow the policy of 'citizenship-through-roots' and the persecution of the rootless.[66] Thus, the industrial revolution encouraged the development of a national culture through education in core skills to enable a mobile, flexible workforce; on the other hand, the concern for roots and heritage was also a product of the alienation fostered by the breakdown in the familial community.

[61] Ernest Gellner, *Nationalism* (London: Weidenfeld & Nicolson, 1997), 64. See also Ernest Gellner, *Nations and Nationalism* (Oxford: Basil Blackwell, 1983); Ernest Gellner, *Culture, Identity, and Politics* (Cambridge: Cambridge University Press, 1987).

[62] Gellner, *Nationalism*, 64–68. [63] *Ibid.*, 67.

[64] Other significant forces were bureaucratisation and Protestant-type religion.

[65] See, generally, Gellner, *Nationalism*, 25–30. [66] *Ibid.*, 74.

The social and political changes that came with industrialisation and modernity provoked nationalist sentiments in other fronts, too. Eric Hobsbawm identifies three such social developments that helped to invent imagined or actual communities as nationalities: traditional communities' resistance to the onrush of modernity, the rapid growth of non-traditional middle classes in the urbanising societies of the developed countries, and the unprecedented migrations that juxtaposed various communities not yet ready to peacefully coexist.[67] Benedict Anderson, on the other hand, traces the emergence of the nationalist ideology in the demise of appeal of three fundamental cultural conceptions of great antiquity: religious script languages that created transcontinental solidarities, hierarchical and centripetal social structure, and a conception of temporality in which cosmology and history were indistinguishable. In the face of the decline of these certainties, print capitalism precipitated the search for a new way for rapidly growing numbers of people to think about themselves and to relate themselves to others.[68] Print capitalism laid the foundation of national consciousness in two ways: by creating unified fields of exchange and communication through which a wide range of people belonging to that language group could communicate with each other and by giving the language a more or less fixed shape, linking it to antiquity.[69] If the nation is an imagined community, in Anderson's term, then this process of vernacularisation through print capitalism was the principal method of imagining a community as a 'nation' in nineteenth-century Europe. Then, once created or imagined, the cultural community readily claimed homogeneity, and culture served as the criterion for the exclusion of all who did not share it. In the words of Gellner: 'Nations, unlike the brotherhood of man favoured by the Enlightenment, are exclusive clubs'.[70]

The Romantic response to the Enlightenment had its root in the German tradition. To the Germans, the authentic *Kultur* of the

[67] Eric Hobsbawm, *Nations and Nationalism since 1780*, 2nd edn (Cambridge: Cambridge University Press, 1992), 109.

[68] Benedict Anderson, *Imagined Communities*, rev edn (London: Verso, 2006), 36. Other major approaches to nationalism include, among others, Anthony D. Smith, *Nationalism in the Twentieth Century* (Oxford: Martin Robertson, 1979); A. D. Smith, *The Ethnic Origins of Nations* (Oxford: Basil Blackwell, 1986); John Breuilly, *Nationalism and the State*, 2nd edn (Chicago, Illinois: University of Chicago Press, 1994); Liah Greenfeld, *Nationalism: Five Roads to Modernity* (Cambridge, Massachusetts: Harvard University Press, 1992). See also A. D. Smith, *Nationalism and Modernism: A Critical Survey of Recent Theories of Nations and Nationalism* (London: Routledge, 1998).

[69] Anderson, *Imagined Communities*, 44.

[70] Gellner, *Nationalism*, 68.

German people was to be preferred to the French notion of rational, scientific, and universal civilisation – the Enlightenment.[71] One of the key proponents of this emergent Romantic nationalism was the eighteenth-century German philosopher Johann Herder, who, despite acknowledging that all mankind shared the same basic attributes, claims that nations have modified their characters according to their specific cultural condition.[72] The link to the specificity is so strong that Herder sees all the aspects of the population within a nation – the constitution of their body, their way of life, the pleasures and occupations to which they have been accustomed from infancy, and the whole circle of their ideas – as climatic.[73] And then he concludes, '[d]eprive them of their country, you deprive them of everything'.[74] For him, the nation is like an enlarged family, and the most natural state is one that is composed of a specific people with a unique national character.[75] It is therefore opposed to the verdict of nature, he argues, to expand the nation beyond its natural limits and thereby cause the indiscriminate mingling of various nations and human types.[76] A nation, in the Herderian sense, is thus a unique and specific ethnic connotation.

Like Herder, German political theorist Johann Fichte inclined to the uniqueness of the German *Kultur* despite his strong faith in the universal solidarity enshrined in the French Revolution. This shift from liberal universalism to the locality of culture was caused by the increasing French expansionism under the pretext of liberalism at the dawn of the nineteenth century.[77] His perception of the international order and international law in the face of expansionism thus begins from the idea of mutual recognition of nations as well as mutual guarantees of security.[78] His late works clearly reveal this shift from liberalism to Romanticism. In his celebrated work, *Address to the German Nation*

71 Adam Kuper, *Culture* (Cambridge, Massachusetts: Harvard University Press, 1999), 6–9.
72 Johann Gottfried von Herder, 'Reflections on the Philosophy of the History of Mankind (1791)' in *The Nationalism Reader*, ed. Omar Dahbour and Micheline R. Ishay (Atlantic Highlands, New Jersey: Humanities Press International, 1995), 48–57.
73 *Ibid.*, 51. 74 *Ibid.*
75 Johann Gottfried von Herder, 'Ideas towards a Philosophy of the History of Mankind (1785)' in *Modern Political Doctrines*, ed. Alfred Zimmern (Oxford: Oxford University Press, 1939), 165.
76 *Ibid.*
77 See Johann Gottlieb Fichte, 'An Outline of International and Cosmopolitan Law (1796–97)' in *The Political Thought of the German Romantics*, ed. H. S. Reiss and P. Brown (Oxford: Basil Blackwell, 1955), 73–84.
78 *Ibid.*, 75.

(1808), written less than a decade before he died, he portrays the German nation as an authentic entity with all its peculiar natural characteristics. The original and truly natural frontiers of all states, he asserts, are undoubtedly their inner frontiers, in that '[t]hose who speak the same language are linked together, before human intervention takes a hand, by mere nature with a host of invisible ties; they understand each other and are capable of communicating more and more closely with one another, they belong together, they are by nature one indivisible whole'.[79] These features are so peculiar to that particular nation that any nation of a different origin and language that would try to appropriate and absorb such a people would inevitably confuse itself in the process and profoundly disturb the uniform progress of its own education.[80] Fichte then concludes that only such a culturally specific inner frontier, drawn by the spiritual nature of man, 'first gives rise to outward frontiers of territories as a direct consequence'.[81] Accordingly, he saw Germany as a culturally and linguistically unified entity, sufficiently distinct from all other nations, and located at the centre of Europe as a 'dividing wall' between the unrelated tribes surrounding this great nation.[82]

Within this Romantic framework, not surprisingly, Fichte found the idea of universalism quite problematic or, to take his words, 'despicable' and 'irrational'.[83] He contends that the phenomenon of divinity reflects on a nation only when each nation develops and takes shape in accordance with its own peculiarities; it is this peculiarity that guarantees the present and future dignity, virtue, and merit of nations. In contrast, he warns, 'if these qualities are dulled by mixture and disintegration there arises from this lack of peculiarity a separation from spiritual nature, and from this there arises the fusion of all in uniform and conjoint ruin'.[84] Thus, his vision of the world comprises culturally specific nations.

Compared to Herder and Fichte, the nineteenth-century scholars of the German Historical School, such as Leopold Ranke, took a more conservative stance. For Ranke, the greatness of a nation lies not in the extent of its possessions or the power of its troops or the amount of wealth it has or its share in the general civilisation but in the moral strength of the nation and its sense of nationality – the two most important elements but for which a state cannot exist.[85] In the face of

[79] Johann Gottlieb Fichte, 'Addresses to the German Nation – Thirteenth Address (1808)' in *The Political Thought of the German Romantics*, 102.

[80] *Ibid.* [81] *Ibid.*, 102–103. [82] *Ibid.*, 103. [83] *Ibid.*, 108. [84] *Ibid.*

[85] Leopold von Ranke, 'The Great Powers (1833)' in *The Nationalism Reader*, ed. Dahbour and Ishay, 158.

the ever-increasing influence of the French philosophy of rationality and materialism, Ranke advocated for a counter-spiritual force – nationalism – to contain that influence: 'The dominion which another nation threatens to gain over us can only be combated by developing our own sense of nationality'.[86] And while explaining this nationalist spirit, he actually refers to 'the real, existing one' – not merely an invented, illusionary nationality – which is expressed in the state.[87] The implication, therefore, is that the authentic root of the German nation-state needs to be traced; nothing could be a better tool to this end than the idea of 'race'. The German Historical School jurists, especially von Savigny, had significant influence, as we shall see later, on nineteenth-century German international law as advanced by Bluntschli and others.

It was always evident, however, that the notion of an authentic German nation would be easily exposed as a myth. As nineteenth-century French philosopher Renan demonstrates, as in all the 'noblest' countries of Europe (England, France, and Italy), in Germany people were mixed in that the entire South was Gallic and all the East, starting from the Elbe, was Slav.[88] Until a few centuries before Jesus Christ, the Germans possessed no distinctive character when mingled with the Slavs in the great shadowy mass of Scythians.[89] The German race is in fact, Renan asserts, the creation of the sciences of philology and history and not of actual human descent.[90] Nevertheless, so far as the Romantic quest for tracing roots is concerned, it is not the actual science of biology that in effect occupies people's psyche. As Max Weber indicates, the 'nation' has in common with the sentiment of solidarity of ethnic communities the notions of a subjective belief in their common descent, whether or not an objective blood relationship exists.[91] In this important shift, therefore, those aware of the specious character of claims to biological homogeneity on the part of nations started to conceive of the idea of community in a rationalistic or sentimental way.

However, it is not only race that Renan refutes as the sole element of a nation; dynastic history, language, religion, community interest, geography – each comes under his critical scrutiny. And finally, he defines the nation as a 'soul' and a spiritual principle – which merge together to form a unitary

86 *Ibid.*, 159. 87 *Ibid.*
88 Ernest Renan, 'What Is a Nation? (1882)' in *Modern Political Doctrines*, ed. Zimmern, 195.
89 *Ibid.*, 196. 90 *Ibid.*
91 Max Weber, *Economy and Society*, ed. Guenther Roth and Claus Wittich (New York: Bedminster Press, 1968 [1922]), 389.

whole: 'One of these things lies in the past, the other in the present. The one is the possession in common of a rich heritage of memories; and the other is actual agreement, the desire to live together, and the will to continue to make the most of the joint inheritance'.[92] Renan advances Romanticism as against materialism by perceiving a nation as a great solid unit, a moral consciousness, which is formed by the people who count on their glorious, heroic events or the painful memories of the past and demonstrate a readiness to sacrifice for the nation in the present.[93] In his words:

> That moral consciousness which we call a nation is created by a great assemblage of men with warm hearts and healthy minds: And as long as this moral consciousness can prove its strength by the sacrifice demanded from the individual for the benefit of the community, it is justifiable and has the right to exist.[94]

Now, if the nation must have a 'root', it must be this kind of exclusive psychological community. Throughout the transition from ethnic 'otherness' to 'selfness', as the concept of the ethnic nation emerged, it was, therefore, destined consistently to play an exclusionary role: while being 'ethnic' originally meant being the derogatory 'other' and therefore 'excluded', the nineteenth-century German Romantic nationalism that was premised on ethnicity – in the forms of culture and race – was designed to depict the unique image of the 'self' and, thereby, exclude the 'other'. As Weber says, 'the significance of the "nation" is usually anchored in the superiority, or at least the irreplaceability, of the cultural values that are to be preserved and developed only through the cultivation of the peculiarity of the group'.[95] Such preservation necessarily means the exclusion of all who do not share this uniqueness. However, what needs to be underscored here is that this version of nationalism, that is, the way of defining the self, is *one* category within the broad discourse on the subject. Nationalism understood in this way appears as the Romantic response to liberal nationalism, to which we return to examine the treatment 'ethnicity' had received in that construction.

Ethnicity in the liberal construction of the nation

The liberal doctrine, developed in the eighteenth century during the French Revolution, not only advocated individual liberties such as the

[92] Renan, 'What Is a Nation?' 202–203. [93] *Ibid.*, 203. [94] *Ibid.*, 205.
[95] Max Weber, 'The Nation' in *From Max Weber: Essays in Sociology*, trans. and ed. H. H. Gerth and C. Wright-Mills (London: Routledge and Kegan Paul, 1948), 177.

right to private property, freedom of speech, political participation, and equality before law but also propagated international cooperation based on commerce and on the spread of republican institutions. However, as a doctrine it had to encounter two major developments already in place, which encouraged thinking in 'national' terms: first, with the weakening of the influence of the church, absolute monarchs consolidated political unity into nation-states, and secondly, the growth of mercantilism strengthened the national economic unit and thereby promoted national solidarity.[96] Nevertheless, as Hobsbawm notes, such a 'nation' basically meant a political body of citizens inhabiting a specific territory and constituting a sovereign political unit irrespective of their ethnic, linguistic, or other similar characteristics.[97] In this sense, nations were to be equated with states.

The post-revolution philosophy of the Enlightenment and liberalism heavily relied on individualism and international solidarity in its endeavour to contain the sense of national loyalty. Locating the individual within the universal realm is the essence of the Enlightenment idea. German philosopher Immanuel Kant was the most prominent propagator of this idea. For Kant, a state is a union of an aggregate of men. The act by which a people constitutes a state for itself is the original contract through which all individual members of the people sacrifice their freedom, which exists in the state of nature, in order to receive civil rights in return.[98] Since all rights emanate from the legislative power, insofar as the laws reflect the wills of the individuals, the form of the state will be the one that the principle of right requires.

In Kant's republican political structure, individuals, in their capacity as citizens, enjoy freedom from the perils of an unjust war by remaining their own lawmakers: 'For a citizen must always be regarded as a co-legislative member of the state (i.e., not just as means, but also as an end in itself), and he must therefore give his free consent through his representatives [...]. Only under this limiting condition may the state put him to service in dangerous enterprises'.[99] At the same time, given that law is the reflection of the will of the individuals, Kant concludes that laws cannot be unjust.[100]

[96] Micheline R. Ishay, 'Introduction' in *The Nationalism Reader*, 3.
[97] See Hobsbawm, *Nations and Nationalism*, 18–19.
[98] Immanuel Kant, 'The Metaphysics of Morals (1797)' in *Kant: Political Writings*, ed. H. S. Reiss, trans. H. B. Nisbet (New York: Cambridge University Press, 1970), 140.
[99] *Ibid.*, 166–167. See also Kant, 'Perpetual Peace: A Philosophical Sketch (1795)' in *Kant: Political Writings*, 99–102.
[100] Kant, 'The Metaphysics of Morals', 139.

His analogy continues to the extent that he refuses the idea of the people's right to resistance against the legislative head of the state, for if the latter is the expression of citizens' will, citizens cannot simultaneously have the right to stand against their collective will.[101]

For Kant, human beings not only make up a nation but also belong to an international community, of which all the nations are members.[102] Thus, by analogy with the way individuals have to sacrifice their lawless state of nature to join the republic, he proposes that states must for the same reason relinquish some of the freedoms they have in their savage natural condition for the sake of the universal good.[103] And the vision of the rights that states ultimately enjoy among themselves is 'cosmopolitan' insofar as they contribute to the union of all nations for the purpose of certain universal laws to regulate the intercourse they may have with one another.[104]

Kant's cosmopolitanism is an effort to transcend the natural geographic confinements of nations. He finds such geographic demarcation of nations obvious, given that nature has confined nations within an area of definite limits through the spherical shape of the planet they inhabit. But, on the other hand, his cosmopolitanism conceives of the specific geographic demarcation as an act of possessing a part within a determinate whole in which everyone has an original right to share, and in this sense, 'all nations are *originally* members of a community of the land'.[105] This is a cosmopolitan community formed not by legal rights of possession or ownership but by the mutual activities of commerce.[106] In the political sphere, Kant projects such a union of nations in the form of a confederation of nations that would maintain peaceful international order.[107]

As noted, Kant's proposition received criticism from Herder, who advocated Romantic ideas of cultural specificity and held the view that the rights of cultural nations should supersede the natural rights of all. Within the liberal stream, Hegel adopted a different approach to oppose Kant's proposition. Like Herder, Hegel believed that the individual exists within a general consciousness, that is, the national consciousness. The individual is brought up within the atmosphere of this consciousness – the substance that underlies the spirit of the nation, that informs all the aims and interests of the nation as well as determines the nation's rights, customs, and religion.[108] But, for Hegel, the spirit of the nation, which is

101 *Ibid.*, 144–145. 102 *Ibid.*, 165. 103 *Ibid.*, 165, 171. 104 *Ibid.*, 172.
105 *Ibid.* Italics in original. 106 *Ibid.* 107 *Ibid.*, 171.
108 George Wilhelm Friedrich Hegel, *Lectures on the Philosophy of World History* (1837), ed. D. Forbes and H. B. Nisbet (New York: Cambridge University Press, 1975), 76–77, 80.

particular in essence, is identical with the universal spirit that is revealed through the human consciousness, corresponding to the divine, hence absolute, spirit. The spirit of the nation, Hegel continues, is therefore the universal spirit in particular form, but the latter is dependent on the former for its actual being or existence. Although the particular spirit of a particular nation may perish, it disappears as a 'particular moment' of the development of the world spirit, which is absolute, hence omnipresent.[109] What is implied, therefore, is an evolutionary process to reach the absolute universal spirit, wherein particular national spirits fuse to supplement each other; some disappear in the process, but an advanced new spirit also appears. In the words of Hegel:

> Each new individual national spirit represents a new stage in the conquering march of the world spirit as it wins its way to consciousness and freedom. The death of a national spirit is a transition to new life, but not as in nature, where the death of one individual gives life to another individual of the same kind. On the contrary, the world spirit progresses from lower determinations to higher principles and concepts of its own nature, to more fully developed expressions of its idea.[110]

This universal spirit that takes a particular national form to come into actual existence as the consciousness within a state is the nation's culture; this is the form into which everything within the state is assimilated.[111] Given that the state embodies a particular spirit, and the law is the objectivity of the spirit as well as the will in its true expression, Hegel concludes that when the subjective will of men subordinates itself to laws, 'the objective and the subjective will are then reconciled, forming a single, undivided whole'.[112] Unlike Herder and Fichte, Hegel thus reconciles liberalism with the Romantic appeals by locating national spirits within the framework of the state and its laws.

The absolute world spirit is then the universal idea of 'civilisation' that is translated within the nation-state as the particular national culture – 'high culture'. As Norbert Elias precisely demonstrates, this construction of culture is distinct from the German tradition of the specific, unique *Kultur*.[113]

See also Timothy C. Luther, *Hegel's Critique of Modernity – Reconciling Individual Freedom and the Community* (New York: Lexington Books, 2009).

109 Hegel, *Lectures*, 81–83. 110 *Ibid.*, 83. See also 147–151. 111 *Ibid.*, 97 112 *Ibid.*

113 For a comparative analysis of the dichotomy of the French 'universal civilisation' and the German 'specific *Kultur*', see Norbert Elias, *The Civilizing Process: The Development of Manners. Changes in the Code of Conduct and Feeling in Early Modern Times* (New York: Urizen Books, 1978 [1939]).

A Frenchman will, for example, 'naively identify his own particular culture with "civilisation" or universal culture'.[114]

Thus, in the liberal nation, ethnicity remains at the sidelines, and the liberal discourse on whether the ethnic 'other' should be assimilated or allowed to maintain cultural distinctiveness is informed by an instrumental understanding of ethnicity. For example, although John Stuart Mill ascribed great value to diversity in human society,[115] he premised such diversity essentially on the proposition that human beings are naturally unique, and hence, individual autonomy engenders diverse opinions and world views.[116] In his words:

> Such are the differences among human beings in their sources of pleasure, their susceptibilities of pain, and the operation on them of different physical and moral agencies, that unless there is a corresponding diversity in their modes of life, they neither obtain their fair share of happiness, nor grow up to the mental, moral, and aesthetic stature of which their nature is capable.[117]

It is therefore imperative that Mill's autonomous 'man' has the right to and also the necessary social environment to freely determine his desirable way of life: 'It is for him to find out what part of recorded experience [of the past] is properly applicable to his own circumstances and character'.[118]

Culture, seen as an obstacle to such full realisation of individuality and autonomy, naturally comes under criticism here: 'The despotism of culture is everywhere the standing hindrance to human advancement, being in unceasing antagonism to that disposition to aim at something better than customary, which is called, according to circumstances, the spirit of liberty, or that of progress or improvement'.[119] For Mill, the appalling conditions in that greater part of the world outside the sphere of civilisation is largely due to this despotism of customs that rule over justice and undermine the value of individual autonomy.[120] It is therefore certain that Mill's notion of diversity emanates from individual choices,

[114] Louis Dumont, *German Ideology: From France to Germany and Back* (Chicago, Illinois: University of Chicago Press, 1994), 3.

[115] For Mill, diversity added richness and variety to the human world, stimulated creativity, led to progress by creating a climate conducive to the emergence of curious minds, and encouraged competition between different thoughts and ways of life. See John Stuart Mill, 'On Liberty (1859)' in *Utilitarianism, Liberty, Representative Government* (London: Everyman's Library, 1964 [1910]), 129–131.

[116] See, generally, Mill, 'On Liberty', 116–126. [117] *Ibid.*, 125. [118] *Ibid.*, 116.

[119] *Ibid.*, 127–128. [120] *Ibid.*, 127.

not cultural peculiarities. As Parekh rightly asserts: 'Since Mill's theory of diversity was embedded in an individualist vision of life, he cherished individual but not cultural diversity, that is, diversity of views and life-styles within a shared individualist culture but not diversity of cultures including the nonindividualist'.[121] It represents, Parekh continues, 'a strange blend of moral egalitarianism and political and cultural inegalitarianism: equality of human beings but inequality of cultures, respect for persons but not their ways of life, rejection of racism but advocacy of cultural domination, equal concern for all as individuals but not as self-determining collective subjects'.[122]

Mill held that the boundaries of government must coincide with those of nationalities for the efficient functioning of a representative government, in that the free institutions necessary to the working of representative government cannot exist in a country made up of a people of multiple linguistic groups and without fellow feeling among them.[123] Nevertheless, he did not see the solution in the creation of German-style ethnic nations by excluding the ethnic 'other'. Instead, he advocated the assimilation of the lower and backward portion of the human race into the higher race: 'The united people, like a crossed breed of animals [. . .], inherits the special aptitudes and excellences of all its progenitors, protected by the admixture from being exaggerated into the neighbouring vices'.[124] And it is an originally inferior and more backward portion of the human race itself, Mill argues, that benefits the most from its absorption into a higher culture. Thus, for him, the interests of the Breton and the Basque of French Navarre or the Welshmen and the Scottish Highlander lie in their assimilation into the highly civilised and cultivated French and British nations, respectively.[125] Thus, when Lord Durham's Report on Canada insisted that the true interests of the 'backward' French Canadians lay in being subject to the 'vigorous rule of an English majority', Mill enthusiastically supported it, glorifying the report as an 'imperishable memorial of that nobleman's courage, patriotism and enlightened liberality' and urging 'all legitimate means' to assimilate the French Canadians.[126] Regarding cases where such smooth assimilation was difficult due to the equal strength of constituent groups in terms of

[121] Parekh, *Rethinking Multiculturalism*, 44. [122] *Ibid.*, 47.
[123] John Stuart Mill, 'Representative Government (1861)' in *Utilitarianism, Liberty, Representative Government*, 361, 362.
[124] *Ibid.*, 364. [125] *Ibid.*, 363.
[126] *Ibid.*, 377. See also Parekh, *Rethinking Multiculturalism*, 46.

demography and elements of power, Mill found the answer in forced-assimilationist measures under a despotic regime.[127]

While Mill prescribes the merger and absorption of one nation into another to secure the homogeneity that is crucial for representative governance, Lord Acton, in contrast, is of the view that '[t]he combination of different nations in one state is a necessary condition of civilised life'.[128] For Acton, this diversity not only results from liberty but also maintains liberty by, among other things, creating a barrier against the intrusion of government beyond the political sphere, supplying the greatest variety of intellectual resources and providing perpetual incentives to progress.[129] Multiculturalism helps the liberal evolutionary process too: 'Inferior races are raised by living in political union with races intellectually superior'.[130] Rejecting the German ideology of 'nation', Acton insists that diversity persists under the same state, for as an instrument of civilisation it will indicate greater advancement and progress than national unity.[131] Nevertheless, he refutes the validity of any claim the nations within the state have to individuals' political allegiance; instead, it is only the nationality formed by the state to which individuals owe political duties and thereby devolve corresponding political rights.[132] In his words:

> The difference between nationality and the State is exhibited in the nature of patriotic attachment. Our connection with race is merely natural or physical, whilst our duties to the political nation are ethical. One is a community of affections and instincts infinitely important and powerful in savage life, but pertaining more to the animal than to the civilised man; the other is an authority governing by laws, imposing obligations, and giving a moral sanction and character to the natural relations of society.[133]

Thus, Acton's proposed diversity is more about a strategic choice to facilitate stability within a multinational state, which is formed in a historical process. The pragmatic tone is expressed in the distinctiveness of the approach that he claims: it aims not at arbitrary change but at careful respect for the existing conditions of political life; it obeys the laws and results of history, not the aspirations of an ideal future.[134]

[127] Mill, 'Representative Government', 366.
[128] John Emerich Edward Dalberg-Acton (Lord Acton), *The History of Freedom and Other Essays*, ed. John Neville Figgis and Reginald Vere L. (London: Macmillan, 1907), 290.
[129] *Ibid.*, 289–290. [130] *Ibid.*, 290. [131] *Ibid.* [132] *Ibid.*, 293. [133] *Ibid.*, 292–293.
[134] *Ibid.*, 289–290.

Thus, in both the liberal approaches to ethnic communities within a state, ethnicity must either be submerged in the state-imposed national identity or silently remain at the periphery for other instrumental purposes such as socio-political stability. In neither case is ethnicity important in its own right – a point that stands in sharp contrast with the salience of ethnicity in ethnic nationalism. What is common between Mill and Acton is their vision of a nation-state that heads towards a progressive, scientific world civilisation – a universal spirit that consistently reflects back on the character of the state. This is such a high level of cultural progression that all other nations should be guided in this direction. The nineteenth-century concept of world civilisation was translated into the theory of modernisation in the early twentieth century and then into the notion of globalisation in the era that followed.[135] Nevertheless, in both approaches, culture – in ethnic (hence backward) terms, that is, low culture – continued to be labelled as a barrier to progression; culture was invoked to explain apparently irrational behaviour and self-destructive strategies directed towards the attributes of advanced societies such as development and democracy.[136]

Ethnicity, therefore, has two different roles in the two different streams of nationalist discourse. In the German Romantic model of nationalism, ethnicity expressed through culture and race defines the specific as well as the unique image of the 'self'. The uniqueness of the 'self' then excludes all others who do not share this specific uniqueness. This understanding of a nation, therefore, rests on exclusion for its existence and vitality. On the other hand, in the liberal model of nationalism, ethnicity is conceived of as an attribute of low culture – one that lags behind in the march towards universal spirit – and as an indicator of backwardness. Therefore, ethnicity has no significant role in the formation of high culture, that is, in the self-image of the liberal state. And the future of ethnicity lies in its assimilation into the high culture or its gradual disappearance.

However, both notions of exclusion and assimilation – the underlying philosophies of these two versions of nationalism – had recourse to another significant concept of the late nineteenth century: social Darwinism. Despite the absence of any causal relationship between social Darwinism and the nationalist programmes, the latter frequently relied on the former for a 'scientific' justification, which was badly needed to fit into the social environment of the time, marked by the loss of faith in abstract ideas such as reason and morality.

[135] Kuper, *Culture*, 10. [136] *Ibid.*

Social Darwinism: the scientific logic of assimilation and exclusion

Although Darwin's evolutionary theory appeared first in *The Origin of Species* in 1859, the discipline dealing with its implications in human social life, which came to be known as social Darwinism, owes more to other early European and American scholars' works than Darwin's own version of social Darwinism, published in *The Descent of Man* in 1871.[137] Not all social Darwinist propositions, despite being treated under this genre, were the same: while Darwin himself reaffirmed the Enlightenment faith in the unity of humankind by acknowledging that all human beings had a common origin and certain groups progressed better than others in the evolutionary process, some of his followers claimed that different races had different origins and thereby advanced the counter-Enlightenment.[138]

Thus, different approaches emerged within the rubric of social Darwinism to explain the human evolutionary process, which can be broadly divided into two main streams. The first one is the monogenic stream that conceives of human races as emanating from a common origin, which despite possessing different ranks in the civilisational process would ultimately survive as the superior whole through the evolutionary continuum. On the other hand, the polygenic stream perceives human races as fundamentally distinct species, whose hierarchical positions are fixed in the evolutionary process, in that the superior must be preserved from any intermixing with the inferior.[139] However, as

[137] For an account of the works by early social Darwinists, see Mike Hawkins, *Social Darwinism in European and American Thought, 1860–1945* (Cambridge: Cambridge University Press, 1997), 61–122. See also Peter Dickens, *Social Darwinism* (Buckingham: Open University Press, 2000), 7–25. Referring to Herbert Spencer as the pioneer of social Darwinism, Greene argues that the historical context of Darwin's work in particular and the interaction between science and society in general tend to emphasise the links between Darwin and Spencer consisting of a network of shared assumptions and viewpoints about God, Nature, society, and history, which rendered Spencer a 'Darwinian before Darwin'. See John C. Greene, *Science, Ideology and World View* (Berkeley: University of California Press, 1981), 134, 140. For a Spencerian account of social evolution, see, generally, John David Yeadon Peel (ed.), *Herbert Spencer on Social Evolution – selected writings* (Chicago: University of Chicago Press, 1972).

[138] Dickens, *Social Darwinism*, 16–17; Hawkins, *Social Darwinism in European and American Thought*, 14–15; Kuper, *Culture*, 11.

[139] Dickens notes that in the 1860s, there was intense debate in Britain between the monogenists, who argued that there was a common ancestor for all human races, and the polygenists, who held the view that different races are indeed separate species. See Dickens, *Social Darwinism*, 14.

a whole, the persuasive force of 'science' gave social Darwinism the opportunity to explain the viability of the merger of different social groups within one political unit or their strict segregation on the basis of biological features. This opportunity was readily grasped by the nineteenth-century protagonists of both liberal-assimilationist and ethnic-exclusionist nationalism to claim scientific justification for their nationalist projects already in operation. The following is a brief account of these two streams of social Darwinism that will demonstrate how they informed the assimilationist and exclusionist logics of nationalism and where 'ethnicity' stood in the process.

The early social Darwinists of the nineteenth century explained human evolution in a way that reinforced the Enlightenment philosophy, which aimed at progression towards a common universal spirit. In general, they relied on the common origin of all human races despite the difference in the level of the races' progress, resulting from the natural selection of some hereditary traits. In this connection, they argued that in the struggle for survival the lower races would ultimately submit to the higher races either through assimilation or complete elimination so as to advance the evolutionary process. For example, Charles Brace asserted that races were varieties of a common origin, not species, and argued that present racial differences were a consequence of the interaction between environmental conditions, natural selection, inheritance, and variations.[140] He argued further that this interaction would initially result in elimination of the weaker, but the stronger would survive and pass their advantageous traits to their descendants until a new type is formed.[141] In this way, Mike Hawkins notes, Brace's Darwinism envisaged a new and a more perfect race in the future through racial intermixture.[142] Likewise, German philosopher Friedrich Buchner claimed in *Man in the Past, Present and Future* (1869) that humans had evolved from an ape-like ancestor through the struggle for existence; the backward races who survived this struggle would only be able to stand up to civilised races by adopting the culture of the latter.[143]

Such monogenic explanations of human progress saw the fruition of the evolutionary process in the Enlightenment and in the liberal

[140] Charles Loring Brace, 'Letter to *The Washington Independent* (September 12, 1861)' in *The Life of Charles Loring Brace Chiefly Told in His Own Letters*, ed. Emma Brace Donaldson (London: Sampson, Low, Marston and Co., 1894), 390.

[141] *Ibid.*, 375. [142] Hawkins, *Social Darwinism in European and American Thought*, 64.

[143] Friedrich Carl Christian Ludwig Buchner, *Man in the Past, Present and Future*, trans. William Sweetland Dallas (London: Asher and Co., 1872), 151, 156, 157.

philosophy of individualism – the highest level of civilisation. This is clearly demonstrated in the writings of Herbert Spencer. He argued that although social and biological organisms exhibited many similarities – unlike natural bodies, which had a single centre of consciousness – in human societies there were as many such centres as there were individual members. Thus, he concluded that there was no separate corporate consciousness independent of and superior to that of the individuals who comprised the social organism.[144] In this sense, society was simply the aggregate of individuals.[145] However, the acts of the individual, which determine the functioning of the society, according to Spencer, are informed by the evolutionary state of the individual:

> The actions of individuals depend on the laws of their nature; and their actions cannot be understood until these laws are understood. These laws, however, when reduced to their simplest expressions, prove to be corollaries from the laws of body and mind in general. Hence it follows, that biology and psychology are indispensable as interpreters of sociology.[146]

In other words, the evaluation of human nature held the key to social evolution, and Hawkins asserts that 'this was the sense in which Spencer's approach can be described as individualistic'.[147]

However, this individualism in Spencer's theory of social Darwinism served a greater purpose; it indicated the direction of progress. In his vision of a perfect society, Spencer envisaged one in which individuals had the liberty to fully realise their potential; governments would not intervene in the process wherein the fittest survived and eventually self-fulfilment would extend right down to the individual; and free trade, a free press, and universal suffrage were to be welcomed towards these ends.[148] Therefore, from the methodological point of view, Spencer had to have recourse to the idea of primitive humans portrayed as immoral, irrational, and aggressive to mark the starting point of the evolutionary process, which then showed how individuality, freedom, and morality – all attributes of a liberal society – emerged during the process of evolution as indicators of higher civilisation.[149]

[144] Herbert Spencer, *The Study of Sociology*, 7th edn (London: Kegan Paul, 1878), 51. See also Peel, *Herbert Spencer on Social Evolution*, 97–101.
[145] Spencer, *The Study of Sociology*, 51.
[146] Herbert Spencer, *Education: Intellectual, Moral, and Physical* (London: Williams and Norgate, 1905), 44.
[147] Hawkins, *Social Darwinism in European and American Thought*, 90.
[148] Dickens, *Social Darwinism*, 23–24. [149] Hawkins, 98.

Another liberal account of social Darwinism is found in the writings of French scholar Clemence-Auguste Royer. She held the view that although human beings had evolved from ape-like ancestors, through evolution, modern men became more individualistic, which for Royer is a sign of progress.[150] However, although in the Preface to her translation of *The Origin*, Royer expressed her lifelong adherence to the Enlightenment ideals of reason, liberty, and progress, she asserted that human inequality is the quite natural result of the struggle for existence; thus, the notion of extreme equality was fallacious and dangerous.[151] Therefore, she claimed that the equality of liberty was the only form of equality consistent with evolution: it allowed each individual to realise his or her own worth, and competition weeded out the unsuccessful.[152] Royer thus concludes: 'The formula for the highest social prosperity is therefore equality of initial liberty for each member of the national group, and the free play of individual capabilities and initiatives'.[153] In other words, Royer reinforces the notion of *laissez-faire* – the essence of liberalism. And consequently, she notes, 'the higher races seem destined to supplant the lower races and to make them disappear or slowly assimilate them'.[154] Linda Clark notes that in the same way Royer supported inequality in international relations, wherein civilised nations were entitled to more rights than the inferior nations.[155] Asserting that only a few ethnic groups had the ability to progress socially, mentally, and intellectually, and most of them advanced only by imitating the superior, she claimed that the absorption of a very inferior race by a superior one was natural and justifiable.[156]

Put in this way, social Darwinism within this monogenic framework of evolution actually goes beyond being a mere parallel of natural evolutionary process. As Peter Dickens persuasively notes, the social Darwinist scholars' descriptions of social evolution included 'progress occurring through evolution, direction to social change, and teleology, an end which is built into social change itself'.[157] Given that this monogenic

150 Clemence-Auguste Royer, *Origine de l'homme et des sociétés* (Paris: Guillaumin, 1870), 169, 215–7, 270–2, cited in Hawkins, 126.

151 See Linda L. Clark, *Social Darwinism in France* (Tuscaloosa, Alabama: University of Alabama Press, 1984), 14. Clark notes that Royer attached forty-five pages of antireligious polemics and pronouncements on the work's philosophical and social significance. Darwin's reaction to this was that her Preface had actually injured his book (12).

152 See Hawkins, 129.

153 Royer, *Origine*, 585, cited in Hawkins, 129.

154 Royer, *Théorie de l'impôt, ou La dîme sociale*, 2 vols. (Paris: Guillaumin, 1862), 141, cited in Hawkins, 125.

155 Clark, *Social Darwinism in France*, 35.

156 *Ibid.*

157 Dickens, *Social Darwinism*, 31–44.

understanding of evolution was informed by the Enlightenment philosophies, it is not surprising that all these concepts – progress, direction, and teleology – are in fact related to the realisation of a civilised society in the Western European sense. Thus, 'progress' is exemplified by modernisation; a modern society is a fully developed one that relies on modern political, educational, and legal systems and also has a value system supportive of economic growth. In contrast, the traditional societies largely depend on clan-based or autocratic systems of government and pre-Newtonian science and technology.[158] Modernisation also exemplifies the concepts of 'direction' and 'end'.[159]

In other words, in the liberal account of evolution, progress is portrayed as cultural attributes which are not 'fixed' but instead are in constant fusion. This sharply contrasts with the inclination towards the fixity and specificity of the notion of culture as demonstrated by the Romantic scholarship. At the same time, culture is perceived as an efficient way of reaching the ultimate destination of progress. Talcott Parsons explains the dynamics in which culture dominates the social system in an integrated relationship between biological, psychological, social, and cultural systems: organisms supply energy to the psychological system, which is then transmitted from the psychological system to the social system, and again from the latter through people's roles to the cultural system of values. But ultimately the cultural system dominates the whole social system by supplying information in reverse order: down to the biological organism through the social system and the psychological system in the middle.[160] What is implied, therefore, is the vision of a culture through which 'progress' would be maintained and thereby the 'end' would be realised. Given that 'high culture', which would lead to liberal progress, comprises selected cultural traits in the social evolutionary process, everything else is arguably destined to submit to this high culture. This explains the logic of assimilation of the low cultural groups,

158 *Ibid.*, 32.

159 For example, Fukuyama famously claimed that liberal capitalism indicates 'the end of the history' by giving every individual a sense of recognition and worth, while simultaneously providing high levels of material well-being. See, generally, Francis Fukuyama, 'The End of History?', *The National Interest* 16 (1989): 3–18. Other writers, such as Kerr and Aron, saw the end in the convergence of different forms of industrialisations. See Dickens, 35–41.

160 Talcott Parsons, *Societies: Evolutionary and Comparative Perspectives* (New York: Prentice Hall, 1966), 26. For the background of Parsons' social science account of culture, see Kuper, *Culture*, 47–72. See also Dickens, *Social Darwinism*, 36.

such as ethnic minorities, into the state-sponsored high culture of a liberal nation.[161]

In contrast to this monogenic stream, the polygenic version of social Darwinism relied on the different origins of various human groups to explain the evolutionary process. In this polygenic understanding of human origin, 'race' was actually equated with 'species'. For example, Gustave Le Bon argues that natural selection formed the different races of mankind, which represent distinct species distinguished by physical characteristics and different mental traits and capabilities.[162] He classifies human races into four groups on a psychological basis – primitive races, inferior races, intermediate races, and superior races; he then concludes that the 'mental gap' which separates them is so obvious that confusion between these groups is absolutely impossible.[163] Likewise, Austrian sociologist Ludwig Gumplowicz explains races as units of evolution, which equate with species defined by durable hereditary characteristics.[164] Similarly, French scholar Georges Lapouge understands race as a discrete biological unit, species in the process of formation, which are created and maintained through the actions of heredity and selection rather than culture and language. Thus, for him, 'race' is a zoological concept.[165] In a similar vein, German zoologist Ernest

[161] While this understanding of social Darwinism advanced by monogenists offers a scientific justification for the French model of liberal-assimilationist nationalism, Clark notes that social Darwinism as a whole did not dominate the French world view of the late nineteenth and early twentieth centuries for a number of factors; among others, republicans needed their rhetoric to stress harmony rather than the struggle for life, and it was not advisable from a patriotic point of view to endorse the social Darwinist view of the survival of the fittest in relation to the loser of the Franco-Prussian War. Thus, social Darwinism was denounced by many French commentators as 'an alien German or Anglo-American doctrine'. See Clark, 180. However, it is to be noted that Clark's general comment on social Darwinism included works of French polygenists, such as Gobineau and Le Bon, which were not compatible with liberal nationalism. As a matter of fact, such writings received official reception in Nazi Germany.

[162] Gustave Le Bon, *L'Homme et les sociétés: leurs origins et leur histoire*, 2 vols. (Paris: Rothschild, 1881), 199–200, cited in Hawkins, *Social Darwinism in European and American Thought*, 187.

[163] Gustave Le Bon, *Les Lois psychologiques de l'evolution des peuples*, 6th edn (Paris: Felix Alcan, 1906), 26, cited in Raymond F. Betts, *Assimilation and Association in French Colonial Theory 1890–1914* (New York: Columbia University Press, 1961), 67.

[164] Ludwig Gumplowicz, *Outlines of Sociology*, trans. Frederick W. More (New York: Paine-Whitman, 1963), 161, 177, 217.

[165] Georges Vacher de Lapouge, *Les Selections sociales* (Paris: Fontemoing, 1896), 1, 11, 5, 8, cited in Hawkins, 192, 193. Lapouge argued that Europe was populated by three major racial groups: *Homo europaeus* – tall, pale-skinned, blue-eyed and long-skulled, *Homo alpinus* – smaller and darker complexioned than the Aryan, with black hair, brown eyes

Haeckel considers races as subspecies; for him, humanity can be divided into twelve species and thirty-six races on the basis of differences in speech and hair type.[166]

An obvious implication of this polygenic notion of human origin is the rigid hierarchy among races and the exclusion of the lower races from any intermixture with the superior races. Thus, Haeckel argues that racial inequalities are biologically determined, and it is not practicable to try to civilise the lower races because the necessary precondition of human culture – 'the perfecting of the brain' – has not taken place.[167] For him, the lower races are destined to perish, while the European races are certain to rule the world, and any interaction between the lower races and the higher one will only accelerate the extinction of the former.[168] Arthur de Gobineau too argues that races are permanent in their characteristics, which can only be affected by hybridisation.[169] Therefore, he is of the view that racial intermixture is an evil, which ultimately causes the destruction of civilisations – though paradoxically a creation of hybridisation.[170] Thus, despite the fact that Aryans are the creators of modern civilisation, he continues, they have become enfeebled through interbreeding with inferior races and are threatened with extinction.[171] Le Bon too believes that the individual always remains representative of his race, which itself is a permanent being; thus, crossings between an inferior and a superior race are disastrous, resulting in the elimination of the latter.[172] Likewise, Scottish anatomist

and brachycephalous heads, and the Mediterranean type – long-headed but possessing the darker skin and shorter stature of *alpinus*.

[166] Ernest Heinrich Philipp Haeckel, *The History of Creation, or the Development of the Earth and Its Inhabitants by the Action of Natural Causes*, rev. trans. E. Ray Lankester (London: King, 1876), 303–310.

[167] *Ibid.*, 363. [168] *Ibid.*, 325, 256.

[169] See Michael Biddis, 'Gobineau and the Origins of European Racism' in *Racism*, ed. Martin Bulmer and John Solomos (Oxford: Oxford University Press, 1999), 50.

[170] *Ibid.*, 51.

[171] Arthur de Gobineau, 'Essay' in *Gobineau: Selected Political Writings*, ed. Michael Biddiss (London: Jonathan Cape, 1970), 175. See also Leon Poliakov, 'Gobineau and His Contemporaries' in *Racism*, 53–55. However, Biddis sympathetically argues that the subsequent treatment of Gobineau's theory was far from what he intended, and he became the inventor of twentieth-century racism by accident. See Biddis, 'Gobineau and the Origins of European Racism', 52. In contrast, Poliakov claims that Gobineau was 'indeed the great herald of biological racism' and his disciples interpreted his works quite rightly. See Polikov, 'Gobineau and His Contemporaries', 56.

[172] Le Bon, *Les Lois psychologiques de l'evolution des peuples*, 12, cited in Raymond Betts, *Assimilation and Association in French Colonial Theory, 1890–1914* (New York: Columbia University Press, 1961), 67. See also Le Bon, *L'Homme et les sociétés*, 199–200, cited in Hawkins, 187.

Robert Knox finds the corruption and collapse of civilisations to be rooted in racial interbreeding.[173]

For Georges Lapouge, the racial differences are inherent as well as permanent; therefore, 'any notion of the unification and integration of races was a mere pipedream, contrary to the elementary laws of biology'.[174] Lapouge's vision of an ideal society is one in which the superior race is not only in complete control but also in strict segregation from the remainder of the population, for '[t]he system of closed, specialised castes, artificial sub-species, is the last-word in evolution'.[175] While dealing with the Poles within Prussia, therefore, assimilation was no longer the solution; instead, it was claimed that for the Germans who wanted to preserve the German type against inferior races, the first rule would be 'No racial mixing with aliens'.[176] Thus, the polygenists conceive of races as being related in a fixed hierarchy, on the one hand, and thereby propose the justification for the exclusion of the lower races from any racial intermixture, on the other. In other words, they perceive evolution 'as preservation rather than change'.[177]

Polygenists further challenged the Enlightenment philosophy by perceiving the individual in biological fixity. For Lapouge, heredity permanently determines not only the physical appearance but also the character of an individual, for traits such as independence and initiative, according to him, can only be acquired through inheritance.[178] Therefore, Lapouge finds the individual constrained by the iron laws of nature: 'The blood that he carries in his veins from birth he keeps all his life. The individual is crushed by his race, he is nothing. The race, the nation, are everything'.[179] Like German theorist Otto Ammon and Italian criminologist Cesare Lombroso, Lapouge seeks to 'quantify physical racial differences and to correlate these with psychological

173 Susan Collinson, 'Robert Knox's Anatomy of Race', *History Today* 40 (1990), 44–49.

174 Georges Vacher de Lapouge, *L'Aryen: Son Rôle Social* (Paris: Fontemoing, 1899), 369, cited in Hawkins, 192.

175 Georges Vacher de Lapouge, *Les Selections sociales* (Paris: Fontemoing, 1896), 484, cited in Hawkins, 196–197.

176 Mark Mazower, *Hitler's Empire – Nazi Rule in Occupied Europe* (London: Penguin Books, 2009 [2008]), 22.

177 Hawkins, 191. Lapouge, for example, adopted an essentialist position on race, contrary to the notion of the ubiquity of change. For him, transformation was possible, but only as corruption and decadence. See Hawkins, 200.

178 Lapouge, *L'Aryen*, 351, cited in Hawkins, 192.

179 Lapouge, *L'Aryen*, 511, cited in Hawkins, 192.

traits'.[180] Thus, relying on biological features for an explanation of human behaviour (i.e., having premised culture upon race), Lapouge continues that modern nation-states, being amalgamations of different races, are artificial entities and hence potential battlegrounds of 'racial conflicts'.[181] In contrast to the liberal understanding of the nation-state, he asserts that 'nations are as real as races, they are biological entities', and therefore the assimilationist idea of turning a foreigner into a national, i.e., naturalisation, is for him 'biological nonsense'.[182]

Having provided the scientific rationale for assimilation and exclusion, social Darwinism thus informs both versions of nineteenth-century nationalism. In other words, as a principle, social Darwinism helped the understanding of the 'self' and the 'other' through an evolutionary paradigm and in the process indicated their future. Social Darwinism provided not only the justification for thinking about society in terms of ethnicity, race, or nation but also a blueprint for social action. In both ways, it set the intellectual scene for colonialism and Nazism, on the one hand, and the evisceration of ethnicity in the form of liberalism, on the other.

Ethnicity, traditions, and nineteenth-century international law

The nineteenth-century nationalist programmes including their elements of evolutionary science were reflected in the construction of international law along the liberal and conservative streams as a way of dealing with the non-European 'other'. As British philosopher Henry Sidgwick noted, in the theory of progress the 'otherness' of the non-Europeans equated to backwardness in the evolutionary process.[183]

[180] See Hawkins, 198, 199. Italian criminologist Lombroso traced the origin of criminals in the evolutionary continuum. He held the view that the interaction of the struggle of survival and the laws of heredity resulted in uneven evolutionary progress; for some, such as born criminals, development was fixed at the level of savages or even animals. See Cesare Lombroso, opening address to the Sixth Congress of Criminal Anthropology, Turin, April 1906, cited in M. Parmelee, 'Introduction to the English Edition' in *Crime: Its Causes and Remedies*, Cesare Lombroso, trans. H. P. Horton (Boston, Massachusetts: Little, Brown, 1911), xxx. It is no accident that psychology as a discipline was established only in the late nineteenth century.

[181] Hawkins, 199. Given that all other psychological aspects of ethnicity outside the biological features are, according to Lapouge, again dependent on biology, an ethno actually equates to race. In this sense racial conflicts here mean what we understand as ethnic conflicts.

[182] Lapouge, *Les Selections*, 225, cited in Hawkins, 199.

[183] Henry Sidgwick, *Philosophy: Its Scope and Relations. An Introductory Course Lectures* (London: Theommes, 1998 [1902]), 174–211.

The categorisation of nations on the basis of their rank in the scale of progress clearly appeared in the writings of Scottish jurist James Lorimer, who asserted in 1883 that '[a]s a political phenomenon, humanity, in its present condition, divides itself into three concentric zones or spheres – that of civilised humanity, that of barbarous humanity, and that of savage humanity'.[184] He hails the emergence of ethnology as a new field of study in the opening statement of his work: 'No modern contribution to science seems destined to influence international politics and jurisprudence to so great an extent as that which is known as ethnology, or the science of races'.[185] However, far from being homogeneous, international lawyers soon followed the parallel streams of liberal and conservative understandings of the role of ethnicity in the construction of the national self-image; hence, there appeared contrasting images of state and sovereignty – the foundational notions of nineteenth-century international law.

Liberal international lawyers of the nineteenth century related their nationalism to a wider vision of European civilisation, sometimes within a cosmopolitan framework.[186] For Pasquale Fiore, law was a spontaneous outgrowth of society rather than an effect of sovereign decision. At the same time, he firmly believed that given the unity of the human species, the law governing humanity must also be universal. Thus, to reconcile the undeniable and constant experience of cultural difference with the idea of a single universal law, Fiore, like most other international lawyers of his time, adopted the evolutionary theory of progress in that only fully civilised states could be members of the *magna civitas*, the juridical community.[187] To quote him: 'This community is already a product of civilisation. To the extent that it expands to savage countries, it gives rise to needs and interests that unite the civilised nations with barbaric or other peoples less advanced in the path of progress'.[188] It was the possession of 'a certain level of culture', according to Fiore, which determined full membership in the international legal community. However, his liberal, assimilationist thrust was demonstrated when he noted that

[184] James Lorimer, *The Institutes of the Law of Nations: A Treatise of the Jural Relations of Separate Political Communities* (Edinburgh: Blackwood, 1883), 101.

[185] *Ibid.*, 93.

[186] See Martti Koskenniemi, *Gentle Civilizer of Nations: The Rise and Fall of International Law 1870–1960* (Cambridge: Cambridge University Press, 2002), 63.

[187] Pasquale Fiore, *Le droit international codifié et sa sanction juridique* (Paris: Predone, 1890), 74, cited in Koskenniemi, *The Gentle Civilizer of Nations*, 55–56.

[188] Fiore, 74, 82, quoted in Koskenniemi, 56.

despite being the attribute of European societies, such culture was slowly spreading through commerce and other contacts.[189]

The backwardness of the non-European 'other' was substantiated by defining the concepts of the state and sovereignty as attributes of 'civilisation' and, as endorsed by evolutionary 'progress', by asserting that Europeans had the monopoly of claim to the notion of civilisation. Hence, international law, being the law among states (read civilised states), was perceived as the domain of European nations. For instance, William Hall claimed that international law was a product of the special civilisation of modern Europe, and therefore only European states could be presumed to be subject to it as 'inheritors' of that civilisation.[190] Thus, according to him, international law consisted of 'certain rules of conduct which modern civilised states regard[ed] as being binding on them in their relations with one another with a force comparable in nature and degree to that binding the conscientious person to obey the laws of his country, and which they also regard[ed] as being enforceable by appropriate means in case of infringement'.[191] This legal conscience is an indication of civilisation, which non-Europeans essentially lack. To be a part of international law, then, Hall argued, they may only progress with the acquiescence of the Europeans.[192]

Thomas Lawrence, noting that only 'sovereign' states were the subjects of international law, qualified the notion of sovereignty in that before a sovereign state could become a subject of international law it must possess a certain degree of civilisation.[193] The necessary degree of civilisation for this purpose was never ascertained; however, Lawrence was assured that there were nations who would never be able to exhibit this mark of civilisation: 'It would, for instance, be absurd to expect the king of Dahomey to establish a Prize Court, or to require the dwarfs of the central African forest to receive a permanent diplomatic mission'.[194] Lawrence, thus, defined international law 'as the rules which determine the conduct of the general body of civilised states in their dealings with one another'.[195] For him, 'civilisation not only provides men with many interests in common, but it also tends to remove man's suspicion of his

[189] Fiore, 75, 81–82, cited in Koskenniemi, 56.
[190] William E. Hall, *A Treatise on International Law*, 2nd edn (Oxford: Clarendon Press, 1884 [1880]), 40.
[191] *Ibid.*, 1. [192] *Ibid.*
[193] Thomas J. Lawrence, *The Principles of International Law* (London: Macmillan and Co., 1895), 58.
[194] *Ibid.*, 58. [195] *Ibid.*, 1.

brother man', among countless other advantages, and thereby civilisation tends 'to knit states together in a social bond somewhat analogous to the bond between the individual man and his fellows'.[196]

Henry Wheaton advanced Lawrence's proposition that sovereignty was an attribute of civilisation by emphasising recognition from civilised nations as a mode for the uncivilised to acquire sovereignty. For him, the terms 'state' and 'sovereign' are synonyms, but the nature of sovereignty – internal or external – determines the fate of the state in international relations. While the internal sovereignty of a state may be acquired by the fact of its mere existence, the external sovereignty of any state requires recognition by other states in order to render it perfect and complete.[197] In his words:

> [I]f [a new State] desires to enter into that great society of nations, all the members of which recognise rights to which they are mutually entitled, and duties which they may be called upon reciprocally to fulfill, such recognition becomes essentially necessary to the complete participation of the new State in all the advantages of this society.[198]

Therefore, unless such recognition is granted, the uncivilised remains 'uncivilised' and does not exist as a member of the international society, though it can well exist as a sovereign so far as its internal affairs are concerned. Classifying sovereignty as internal and external, Wheaton thus reinforces the image of a world composed of a family of civilised nations as well as a group of states that lack the necessary external sovereignty to be a part of the civilised family. In this complex setup, the latter exists as a state in relation to its internal affairs but, at the same time, does not exist in relation to international law in the absence of recognition from the civilised states.[199]

Lawrence offered a rationale behind such privileges for civilised nations when he asserted that operating areas of the law of nations and civilisation are supposed to coincide.[200] Presenting his claim that international law is what the civilised nations practice among themselves in

[196] *Ibid.*, 3.

[197] Henry Wheaton, *Elements of International Law*, 8th edn (Boston, Massachusetts: Little, Brown, and Company, 1866), 28.

[198] *Ibid.*

[199] Wheaton found the supremacy of the international law of Christian, civilised nations in the fact that the Mohammedan and Pagan nations of Asia and Africa, in their interaction with the Europeans, renounced their peculiar international usages and adopted those of Christendom (18).

[200] Lawrence, *The Principles*, 59.

this way, he then asserts that for a new state to be admitted to this common sphere of international law, as well as civilisation, it needs to obtain a kind of 'international testimonial of good conduct and respectability', which the European nations have developed over centuries.[201] To quote him:

> Modern international law grew up among them. There never was a time when they were outside its pale. Their influence helped to mould it. Many of them existed before the great majority of its rules came into being. There was no need for them to be formally received among its subjects.[202]

But whenever other nations desire to join this European group, they must have the group's approval. This fully justified the notion that the European nations possess the right to decide on the membership of the civilised family of nations.

John Westlake had a more pragmatic approach, one that reconciled his perception of international law as rules applicable among the members of international society with the actual interactions between European–American states and certain Asian powers such as Japan and China that took place against the backdrop of international legal norms. He advanced the idea that international society exercised the right to admit non-European nations to only 'parts of its international law without necessarily admitting them to the whole of it'.[203] Accordingly, many of the relations between them, Westlake notes, were conducted on the footing of 'ordinary' international law, but European–American states enjoyed in the 'other' a consular jurisdiction that replaced the rules of jurisdiction belonging to the ordinary international law.[204] He deviated from the general notion of equality of nations as advanced by naturalist international lawyers in his conviction that the equality of states within a legal framework would depend on the presence of civilised institutions, such as a Western-style government, in those states. 'Can the natives furnish such a government, or can it be looked for from the Europeans alone? In the answer to that question lies, for international law, the difference between civilisation and the want of it'.[205] Thus, he concluded that the general rules of international law applied in their fullness only to those states which were sovereign and independent constitutionally as well as internationally, such as France and the UK, and also to those

[201] *Ibid.*, 59. [202] *Ibid.*, 84.
[203] John Westlake, *Chapters on the Principles of International Law* (Cambridge: Cambridge University Press, 1894), 82.
[204] *Ibid.* [205] *Ibid.*, 141.

which other states accepted in their dealings as being sovereign and independent, a privilege that the states of the Holy Roman Empire formerly enjoyed despite their weak constitutional tie. According to Westlake, these were the only states that were entitled to normative equality; the international law which they recognised among themselves was a body of general rules and not of particular solutions.[206] As we shall see in the following chapter, Westlake relied on this logic of a hierarchical system of international law to justify colonial projects.

Thus, what appeared from the liberal doctrines of international law was a liberal universalist vision of the world but essentially within the social Darwinist framework of 'progress', which broke with the Enlightenment ideology of 'equality'. The non-European 'other', therefore, always remained at a distance from, but set to follow, European nations. In other words, the liberal notion of evolutionary 'progress' would 'civilise' the non-European communities in the light of European civilisation, and therefore international law, being the law of civilised nations, would accommodate the 'other' as soon as they reached a level of spirituality comparable to Europeans, as Swiss jurist Alphonse Rivier noted.[207]

The liberal universalist version of international law was fundamentally different from the Romantic version, which largely relied on the cultural peculiarity (in the conservative ethnic sense) of the state. Although Bluntschli's liberalism dreamed of a universal unity and spirit, which for him was an inner necessity of a nation, and envisaged a universal empire as the ideal of human progress, he thought of the nation as essentially within the purview of the state.[208] Such a salient image of the state in nineteenth-century German jurisprudence had its root in Hegelian thought, which, as we have seen earlier, sought refuge in the concept of the state to reconcile Kantian cosmopolitanism with Romanticism.[209] Jacques Dampierre, for example, claimed that the

[206] *Ibid.*, 87–89.

[207] Alphonse Rivier, *Lehrbuch des Völkerrechts* (Stuttgart: Enke, 1889), 5, quoted in Koskenniemi, *The Gentle Civilizer of Nations*, 135.

[208] See, generally, Johann Kaspar Bluntschli, *The Theory of the State* (Kitchener, Ontario: Batoche Books, 2000 [1885]), 30–38, 228.

[209] Jacques Marquis de Dampierre, *German Imperialism and International Law – Based Upon German Authorities and the Archives of the French Government* (New York: Charles Scribner's Sons, 1917), 23. Publicists of our time, such as Koskenniemi and Carty, also hold the same view. See Anthony Carty, *The Decay of International Law? A Reappraisal of the Limits of Legal Imaginations in International Affairs* (Manchester: Manchester University Press, 1986), 71–86; Koskenniemi, *Gentle Civilizer of Nations*, 268.

idolatry of the state in the sphere of politics and sociology, as well as the most extreme forms of nationalism and utilitarian dogmatism, was contained in the philosophic teachings of Hegel – ideas that were reflected in the conception of the historic role of the German race drastically advanced by the pan-Germanists of the late nineteenth and early twentieth centuries.[210]

However, while Hegel solemnised the state as a reservoir of the absolute spirit in its temporal form, it is the German Historical School that not only constructed German nationalism as culturally specific to counter the force of universalism but also instated 'life' into the state so that it would accommodate such an idea of the nation. Under the influence of the Historical School, Bluntschli's criticism of Hegel was that although Hegel, in his theory of law, recognised the historical formation of states more than the earlier theorists of natural law, he emphasised the moral significance of the state and, 'in opposition to the wretched idea that it was only a necessary evil, praised it as the highest and noblest realisation of the idea of right'. His notion of

> State is however only a logical abstraction, not a living organism, a mere logical notion, not a person. Hegel, by founding the State and law merely upon will, overlooks the fact that in the State not merely is the collective human will operative, but all the powers of human spirit and feeling together.[211]

The Historical School, as Anthony Carty notes, rejected the idea that a standard of conduct could be imposed from without; instead, it had to develop organically from within the national culture.[212] One of the founding historians of the school, von Savigny, stressed in particular that 'the positive law lived in the common consciousness of the people', which denoted a real, supra-individual historical process.[213] He declared the state to be 'the bodily form of the spiritual community of the nation or the organic manifestation of the nation'.[214] Yet, given von Savigny's proposition that civilised nations developed legal rules to regulate their relations with each other and occasionally with other nations, the idea of international law gained relevance despite his perception that law is an expression of community spirit and that there is no universal community.[215]

[210] Dampierre, *German Imperialism and International Law*, 23.
[211] Bluntschli, *The Theory of the State*, 69.
[212] Carty, *The Decay of International Law?* 33. [213] See Koskenniemi, 43.
[214] See Bluntschli, 68.
[215] Koskenniemi, 44. Related to von Savigny's idea of law was that of von Kaltenborn, who argued that a relative human freedom has its own inner ground in human consciousness

Von Savigny had a profound influence on his young Swiss pupil, Johann Bluntschli. Later in his autobiography, Bluntschli wrote that upon the recommendation of his professor of Roman law, at the Political Institute of Zurich, who was a former student of von Savigny – Professor Keller – he went to the University of Berlin to study under von Savigny.[216] It is therefore no surprise that in his chief work, *The Theory of the State*,[217] Bluntschli wholeheartedly declared that the 'State is in no way a lifeless instrument, a dead machine: it is a living and therefore organised being'.[218] And he did not hesitate to give full credit to the German Historical School for recognising the organic nature of the nation and the state; this was an idea that according to Bluntschli refuted both the mathematical and mechanical views of the state and the atomistic way of treating it, which forgets the whole in the individuals.[219] Bluntschli himself claimed that the French contractualist notion of the state – which had enjoyed great popularity since the time of Rousseau, gained impetus during the years of the revolution, and finally came to claim universal validity by depicting each individual as an 'equal' constituent of the state – is not supported by a single incidence in history. To take his words:

> The evidence of history is [...] absolutely opposed to this theory. Even at the time when the doctrine of social contract was most widely accepted and exercised most influence, it was contradicted by manifest facts. The people was broken up into 'free and equal citizens', but even in the primary assemblies the minorities did not contract with the majorities, who carried out their will as if it had a superiority and validity of its own. [...] People adopted a fiction of contract, and deceived themselves and others by speaking of the consent of individuals, where the majority, as

and will; this consciousness is found in the common will of the *Volk*, and not in the individual man; that would lead to arbitrariness. See Carl von Kaltenborn, *Kritik des Völkerrechts* (1847), 231–234, cited in Carty, 32.

216 During his stay in Berlin, Bluntschli often visited von Savigny's house and worked in his private library. In his first book published in 1829, he thanked his master for materials found in his private library. See Herbert Baxter Adams, *Bluntschli's Life-Work* (Baltimore, Maryland: Privately printed, 1884), 6.

217 It took final shape in 1875 in three volumes. Adams claimed that this was Bluntschli's chief work, representing not only the union of the historical and philosophical methods but also the rich fruit of the author's political experience. Another prominent nineteenth-century German international lawyer, Hohzendorff, asserted that since Montesquieu no work had appeared in the field of public law which could be compared with this treatise of Bluntschli in 'readability, suggestive power, ideal worth, practical sense, political insight, and historical breadth of view'. See Adams, *Bluntschli's Life-Work*, 11–12.

218 Bluntschli, *The Theory of the State*, 24. 219 *Ibid.*, 25.

organ of the whole, was exercising an authority which was often an intolerable tyranny.[220]

With the perception of the state as a unitary whole, it was obvious that Bluntschli would instate sovereignty in the state, not in individuals. The German understanding of 'sovereignty', as Bluntschli denoted, meant both the power and the dignity of the state. As the highest authority in, and also the necessary condition of, a state, 'sovereignty' implied that international law would not restrict a state any more than its own constitution; the state would enjoy 'supreme public dignity', and most importantly, sovereignty was not a mere sum of particular rights but a general and common right, understood as a 'central concept' above everything else.[221] His criticism of the French notion of 'sovereignty' of individual citizens or of reason and justice, therefore, relied on the view that political supremacy could only be ascribed to a political entity and must then be exercised on the basis of reason and justice. Therefore, it is the state that functions as a person in possessing sovereignty, expressed in its independence, honour, power, supreme authority, and unity.[222]

However, despite being immensely influenced by the Historical School, Bluntschli criticised it for its overt inclination to perceive the state as merely national and to overlook, or even dispute, the state's

220 *Ibid.*, 241. Bluntschli, however, carefully avoided any endorsement of the absolutist notion of state, which regarded states as being essentially the sphere of power of a superior and wherein 'the subjects were looked on as mere mass, to be managed and governed from above, but with no claims to govern themselves, or to share the government, or to control the rules of their conduct' (65–66).

221 *Ibid.*, 389.

222 *Ibid.*, 391–393. Such a view was later refuted by Westlake, who despite being deeply influenced by the Historical School ultimately moved to the conviction that states were merely the immediate members of international society, and its ultimate members were men within states. Thus, it was among men that international society existed; hence, the rights and duties of states were only those of the men who composed them. See Westlake, *Chapters*, 78. Having defined international law as the body of rules prevailing between states, Westlake argued that states form a society, in which members observe certain rules with more or less regularity, and mutually compel the observance of such rules, by force if necessary (1–2). And then it followed: 'The consent of international society to the rules prevailing in it is the consent of the men who are the ultimate members of that society' (78). Claiming that international society comprised all European states and American states in that the latter share a common civilisation with the former, Westlake held the view that in order to invoke any rule of international society against a state, it was not necessary to show that the state in question had assented to the rule either diplomatically or by having acted on it. Rather, it would suffice to show that 'the general *consensus* of opinion within the limits of European civilisation [was] in favour of the rule' (78–102).

human significance.[223] Too much involvement of the Historical School with the ancient past, Bluntschli's criticism continued, made it harder to understand and improve the contemporary public conditions but, at the same time, conceived the state as 'fast bound to traditional authority and hereditary prejudices'.[224] As a matter of fact, Bluntschli was writing at a time when the traditional conflict between the ideological and the Historical School in Germany had already come to an end; he himself wrote that since 1840, concerned groups realised that 'the experiences and phenomena of history must be illuminated with the light of ideas, and that speculation is childish if it does not consider the real conditions of the nation's life'.[225]

Within this reconciliatory framework of his time, Bluntschli endeavoured to strike a pragmatic balance between history and ideology in a number of ways. On the one hand, he sincerely believed in individual liberty but, on the other, claimed that in the face of the supreme right of a people to that people's existence and development, all rights of its individual members and/or of its princes would fall into insignificance.[226] Despite his firm conviction that it would be a great advantage to unity if the nation was based on a distinct nationality, he nonetheless accepted the idea of a multinational state in that humanity was for him a more important foundation of a nation than its national and cultural peculiarities.[227] Bluntschli was an active supporter of Bismarck's unification policy; he found it necessary to integrate Schleswig-Holstein into the German Confederation in 1863 on the basis of the nationalist idea even if the population opposed it, and in this regard he justified recourse to war to defend German honour.[228] Nevertheless, in *The Theory of the State* he acknowledged that a national state need not include an entire people; it must only accommodate

223 Bluntschli, *The Theory of the State*, 68. 224 *Ibid.*

225 *Ibid.*, 70. Bluntschli was not the only liberal international lawyer who set for himself the task of reconciliation. Koskenniemi notes that the presence of nationalism was so powerful in the political reality of the time that any legal doctrine with cultural underpinnings could hardly ignore it. See Koskenniemi, 63.

226 See Bluntschli, 93. Koskenniemi claims that Bluntschli certainly never imagined that there was any conflict between his nationalism and individual rights, in that each was defined in terms of the other; the defense of individual liberty went hand in hand with his moderate conception of nationalism. See Koskenniemi, 64.

227 Bluntschli, 94. For him, the true end of the state is the development of the national capacities, the perfecting of the national life, and, finally, its completion, provided that the process of moral and political development shall not be opposed to humanity (262).

228 See Koskenniemi, 64.

a sufficiently large and strong portion of it to assert its character and spirit effectively in the state. But at the same time, he projected the limits of a national state as wide and shifting as the language of its people and thereby opened up possibilities for further adjustment of the territorial domain of state power.[229]

Being a moderate-liberal politician, Buntschli demonstrated his reconciliatory approach most profoundly while dealing with social Darwinist notions of human evolution. He was aware, and to some extent convinced, of the monogenic claim of a common human origin – the relationship between pre-historic men and ape-like animals. But then, his argument took a different course by asserting that although the history of man's creation might go back to far earlier times, it would be inappropriate to extend the history of civilisation as far back. It was only with the appearance of a higher race – whites, the children of light – and the ensuing perfection of mankind that universal history began.[230] Carefully relying on the failure of science to discover the mysterious origin of differences among races, he comfortably lived with the 'fact' that since the beginning of the history of human development, the major races demonstrated differences in mental capacity and also in build and colour, as 'white, black, yellow, and perhaps, red', a significant diversity that remained essentially the same despite racial intermixing and some loss of racial purity.[231]

Bluntschli disagreed with many of his contemporary thinkers who in theory denied the mental inequality of different races, claiming that there was scarcely anyone who did not constantly recognise such differences in practical life.[232] Having agreed that a belief in the unity of the family of men was essential to higher religious sense and sympathising with the fact that the civilised states assumed the unity of mankind and recognised a common human nature even in lower races and tribes, Bluntschli nevertheless asserted that 'the diversity of races is of the highest importance for the State and for public law, for in the State men appear in an order, and order cannot be imagined without difference'.[233]

However, while accepting this diversity of races as a natural phenomenon, Bluntschli saw nations, which often accommodated these races in the process of racial separation as well as fusion, as products of human history. Unlike many polygenists of his time, he believed that the mixing of races was not the real reason for the fall of a state and many states had in fact become great and powerful despite such mixing.[234] Consequently,

229 Buntschli, 94. 230 *Ibid.*, 55. 231 *Ibid.*, 74. 232 *Ibid.*, 75. 233 *Ibid.*, 74.
234 See *ibid.*, 228.

nations being the creation of historical process, their distinctiveness, according to him, gradually shifted from their physical appearance to their spirit, character, language, and law – in short, to their culture.[235] He thus concluded: 'The whole history of the world bears witness to the different endowment of races, and even to the unequal capacity of the nations which have grown out of them'.[236] One direct implication of this is the claim of a hierarchical world order wherein the Aryan nations of Europe would politically lead the 'other' and perfect the organisation of mankind by their ideas and institutions.[237]

Whereas Bluntschli consistently struck a balance between the Romantic and the liberal notions of the German self-image in the form of the state, his contemporary jurists decidedly allied themselves with the conservatives. Dampierre summed up the basic philosophy behind their construction of the German 'self': '[T]he individual rises in the scale of being in proportion to the degree of his voluntary submission to the community'; the tendencies of all communities, and therefore all individuals, ought to be directed to the goal of the supreme community – the state. And since the Germanic race excels beyond all other races in its faculty of conscious subordination to a community of discipline and organisation, 'it has been reserved for the Germanic race to realise the supreme ideal of collective human organisation'.[238] In this way, the idea of racial hierarchy took refuge in the German notion of the state that was entrusted with not only absolute sovereignty but also the life and the spirit of the whole people. Such a formulation of the 'self' could only be the best breeding ground for the social Darwinist justification for struggle on a world scale. Rudolf Jhering, breaking with the Historical School, thus claimed that struggle, through which a nation

[235] *Ibid.*, 77. [236] *Ibid.*, 75. [237] *Ibid.*, 77.

[238] Dampierre, *German Imperialism and International Law*, 23. However, the proposition advanced by Dampierre and other French and British scholars, such as Le Fur, Brierly, and Lauterpacht, that absolute doctrines of sovereignty and theories of the will of the state and of the right of the war were responsible for Germany having launched major wars has been challenged by Carty. According to him, the substantive and authoritative German international law doctrine both before and after the war took it for granted that wars of conquest, therefore of aggression, were illegal – a fact which significant English and French international law doctrine did not realise; hence they erroneously assumed that German international law doctrine was part of the German intellectual consensus urging Germany to wage wars of conquest. See, generally, Anthony Carty, 'The Evolution of International Legal Scholarship in Germany during the Kaiserreich and the Weimarer Republic (1871–1933)', *German Yearbook of International Law* 50 (2007), 29–90.

creates self-awareness and a sense of attachment to its rights, was the core of law.[239]

Such a perception of the state and its position in international relations was more evident in the writing of Adolf Lasson. For him, among states there could be no law; since law is only the fruit of the power of the unquestioned superior, a state that recognises any law emanating from another state would thereby confess its weakness. It thus followed: 'Between States, there is only one force of right, the right of the strongest. It is perfectly reasonable that wars should arise between States'.[240] It is, therefore, no surprise that while tracing the root of German imperialism and its brutality to the German philosophy of the nation-state and racial superiority, Dampierre, in his book written in the midst of the Great War, quoted paragraph after paragraph from the writings of Lasson without much analysis.[241] One such quotation read: 'The State which is only organised for peace is not a true State; the State only reveals its whole significance by its preparations for war. [. . .] Law is the friend of the weak'.[242] Lasson further claimed that being the highest expression of the culture of its race, the national state could only come into being by means of the violent destruction of other states.[243]

While writing about international law in the politico-legal environment of late-nineteenth-century Germany, Heinrich von Treitschke maintained that '[t]he existence of international law is precarious; it is a *lex imperfecta*, because there is no higher power to control States as a whole. All depends on the sense of reciprocity between nations, and here, in default [. . .] of a supreme authority, learning and public opinion may play a great part'.[244] Thus, in his perception, international law was motivated primarily by states' self-interest in maintaining a European balance of power, which, as he envisaged, ought to be ultimately directed towards curbing the monopoly of power of any particular state and not towards bringing equality among nations.[245] For him, the preservation of sovereignty amid the general community of states was the highest duty of

239 See Koskenniemi, 36–37. However, Koskenniemi notes that perhaps Jhering was dimly aware of the social Darwinist tone of his argument.

240 Adolf Lasson, *Das Kulturideal und der Krieg* (1868), quoted in Dampierre, 51.

241 See Dampierre, 50–53.

242 Lasson, *Das Kulturideal und der Krieg*, 29, quoted in Dampierre, 52.

243 Lasson, 66, quoted in Dampierre, 52.

244 See Adolf Hausrath (com. and trans.), *Treitschke: His Doctrine of German Destiny and of International Relations Together with a Study of His Life and Work* (New York: G. P. Putnam and Sons, 1914), 162.

245 *Ibid.*, 163.

the state; therefore, a sphere of international law must never encroach upon state sovereignty.[246] Treitschke undoubtedly perceived 'sovereignty' in the conservative German sense of 'honour' when he asserted that '[t]o lay a finger on the honour of a State is to contest its existence'.[247] Therefore, he had no difficulty in prescribing war to maintain national prestige; also, according to him, war was just and moral, unlike the ideal of eternal peace.[248]

Treitschke's foundational notion of international law was well reflected in his assessment of international treaty obligations: all the limitations which states impose on themselves in treaties are merely voluntary; no state can pledge itself to the unlimited observance of treaties, for that would limit its sovereign power and relinquish the 'ego' of its sovereignty.[249] To a great extent, this understanding of international law echoed the auto-limitation theory of international law advanced by another nineteenth-century German international lawyer, George Jellinek. Holding the same belief that the sovereign will of a state could not be subjected to any restriction not imposed by that state itself, Jellinek contended that international law was nothing more than the results of voluntary acts of self-obligation committed by states, and when the observance of a rule conflicts with state interests, the self-imposed obligation disappears.[250]

Treitschke's philosophy of the state and sovereignty lived on, indeed in a more extreme form, in the writings of his disciples. Friedrich von Bernhardi, one such disciple, conceived of war from the standpoint of civilisation and thus claimed that war was not only a necessary element of national life but also an indispensable aspect of its culture. Since a truly civilised nation finds the highest expression of strength and vitality in its culture, and the German people were destined to be the greatest civilised people known to history, he argued that war was an essential element for the existence of Germany as a great race.[251] In such struggles for existence, the extinction of the weaker was essentially the verdict of nature.[252] Carl Peters was also among Treitschke's disciples and, as we shall see in the following chapter, emerged as one of the most prominent figures in

246 *Ibid.*, 165–166. 247 *Ibid.*, 166. 248 *Ibid.*, 169. 249 *Ibid.*, 166–167.

250 Lawrence Preuss, 'National Socialist Conceptions of International Law', *The American Political Science Review* 29, no. 4 (1935), 599.

251 See, generally, General Friedrich von Bernhardi, *Germany and the Next War*, trans. Allen H. Powels (New York: Chas A. Eron, 1914), 14–19.

252 *Ibid.*, 18–19.

popularising the idea of German colonial settlements in Africa to protect the unique German cultural spirit in the face of massive emigration.

Thus, in the discourse on German international law of the nineteenth century, we see a gradual shift from a reconciliation between liberal internationalism and Romanticism to a strong inclination towards a conservative notion of the state that allegedly stood above everything else. With the strengthening of the sense of ethnicity and race as foundations of the national 'self', international law came to be perceived as only an optional extra. As Treitschke once said, '[t]he only principles of international conduct which are seldom broken and may claim to be fixed are those which do not touch this sovereignty, those namely which concern the formal and ceremonial rules'.[253] As in the discourse on nationalism, in international law, too, social Darwinism offered Germany the vision of a racially superior nation and accordingly the mission to accomplish the task of securing its due position in world history by way of violent imperialism. Indeed, the science of human evolution that gained popularity in nineteenth-century Germany justified the extinction of the inferior race in this struggle for survival.

Conclusion

Throughout history, the ethnic 'other' has been regarded as barbarian or savage for not being Greek, Roman, Muslim, Christian, Chinese, European, and so on. However, in the Romantic literature of the nineteenth century, ethnicity came to encapsulate the 'self-image' of a nation. Although, in contrast, the liberal image of the national 'self' referred to ethnicity only in an instrumental sense, ethnicity remained salient in both versions of nationalism to identify the 'other' within the nation and also to set the agenda for the other's exclusion or assimilation. In the latter part of the nineteenth century, social Darwinism came to offer a 'scientific' rationale based upon biological determinism for this nationalist agenda of exclusion in the form of exclusive ethnic homogeneity, or assimilation in the name of liberal universalism.

Being a product of this nineteenth-century socio-cultural environment, international law too developed within this framework of the ethnic dichotomy of 'self' and 'other' expressed in the liberal and conservative traditions. While the German tradition of perceiving the 'self' and its ensuing approach to international law developed in this way as the

[253] Hausrath, *Treitschke*, 165.

nineteenth century progressed, the liberal self-image of a nation within the Enlightenment tradition was reflected, as we have seen, in an understanding of international law that went beyond the notion of ethnic culture to envision a universal cultural domain. Yet, such cosmopolitanism was essentially refined by the social Darwinist concept of progress; hence, international law came to be understood as a sphere of the civilised nations alone. In this way, ethnic 'otherness' emerged within the liberal discourse on international law to safely isolate the European cultural 'self' from the non-European 'other'. In other words, while nineteenth-century international law within the Romantic tradition was shaped by the image of the 'self' as a racially superior nation, within the liberal discourse, international law was the reflection of a universal, yet confined to European civilisation, notion of the 'self' vis-à-vis the uncivilised, non-European 'other'.

Our story of ethnicity in relation to international law, which started in the nineteenth century, goes far beyond this period. The modern versions of minority protection and ethnic conflicts are intimately related to the rise of nationalism in the nineteenth century. Nationalism developed a very clear sense of 'self' and 'other', and the liberal and conservative philosophical traditions in the nineteenth century had very different approaches to conceptualising and managing this relationship between 'self' and 'other'. As we shall see soon, these two traditions have had enduring significance for the creation of international legal regimes devoted to managing ethnic tension expressed through minority problems or ethnic violence. Using the narrative in this chapter as a framework, this book demonstrates how the treatment of ethnicity in these philosophical traditions critically shaped the way international law developed to deal with these issues as history progressed.

However, before getting into a discussion of the peculiarities of international legal engagement with ethnic minorities and ethnic conflicts, in the following chapter I demonstrate how this ethnic dichotomy of 'self' and 'other' in liberal and conservative traditions, as a normative framework, exposes another key element of the nineteenth-century construction of international law, colonialism, in a new light. An understanding of international law in relation to the nineteenth-century moment of nationalism and colonialism within this framework then sheds light on the politics and practices of international law regarding ethnic minorities and ethnic conflicts in subsequent epochs of international legal history.

2

Colonialism and international law

A story of two traditions

Introduction

The nineteenth-century European discourse on nationalism within the framework of liberal and conservative traditions of understanding ethnicity can be seen in the conception of the non-European 'other'. This proposition is best substantiated by the colonial projects, wherein one can trace separate but simultaneous streams of liberal and conservative justifications for colonial missions in light of the corresponding concept of the 'nation' in the metropolis. This framework also exposes the parallel streams of monogenic-assimilationist and polygenic-exclusionist policies vis-à-vis the natives in the colonies.

In this chapter, I examine the colonial policies of nineteenth-century France and Germany to explore how their respective liberal and conservative treatments of ethnicity in relation to the construction of the national 'self' distinctively informed their understanding of colonialism as well as their actual execution of colonial policies. Though based on the philosophies and practices of two particular states, this account represents the contrast between the liberal and conservative notions of colonialism and native relations and exposes how such interactions with the colonial 'other' were reflected back in the dynamic process of the construction of the 'self' in the metropolis. While providing this narrative, I also demonstrate how nineteenth-century international lawyers' perceptions of the state within the liberal and conservative traditions were essentially reflected in both their justifications for colonialism and the atrocities associated with it.

It is to be noted here that colonialism is by no means a unique event of the nineteenth century but a much older phenomenon. However, while dealing with colonisation in this chapter, I do not intend to present a history of colonisation per se; instead, this chapter focuses on the historical juxtaposition of two powerful philosophical traditions in nineteenth-century Europe through which I offer my narrative of the colonial encounter. Given that nationalism, a central element of this juxtaposition, is essentially a product of the nineteenth century, this particular moment of history is the best point of departure for this chapter. In short, rather than presenting a history of colonisation, my aim is to demonstrate how the nineteenth-century discourses on ethnicity, nationalism, and social Darwinism and their relationship with international law were translated into colonial policies and practices during that moment of history.

This chapter is divided into two major sections. The first section deals with the German colonial policies in the nineteenth century, highlighting their conservative ethnic-exclusionist underpinning vis-à-vis the colonial other. It also explains how such interactions with the colonial 'other' were reflected back in the dynamic process of the construction of the ethnic 'self' in the metropolis. This section then discusses how international lawyers with a conservative Romantic understanding of nationalism endorsed such exclusionist colonial policies. In the second section, I juxtapose the German model of colonialism with the French model, which is often understood as a liberal assimilationist project, a 'civilising mission', to underscore the distinctiveness of these approaches to the ethnic 'other'. I also explain how, being fuelled by social Darwinist ideas, such a liberal project, despite its premise of universal equality, could hardly break with the notion of racial hierarchy. In this connection, I also discuss the engagement of liberal international lawyers in this civilising project. In both sections, I take care to consider the socio-economic as well as political contexts against which the colonial projects were advanced in nineteenth-century France and Germany.

The ethnic 'other' in German colonialism and international law

The background of German colonialism

The nineteenth-century German idea of the 'self' – the ethnic nation – informed its relationship with colonies in a number of ways. Although colonial proposals were discussed in the Frankfurt National Assembly in 1848, no major interest groups supported colonial expansion. The state governments, namely, Prussia, Hamburg, and Bremen, which were in the best position to effect a colonial policy, were against the idea of colonisation.[1] However, a majority of western German liberals remained

[1] Woodruff D. Smith, *The German Colonial Empire* (Chapel Hill, North Carolina: University of North Carolina Press, 1978), 5.

an exception to this general trend. As a matter of fact, the liberals advocated a colonial policy in 1848 in the face of massive German emigration from south-western Germany, which intensified with the growth of industrialisation and ensuing socio-economic changes. German overpopulation, especially in rural areas, was also said to have boosted emigration.[2] Between 1830 and 1860, over one million Germans left for the United States; others went to Brazil and Chile.[3] By the 1890s, a fresh exodus of staggering proportions was under way. Within just ten years, 1,445,181 German immigrants arrived in New York alone.[4] After 1895, an estimated 830,000 Germans emigrated from Prussia only, making depopulation a great threat to German nationalism.[5]

Nevertheless, the liberals of 1848, whose prominence in politics at that time was temporary, considered colonisation as a policy option in non-nationalist terms. Their concern was that lower-class people, who had been displaced by changes in German agriculture, would become criminals and possibly revolutionary; thus, having colonies would create a good option: exporting those people to colonies.[6] Despite the fact that Bismarck allowed his political allies to appeal to sentiment in favour of colonies in order to rally support for unification in western Germany, he himself remained publicly opposed to overseas colonies until the 1880s, mainly due to the projected financial burdens of maintaining overseas colonies and the strategy of avoiding any serious confrontation with other major colonial powers.[7] Therefore, it was no surprise that most of

2 However, Smith argues that seen from a more modern standpoint, 'emigration was the product, not of absolute overpopulation, but of the development of German agriculture towards large-scale capitalist forms under severe economic pressure, compounded by a gradual reduction in the size of independent farms through their division among sons of farmers'. See Smith, *The German Colonial Empire*, 10.

3 Edward J. Neather, 'Introduction to the English Edition' in *Genocide in German South-West Africa*, ed. Jurgen Zimmerer and Joachim Zeller, trans. E. J. Neather (Monmouth: Merlin Press, 2008 [2003]), xix.

4 David Olusoga and Casper W. Erichsen, *Kaiser's Holocaust* (London: Faber & Faber, 2011), 87.

5 Mark Mazower, *Hitler's Empire – Nazi Rule in Occupied Europe* (London: Penguin Books, 2008), 21.

6 Smith, *The German Colonial Empire*, 4.

7 In a letter to the minister for war, Bismarck wrote: 'On the one hand the advantages for trade and industry of the motherland, which are expected from the possessions of colonies, for the most part are based on illusions. Because the costs caused by the establishment, support and maintenance of colonies, often exceed the benefit enjoyed by the motherland, as the experiences of England and France prove [. . .]. On the other hand, our navy is not yet sufficiently developed to take responsibility for the protection in distant states. Finally, the attempt to found colonies in regions claimed by other states, no matter if with or

Germany's acquisition of colonies took place quite late, between April 1884 and February 1885.[8]

However, German ethnic nationalism soon emerged as a uniquely dominant factor in German politics in the discourse on the viability of colonial projects. German unification, its appearance as the Great Power in the middle of Europe, and intense international economic competition enhanced by the depression of 1873 – all contributed to increased support for Germany's participation in the colonial mission. At the same time, the depression gave the German middle class, who suffered the worst of it, a fresh impetus for further emigration, jeopardising the vision of a unified, ethnic German nation.[9] The urge to protect German culture by preventing de-Germanisation put the idea of emigrationist colonialism in a nationalist light, conveniently reconciling the needs of emigration with the protection of culture. In the words of Smith:

> Freedom to emigrate if conditions should become too unbearable was widely accepted as the ultimate recourse of the lower orders of respectable society, and parties [. . .] that emphasised continued freedom of emigration were supported by these groups. The same group also tended to support emigrationist colonialism, since colonies offered an alternative to normal emigration that preserved both the German culture of the emigrants and their contributions to the German economy. Especially after 1871 and the growth of lower-middle-class nationalism, colonialism attained some popularity because it reconciled patriotism with freedom to desert Germany.[10]

Thus, the shift from a liberal vision of emigrationist colonialism to a more culturalist project not only accommodated nationalist passion but also allowed Bismarck, who always kept alive his instrumental considerations for colonisation, to manoeuvre the middle class to subjugate the left liberals' electoral support in the 1870s and 1880s.[11]

without legitimation, would cause manifold, undesired conflicts.' See Hans Spellmeyer, *Deutsche Kolonialpolitik im Reichstag* (Stuttgart, 1931), 3, cited in Neather, 'Introduction to the English Edition' in *Genocide in German South-West Africa*, xxii.

[8] This timeline categorically applies to the African colonies of South-West Africa (April 1884), Togo (4–6 July 1884), Cameroon (14 July 1884), and East Africa (February 1885). However, the official acquisition of colonies in the Pacific and in China took place in 1899 and 1888, respectively. See Elise von Joeden-Forgey, 'Nobody's People: Colonial Subjects, Race Power and the German State, 1884–1945', unpublished PhD dissertation, University of Pennsylvania (2004), ch. 1, fn. 1 at 52.

[9] At the same time, economic groups within Germany related their projected fortune to Germany's success in colonial affairs. See Smith, 7.

[10] *Ibid.*, 10–11. [11] *Ibid.*, 18.

During the period of 1879–1884, colonialist organisations played pivotal roles in popularising colonialism, and the intellectual figures behind institutional campaigns mostly put their arguments in ethno-nationalist terms. For example, one of the foremost German colonial activists, missionary Friedrich Fabri, although initially premising his arguments in favour of colonies on economic considerations favoured by big businesses, ultimately claimed that the population overflow caused by the natural vigour of the German race could be directed to the colonies.[12] With his nationalist passion, Fabri 'demonstrated graphically and alarmingly how the constant loss of youth, talent, skill, business ability and initiative (for it is always the best who go), was constantly depleting Germany of her vitality'.[13] Thus, his argument followed that settlement colonies would not only accommodate German farmers and small bourgeois, with an agricultural economy and a traditional middle-class society, but also retain the emigrants' capabilities for Germany and prevent their de-Germanisation.[14]

Another colonialist, Wilhelm Hubbe-Schleiden, shared Fabri's view of emigrationist colonialism in more aggressive terms. Despite his financial interests in a number of tropical trading concerns, his colonialist writings were devoted to downplaying the commercial and industrial sides of German life and emphasising the heroic, cultural, and agricultural aspects.[15] For him, colonies were necessary to prevent the degeneration of the German people through industrialisation and the sapping of Germany's strength through emigration and thereby to maintain German culture and prevent its decline. Germany should stand in contrast to England, 'where the typical person had become a crass material and a cog in an industrial machine'.[16] Depicting industry as a necessary evil that caused social and cultural damage, Hubbe-Schleiden found essentials of national 'health' and 'power', such as human traits and social organisations, in the traditional agrarian economy. Thus, he envisaged that the 'heroic' German with his agrarian culture would prosper in the colonies and thus help Germany continue on its road to greatness and dominance.[17]

[12] Friedrich Fabri, *Bedarf Deutschland der Kolonien?* (Gotha, 1879), 1–13, 20–32, cited in Smith, 23.

[13] Mary Evelyn Townsend, *Origins of Modern German Colonialism, 1871–1885* (New York: Columbia University Press, 1921), 92.

[14] Fabri, *Bedarf Deutschland der Kolonien?* 1–13, 20–32, cited in Smith, 23.

[15] Wilhelm Hubbe-Schleiden, *Uberseeische Politik, eine Kulturwissenschaftliche Studie* (Hamburg, 1881), 13–14, 74–75, cited in Smith, 24.

[16] *Ibid.*, 24. [17] *Ibid.*, 25.

Nationalists like Hubbe-Schleiden believed that without this bond to the land, the nation would eventually face a spiritual calamity. Therefore, settlement colonies were seen as a pragmatic way of redeeming the whole nation, in that the children of the colonies, immersed from birth in a true Germanic life and bound to the soil, would become 'a living repository of the *Völkisch* spirit'.[18] Even though the soil they would be tilling was that of another continent and not the sacred trust of Germany, they argued, life as a farmer in a distant colony was far preferable to an urban existence in Germany or the United States. In the words of one commentator, nationalists believed that Germany's colonies 'would become the incubators in which those values would be preserved, safe from the forces of modernity and industrialisation that would inevitably continue in Germany'.[19] As Eyre Crowe, a British diplomat in the Foreign Office, noted about the then renewed enthusiasm for colonial settlement in Germany: 'Emperor, statesmen, journalists, geographers, economists, commercial shipping houses and the whole mass of educated and uneducated public opinion continued with one voice to declare: We must have real colonies, where German immigrants can settle and spread the national ideals of the Fatherland'.[20]

A similar approach to the colonial project was taken by Carl Peters, the most famous of all colonialists of that time. Despite his personal interest in overseas trading companies, he nonetheless took a nationalist stance by advocating that Germans living in overpopulated Germany had to move somewhere, and for Germany to retain the productive power of the emigrants and protect their culture, colonies were a necessity.[21] Although Peters and his associates established colonial trading enterprises, Smith notes, their propaganda often endorsed as well as advanced the popular idea of large-scale agricultural settlements.[22]

Such a position on German colonialism was also taken by Heinrich von Treitschke, who, as we saw in the previous chapter, conceived of international relations essentially as self-interested arrangements outside the domain of law. He argued that '[f]or a nation that suffers from

18 Olusoga and Erichsen, *Kaiser's Holocaust*, 89. 19 *Ibid.*

20 John C. G. Röhl, *From Bismarck to Hitler: Problems and Perspectives in History* (London: Longmans, 1970), 61.

21 Carl Peters, *Gesammelte Schriften*, ed. Walter Frank, 3 vols. (Munich, 1943), 1: 332–341, cited in Smith, 26.

22 Carl Peters, *Zur Weltpolitik* (Berlin, 1912), 141–145, cited in Smith, 26. Smith notes that Peters is a difficult character to assess, someone who was genuinely interested in settlement colonies and German empowerment in world politics but at the same time was quite keen to get his own share.

continual over-production, and sends yearly 200,000 of her children abroad, the question of colonisation is vital'.[23] Having predicted that the German emigration would continue for a long while to be an unavoidable necessity even if Prussia resumed the colonisation of its eastern borderlands, he proposed that it was a new duty for Germany to ensure that its 'wandering children' remained true to their nationality and simultaneously to open new channels for its commerce.[24] Thus, he concluded that Germany was justified on the ground of 'national self-preservation' to seek ways and means to divert the stream of German emigrants into lands where they would be able to maintain their nationality.[25]

However, although the nationalist agenda was at the forefront of colonial advocacy in the 1880s, a parallel stream of support from the German government and business interests in favour of colonial acquisition on non-nationalist grounds also emerged. Given the high degree of public support for nationalist notions of settlement colonies, protagonists of economic colonialism often relied on nationalist rhetoric to advance their own projects, while nationalism never displaced economic considerations for the viability of such a mega-project of overseas settlement.[26] Such moderate reconciliation offered Bismarck, who conceived of an ideal German colony in terms of the classic trading-colony model, the opportunity to manage domestic politics. As Smith notes: 'Bismarck's motives in acquiring colonies were complex and varied, but it appears from the available evidence that the basic impetus to expansion is to be found in domestic politics and Bismarck's attempt to manipulate them'.[27] Nevertheless, as the Colonial Society and the Pan-German League sought to strengthen the conservative nationalist voice after 1885, Bismarck was under increasing pressure to change his policy of trading colonialism.[28] It is to be noted here that the Pan-German League was a highly respectable organisation with prominent members who held seats in the Reichstag and academic positions at most respected German universities.[29]

In this sense, the very notion of German colonialism is a product of a series of inter-connected factors – nationalism, large business interests, the government's instrumentalist calculations, and domestic political

[23] Adolf Hausrath (com. and trans.), *Treitschke: His Doctrine of German Destiny and of International Relations Together with a Study of His Life and Work* (New York: G. P. Putnam and Sons, 1914), 205.

[24] *Ibid.*, 207. [25] *Ibid.*, 209. [26] Smith, *The German Colonial Empire*, 27.

[27] *Ibid.*, 33. [28] *Ibid.*, 44. [29] Olusoga and Erichsen, *Kaiser's Holocaust*, 90.

dynamics – though often it appeared to be a dichotomy of economic and settlement models of colonialism. But what we trace in particular is that nationalist elements, premised on middle-class support for initiating German settlements in colonies in order to protect German culture, remained a decisive force behind German colonial expansionism. This force only grew with the passage of time, with Germany's march towards greater expansion until it faced sheer humiliation in successive world wars.

German international lawyers, Koskenniemi notes, started to write about colonialism only after Bismarck had changed his attitude towards colonisation in 1884. But their response to the subject was based on municipal public law, instead of international law, in that they focused primarily on how German protectorates could be fitted into the imperial constitution.[30] For them, colonisation was a natural part of Germany's development into a leading European power. Early commentators on colonialism, such as Paul Heilborn, Karl Heimburger, and Friedrich Geffcken, understood colonisation as an obvious, natural phenomenon; they engaged themselves merely in defending Germany's right as a latecomer to the imperial game or in explaining the legal technicalities of the concepts of 'protectorate' and 'territorial sovereignty', for example.[31] German jurist Heimburger maintained in 1888 that the state's quest for territory is a justified 'expression of its life-energy' under international law and is 'protected as long as it does not conflict with the legal spheres of the other European States'.[32] Such an approach of German international lawyers towards the colonial project, essentially, reflected their perception of the state as a racially superior organic body and of its sovereign authority in an absolute sense, as we have seen in the previous chapter.

Thus, in *The Theory of the State*, Bluntschli argued that the settlement of political communities in an uninhabited and scarcely cultivated country with the intention of founding a new state is a peaceful form of territorial acquisition. And then he maintained that if the 'barbaric natives' remained in the territory of the new colony, the superiority of the 'civilised' over a barbarous people would necessarily lead to the dominion of the former.[33] Elsewhere, while talking about the superiority of the Aryans as a race possessed of rationalism and philosophy, he noted

[30] Martti Koskenniemi, *Gentle Civilizer of Nations: The Rise and Fall of International Law 1870–1960* (Cambridge: Cambridge University Press, 2002), 109.

[31] *Ibid.* [32] Cited in *ibid.*

[33] Johann Kaspar Bluntschli, *The Theory of the State* (Kitchener, Ontario: Batoche Books, 2000 [1885]), 219.

that the Aryan races were superior in that they emphasised the dignity and honour of the human being in contrast to the Negro, who 'allowed his master to enslave him, even threw himself on the ground before his master, and lifted the master's foot himself on his head'.[34] Of the Aryan races with unparalleled political excellence, Bluntschli continued, it was the Germanic people who flourished most in the elevation and clarity of ideas regarding the theory of state. His conclusion followed that the Aryans were under a great historical responsibility to educate other races in political theory and statehood and to teach them 'to develop and complete the domination of the world which already lies in the hands of the Aryan peoples in a consciously humanistic and noble way so as to teach civilisation for the whole mankind'.[35]

This sense of Germanic racial superiority, Dampierre noted in *German Imperialism and International Law*, was offered a scientific basis by Darwinism. Evolutionary thinking rationalised the imperialistic tendencies of intellectual Germanism not only by corroborating the idea of the inherent superiority of certain races but also by scientifically justifying the elimination of the weak by the strong.[36] This principle of unequal evolution implied that among all the human races it was the Germanic race that had undergone the most perfect evolution. Thus, German intellectuals believed that from the point of view of Germany's aptitude for expansion as an organised community, it had reached 'a stage of its evolution at which it was incumbent upon all the others to submit to its sovereignty'.[37] Treitschke's disciple, Bernhardi, therefore, declared on the eve of the First World War that

> [t]he struggle for existence is, in the life of Nature, the basis of all healthy development. All existing things show themselves to be the result of contesting forces. So in the life of man the struggle is not merely the destructive, but the life-giving principle. The law of the stronger holds good everywhere. Those forms survive which are able to procure themselves the most favourable conditions of life, and to assert themselves in the universal economy of Nature. The weaker succumb.[38]

[34] Johann Kaspar Bluntschli, 'Arische Völker und arische Rechte' in *Gesammelte Kleine Schiften*, 2 vols. (Nordlinger: Beck, 1879), 74–77, cited in Koskenniemi, 103.

[35] Quoted in Koskenniemi, 104.

[36] Jacques Marquis de Dampierre, *German Imperialism and International Law – Based Upon German Authorities and the Archives of the French Government* (New York: Charles Scribner's Sons, 1917), 32.

[37] *Ibid.*, 32–33.

[38] General Friedrich von Bernhardi, *Germany and the Next War*, trans. Allen H. Powels (New York: Chas A. Eron, 1914), 18.

Bernhardi, thus, conceived of colonisation essentially as a matter of recognised right, for through colonisation 'vast territories inhabited by uncivilised masses are occupied by more highly civilised States, and made subject to their rule. Higher civilisation and the correspondingly greater power are the foundations of the right to annexation'.[39] Given that Germany was a latecomer in the imperial game and burdened with a surplus population, which the mother country could no longer feed, Bernhardi proposed that the only course left to Germany was to acquire the necessary territory by war: 'Thus the instinct of *self-preservation* leads inevitably to war, and the conquest of foreign soil. It is not the possessor, but the victor, who then has the right'.[40] He maintained further that since might is the supreme right, and the dispute as to what is right is decided by war, might gives the right to occupy or to conquer. War, according to him, was a biological determinant between just and unjust, for its decisions rested on the very nature of things.[41]

The projection of the ethnic 'self' on the colonial 'other' through exclusion

While the German notion of the ethnic 'self' constituted a major force behind the German colonial mission in the internal context, in the external context, that is, in the relationship with the colonial 'other', Germany demonstrated an inherently polygenic as well as exclusionist attitude towards the natives. It is to be noted from the outset that in the dichotomy of nationalist-settlement and instrumentalist-trading model of colonialism in German politics, Bismarck's inclination for the latter offered only South-West Africa, present-day Namibia, as a suitable venue for large-scale German settlement.[42] South-West Africa thus became the

[39] *Ibid.*, 22. [40] *Ibid.*, 22. Emphasis added. [41] *Ibid.*, 23.

[42] Although Togo was considered as the 'model colony', Rohrbach argues that it was so from a merely economic point of view as a market and source of raw materials, for its tropical climate was not suitable for mass German settlement. See Paul Rohrbach, *Der deutsche Gedanke in der Welt* (Dusseldorf; Leipzig: Karl Robert Langewiesche, 1912), 133–160, cited in Smith, 67. Similarly, in the case of Cameroon, the Pan-German League's approach contrasted a business-oriented colonial policy with a more patriotic settlement one. Foerster notes that given the absence of a white agricultural population in Cameroon, Pan-German spokesmen sometimes supported a black peasantry as a substitute for industrialisation. See E. Th. Foerster, *Das Konzessionsunwesen in den Deutschen Schutzgebieten* (Berlin: Gross-Lichterfelde, 1903), 18, cited in Smith, 83. As a matter of fact, the Pan-German League continually attacked the government for its unwillingness to support settlement anywhere except South-West Africa, and also for its concession-company policy along with the lack of vigorous efforts to expand the empire. See Smith, 144.

focal point of radical Rightists' nationalist campaign for German settlement. In retrospect, it also offers us an opportunity to explore how the German nation, juxtaposed with the African natives in order to protect its ethno-national 'self' in the face of massive emigration, simultaneously endeavoured to 'distance' itself from the natives, paradoxically to protect its racial superiority from any undesired racial intermixing. The exclusion of the 'other' in the form of strict racial segregation on polygenic grounds was the obvious policy option to that end.

Consequently, to combat the increasing trend of marriage between whites and African women,[43] the colonial government of South-West Africa opted for legislation that would erect a significant barrier between natives and non-natives with a view to protecting 'the ranks of Europeans against an influx of coloured blood'.[44] When Governor Tecklenburg banned mixed marriage in 1905 in defiance of directives of the Department of Colonial Affairs in Berlin, he evidently relied on racial, exclusionist logic against mixed marriages:

> Not only will the preservation of the purity of the German race and of German civilisation be very significantly harmed, but also, and above all, the authority of the white man will be endangered. [...] experience had long shown, and not only in Africa, that when a white person lives for an extended period with a number of a subordinate race, it is not the latter who is elevated by the contact but the white person who is dragged down and 'goes native' as they say here. In the same way, experience shows that such relationships do not improve the race but cause it to deteriorate.[45]

Segregation was also advanced by three notorious native ordinances of 1907 – the Control Ordinance, the Pass Ordinance, and the Master and Servant Ordinance – which together established a racist and interventionist state within the framework of law. Jurgen Zimmerer notes that such a 'policy of total control over the natives was at the very heart of German colonial rule from the very first consideration of how working relationships should be regulated as early as 1894'.[46]

For example, Paul Rohrbach, who was sent to South-West Africa in 1903 by the Colonial Department as the Commissioner for Settlement, most forcefully promoted social Darwinist theories there. In *Deutsche*

[43] Although the white Europeans in most cases looked down upon African women as racially subordinate, they maintained relationships with the latter due to a lack of white women or the possibility of gaining economic benefits from an elite African family.

[44] Jurgen Zimmerer, 'The Model Colony? Racial Segregation, Forced Labour and Total Control in German South West Africa' in *Genocide in German South West Africa*, 19–21.

[45] Quoted in *ibid.*, 21. [46] *Ibid.*, 29.

Kolonialwirtschaft (German Colonial Commerce) published in 1907, he argued that '[i]n order to secure the peaceful White settlement against the bad, culturally inept and predatory native tribe, it is possible that its actual eradication may become necessary under certain condition'.[47] In support of his extermination policy, he reiterated in 1912 that

> [i]t is not right either among nations or among individuals that people who can create nothing should have a claim to preservation. [. . .] Should the German people renounce the chance of growing stronger and of securing elbow room for their sons and daughters, because [. . .] some tribe of negroes [. . .] has lived its useless existence on a strip of land where ten thousand German families may have a flourishing existence and thus strengthen the very sap of our people?[48]

The German colonial administration's exclusionist approach to the natives of South-West Africa was demonstrated with utmost brutality in the events of the Herero genocide between 1904 and 1907, events that in many ways appear as the prelude to the Holocaust during World War II. The Herero war offered the colonial administration an excuse to exterminate the whole Herero community; the commander-in-chief and the man in charge of this campaign – Lieutenant-General Lothar von Trotha – was very close to completing this task when he was called back to Germany in the face of controversy in the metropolis over his policy. As a matter of fact, von Trotha issued an Extermination Order on 3 October 1904 in which he declared that

> the Herero people must leave the country. If they do not do so I shall force them with a big gun. Within the German frontiers every Herero, armed or unarmed, with or without cattle, will be shot dead. I shall take in no more women and children. I shall drive them back to their people or have them fired on.[49]

Nearly 80 percent of the Herero people, that is, 60,000 Herero, were annihilated by the Germans during this campaign: some in battles and some deprived of food and water when driven to the Omaheke desert by the colonial army and blocked there.[50] In order to prevent the Herero from

[47] Quoted in Clarence Lusane, *Hitler's Black Victims* (London: Routledge, 2002), 43.
[48] Paul Rohrbach, *Der Deutsche Gedanke in der Welt* (Dusseldorf: Langewiesche, 1912), 141–142, quoted in Olusoga and Erichsen, *Kaiser's Holocaust*, 112.
[49] Quoted in Jurgen Zimmerer, 'War, Concentration Camps and Genocide' in *Genocide in German South West Africa*, 48.
[50] For an account of the major causes behind the Herero war and the atrocity committed by the German colonial army, see Zimmerer, 'War, Concentration Camps and Genocide', 41–60; Smith, *German Colonial Empire*, 60–65; Von Joeden-Forgey, 'Nobody's People', 442.

slipping westwards, back into the colony where they could find water and food, von Trotha issued orders to his troops on 16 August and again on 26 August 1904 to cut off waterholes and set up patrols along the perimeter of the Omaheke.[51] A German private named Adolf Fischer wrote about the plight of the Herero as they were pushed into the Omaheke desert:

> The greater part of the Herero nation and their cattle lay dead in the bush, lining the path of their morbid march. [. . .] Vultures and jackals had already filled themselves to their bellies' content. They had an infinite supply of meat, more than they could possibly consume. [. . .] Whenever we dismounted, our feet would hit against the human bodies. There was a young woman with wilted breasts, her frozen face covered with flies and curled up next to her hip an aborted birth. [. . .] There was a boy. He was still alive; staring into the night with a stupid grin from an empty mind. [. . .] Whoever took part in the chase through the Sandveld lost his belief in righteousness on Earth.[52]

The extermination order was finally lifted by Kaiser Wilhelm, with a significant degree of hesitation, in the face of increasing criticism in international media and ensuing pressure from the chancellor, von Bülow. However, von Trotha's policy was endorsed by the German chief-of-staff, von Schlieffen, who wrote to the chancellor in the following words:

> One can agree with him (von Trotha) in wishing to exterminate the whole nation or drive them out of the country [. . .]. The racial war which has flared up can only be brought to an end by the extermination or total subjugation of the one party. The latter option is however not feasible in the long term, judged on currently valid assessments. Therefore the objective of General von Trotha can be approved. But he just does not have the forces to carry it through.[53]

It was this practical limitation that made the chief-of-staff appeal for the lifting of the extermination order. Von Schlieffen reportedly appeased von Trotha, who was enraged upon hearing about the withdrawal of the extermination order, by reassuring him that 'His Majesty has not forbidden you to shoot the Hereros', rather that 'the possibility of showing mercy is to be restored'.[54] The Kaiser himself wrote to von Trotha in

51 Olusoga and Erichsen, *Kaiser's Holocaust*, 147–148.

52 Adolf Fischer, *Menschen und Tiere in Süedwestafrika* (Berlin: Safari Verlag, 1914), quoted in Olusoga and Erichsen, *Kaiser's Holocaust*, 146–147.

53 Quoted in Zimmerer, 'War, Concentration Camps and Genocide', 51.

54 Olusoga and Erichsen, *Kaiser's Holocaust*, 158.

support of the genocidal policy: 'You have entirely fulfilled my expectations when I named you commander of the colonial troops, and I take pleasure in expressing, once again, my utter gratitude for your accomplishments so far'.[55]

What followed the massacre of the Herero in battlefields and the Omaheke is another episode of brutality of even worse character – 'concentration camps'. A local missionary, Heinrich Vedder, recorded the appalling conditions in the Swakopmund Camp, one of five main concentration camps, in the *Swakopmund Missionary Chronicle* of December 1905 in the following words:

> The Herero were placed behind a double row of barbed wire [. . .] and housed in pathetic structures constructed out of simple sacking and planks, in such a manner that in one structure 30–50 people were forced to stay without distinction to age or sex. From early morning until late at night, on weekends as well as on Sundays and holidays, they had to work under the clubs of the raw overseers until they broke down. Added to this food was extremely scarce. [. . .] Like cattle, hundreds were driven to death and like cattle they were buried.[56]

According to official records, approximately 40 percent of the prisoners in the Swakopmund Camp died during their first four months of captivity, and any prisoner who entered the camp was likely to be dead within ten months.[57] For Hans Tecklenburg, the deputy governor of South-West Africa, the high death rate in concentration camps was in Germany's long-term interest, for it would weed out the weak and leave only the stronger Herero. These survivors, necessarily the strongest and fittest, would then become the slaves of the German colonisers.[58] Similarly, in the concentration camp for the Nama people maintained on Shark Island, at least 1,203 prisoners had died by March 1907, of which 460 were women and 274 were children. In December 1906 alone, 263 prisoners died, an average of 8.5 per day. A total of more than 1,900 Nama prisoners died on Shark Island, and Herero prisoners there died in similar numbers.[59]

Recent research by David Olusoga and Casper Erichsen based on new archival evidence reveals yet another horrific aftermath of deaths in concentration camps – the growth of an industry developed around the supply of body parts. Female prisoners in the Swakopmund Camp were

[55] Quoted in Isabel V. Hull, *Absolute Destruction* (Ithaca, New York: Cornell University Press, 2005), 30.
[56] Quoted in Olusoga and Erichsen, *Kaiser's Holocaust*, 163–164. [57] *Ibid.*, 168.
[58] See *ibid.*, 170. [59] *Ibid.*, 229.

forced to boil the severed heads of their own people and process their skulls to be shipped to museums, collections, and universities in Germany. Towards the end of 1906, the camp physician at Shark Island, Dr. Bofinger, decapitated the bodies of seventeen Nama prisoners in the camp, including that of a one-year-old girl, removed and weighed the brains before placing each head in preserving alcohol and sealing them in tins for export to the Institute of Pathology at the University of Berlin. These 'samples' were used by aspiring racial scientist, then a medical student, Christian Fetzer in a 'series of experiments designed to demonstrate the anatomical similarities between the Nama and the anthropoid ape'.[60]

As discussed earlier, the endorsement of von Trotha's genocidal policy was not confined to the military establishment alone. Medardus Brehl shows how the literature of the time perceived the annihilation of the Herero and Nama as 'a legitimate means of dealing with the inevitable and necessary confrontation of "whites" and "blacks", of "civilised" and "uncivilised"' – a phenomenon that can be explained with the nineteenth-century concepts of German entitlement, revolutionary culture, social Darwinism, and historiography.[61] Brehl demonstrates that besides publications from a closed circle of particular social interest groups, works by mainstream authors with immense popularity among the masses in fact portrayed the events in ethno-nationalist terms. Among many authors that Brehl's research reveals, the novel by Gustav Frenssen, entitled *Peter Moors Fahrt nach Sudwest. Ein Feldzugsbericht* (Peter Moor's Journey to the South West. A Campaign Report), published in 1906, is of particular relevance given its Europe-wide reception.[62] In his account of the South-West African massacre, Frenssen portrays the incidents in purely nationalist terms, with the legitimate cause of ensuring German cultural homogeneity. For him, as Brehl notes, extermination of the 'existential other' would not only suppress the threat they posed to the German culture but also allow men of diverse regional and social origins to create a homogeneous community. It is, therefore, legitimate under

[60] *Ibid.*, 224–225.

[61] Medardus Brehl, 'The Drama Was Played Out on the Dark Stage of the Sandveldt: The Extermination of the Herero and Nama in German (Popular) Literature' in *Genocide in German South West Africa*, 101.

[62] Frenssen was an extremely popular writer in Germany; in fact, he was even put forward as a candidate for the Nobel Prize for literature in 1912. This book was a best seller in Germany and abroad. It was translated into English, Danish, Dutch, Afrikaans, and Swedish. For a list of contemporary popular German literature on colonial war, see Brehl, 104.

evolutionary biology and the law of advanced cultural development and, hence, absolutely necessary.[63] In the words of Frenssen, 'these blacks deserved to die, before God and mankind, not because they murdered the two hundred farmers and rose against us, but because they built no houses and dug no springs'.[64]

As for international lawyers, no critical accounts came from them about the extremely brutal response of the German colonial administration to native uprisings, for they considered this a natural consequence of Germany's emergence as a great colonial power.[65] Dampierre argues that in the minds of German intellectuals, the notion of German racial superiority induced the instincts of domination, and Germany's military might, then, relied on the idea of violence with moral comfort.[66] This form of violent domination was unique, in that it differed from the intellectual domination of the Latin races, from the commercial ambitions of the Roman and British empires, and from the species of religious mysticism of the Arabs and artistic mysticism of the Hellenes.[67] Given that 'Germanism' was a civilisation deeply rooted in a particular race, rather than a universal civilisation that had the potential to accommodate other races, Dampierre asserts that German imperialism was a force for elimination, in contrast to that of the Hellenes, the Romans, the Arabs, the British, and the French, which had each been a force for assimilation. It was this original and dangerous characteristic which differentiated German imperialism from the rest of the civilised world.[68] In his words:

> In fact, from the moment that the German becomes possessed with the idea of an innate superiority whether historic, providential or biological imposing on his race the obligation to civilise the world, his conception of the relative rights of nations must undergo a profound modification, the duty of expansion by means of elimination which this mission imposes being scarcely reconcilable with the right to exist of other nations.[69]

[63] *Ibid.*, 106. [64] Quoted in *ibid.* [65] Koskenniemi, 167.
[66] Dampierre, *German Imperialism and International Law*, 43. [67] *Ibid.*, 43.
[68] *Ibid.*, 43–44. In the following section, we shall examine the liberal-assimilationist thrust of French colonialism and its subsequent adjustment with the notion of 'association' in the face of pragmatic needs.
[69] *Ibid.*, 46. Cf. Anthony Carty, 'The Evolution of International Legal Scholarship in Germany during the Kaiserreich and the Weimarer Republic (1871–1933)', *German Yearbook of International Law*, 50 (2007), 29–90.

With this analogy, it was therefore natural that Imperial Germany would adopt brutal means in warfare in order to execute the 'sacred' task of elimination.[70]

Nevertheless, in the political circle of the metropolis, information on the South-West African atrocities created controversy over German colonial policy. Since the very beginning, colonialism had been a fertile source of political manoeuvring for almost all political philosophies. According to Smith, participants in the German political system employed colonialism as a tool to get what they wanted and as a means of overcoming some of the major deficiencies in the system – the government was particularly vulnerable to attack and criticism during the annual budget review by the Reichstag and the Budget Commission.[71] Following the reports of genocide of the Herero and Nama peoples, the Social Democratic Party (SDP) refused any further backing for the colonial war; the refusal initially led to the rejection of part of the supplementary budget submitted by the government to pay for the continuation of the colonial war in South-West Africa and, finally, to the dissolution of the parliament.[72] Paradoxically, in the elections to the Reichstag at the beginning of 1907 that followed the dissolution, nationalist campaigns depicted the SDP and the Centre Party as 'enemies of colonialism, opposed to the national interest and traitors to the fatherland'.[73] This, along with other elements of election engineering, offered the conservative bloc a majority in the Reichstag. Ulrich Heyden notes that the election result had an 'educational influence' on German social democracy, in that it finally led to the development of concepts of 'socialist colonialist policies' in which colonies came to be perceived as an economic necessity and in the public interest of the German Reich.[74]

Another, less complicated response in the metropolis towards German atrocities in the colonies was the outright denial of any guilt, on the grounds that such measures were either necessary or were deviations from the law that were punished. The strongest justification relied on the similar or even worse treatment of natives by other European colonial powers. An archetypical example of such a stance is the works of Heinrich Schnee, a lawyer, former colonial governor, and member of the Reichstag. In the context of Germany's loss of colonies following the Great War, Schnee wrote, 'the natives, satisfied, and more than satisfied,

[70] Dampierre, 134–135. [71] Smith, *German Colonial Empire*, 122.
[72] Ulrich van der Heyden, 'The "Hottentot Elections" of 1907' in *Genocide in German South West Africa*, 114.
[73] *Ibid.*, 116. [74] *Ibid.*, 117–118.

with German sovereignty, desired nothing better than its continuance'.[75] Under the chapter title 'What the Natives Really Want', he claimed that '[i]f a genuine, uninfluenced, and impartial *plebiscite* could be taken, Germany would need to have no fear as to the result of the native vote'.[76] Throughout his writings, one can hardly ignore the racial foundations of his arguments. A similar approach was taken by Matthias Erzberger, who held the view that although Germany had made mistakes in its colonial policy, such mistakes were not greater than those of other colonial powers.[77] For him, colonialism was a matter of national pride as well as an indication of superiority. Thus, in the aftermath of Germany's defeat in the Great War, he declared that

> Germany cannot, for the sake of her honour, submit to be shut out from the ranks of the colonising Powers. If she were struck out of the ranks of colonising nations, it would mean *the moral degradation of Germany*, and she would, from the cultural point of view, be inferior to countries like Portugal.[78]

The ethnic 'otherness' reflects back on the understanding of the 'self'

While Germany's polygenic, exclusionist self-image was reflected in its extreme in the brutal extermination of the natives in South-West Africa, in the metropolis the exclusion of the native 'other' on racial grounds took place through 'distancing'. Late-nineteenth-century German colonial enthusiasts, such as Carl Hagenbeck, Felix von Luschan, and Hilke Thode-Arora, had recourse to the idea of 'colonial exhibitions' (*Volkerschauen*) to highlight the distinctiveness of the natives as well as to educate the Germans about the practicalities of the science of race. Before German race-scientists began to travel to the colonies themselves, such exhibitions offered them access to a steady supply of human subjects to examine and measure and, in return, allowed the organisers of these exhibitions to assure their audience that their living exhibits had been authenticated by men of science and even to claim that their shows were contributing to scientific progress.[79]

[75] Heinrich Schnee, *German Colonisation: Past and Future* (London: George Allen & Unwin, 1926), 169.
[76] *Ibid.*, 171.
[77] Matthias Erzberger, *The League of Nations: The Way to World's Peace*, trans. Bernard Miall (New York: Henry Holt and Company, 1919), 242.
[78] *Ibid.*, 246. Italic in original. [79] Olusoga and Erichsen, *Kaiser's Holocaust*, 92.

In one such exhibition in Hagenbeck's Tierpark, clusters of authentic villages representing the cultures were built on either side of a path; they were numbered, labelled, and cross-referenced in an educational brochure.[80] To sharpen the line of difference between the native show-members and the European visitors, whose mutual communication was restricted, the arrangement in Tierpark and Berlin's Zoological Garden allowed the visitors, as von Joeden-Forgey notes, 'to move from one display of people to the display of animals without leaving the grounds, a geographical fact that suggested a greater link between non-Western peoples and animals than between non-Western and Western peoples'.[81] In 1896, the German state itself organised one of the largest colonial exhibitions in Berlin's Treptow Park; it created the appearance of vast cultural and racial differences between Germans and colonial subjects.[82] It was a joint venture of the government's Colonial Department and the Colonial Society, whose patron was Kaiser Wilhelm's close friend, Prince von Hohenlohe. It was envisaged as a human zoo, in which all the races over whom the Kaiser claimed domination could be viewed in their natural and primitive state.[83] Interestingly, when the Herero and Nama arrived in Berlin wearing trousers, organisers demanded they abandon their Western clothes, which would undermine the authenticity of the show.[84]

This, then, was a moment of understanding the ethnic 'self' through its relationship with the ethnic 'other'. Proponents of political racialism believed that colonial governance had taught the German state 'that "mixing" was a threat to national well being, that race difference was a radical phenomena involving completely opposing cosmic spaces, and that humanity (humanitarianism) must be exercised in conformity with racism's scientific laws'.[85] With the conviction that a colonial model of racially exclusionist governance in the metropolis would secure Germany's cosmic superiority, leading proponents, such as Josef Reimer, Klaus Wagner, and Heinrich Class, juxtaposed colonial scenarios

80 Von Joeden-Forgey, 'Nobody's People', 387. 81 *Ibid.*, 388, 393.

82 *Ibid.*, 388. Interestingly enough, even in June 2005 an African cultural festival, entitled 'African Village', took place in the local zoo of the town of Augsburg in southern Bavaria as the zoo provided, according to the brochure of the event, the 'natural environment' to demonstrate the 'dark continent' in a 'genuine exotic ambience'. This exposition of racism and cultural insensitivity created controversy in Germany. See Charles Hawley, 'African Village Accused of Putting Humans on Display' in *Spiegel Online*, submitted on 9 June 2005; available at: www.services.spiegel.de.

83 Olusoga and Erichsen, *Kaiser's Holocaust*, 92. 84 *Ibid.*

85 Von Joeden-Forgey, 'Nobody's People', 432.

with the Eastern expansion in which the non-Aryan 'other' was excluded from the Germanic image of the 'self' following the pattern of colonial brutalities.[86]

The liberal vision of universalism came under strong criticism here. Reimer found the notion of universal humanity to be a 'bastard-idea' introduced by the 'bastards of [the] Roman Empire', and if the Germanic race accepted it, according to him, alien races 'would be able to "smuggle" themselves into the German body politic by virtue of the political openness fostered by false ideas of humanity'.[87] He therefore hoped that the proper understanding of humanity in racial terms would awaken German youth to the new possibilities as well as necessities of their time: the German state had to expand, and at the same time a strict separation of the races had to take place in the occupied territories as well as at home – the 'civitas Germanica' – into which persons with only Germanic blood would be incorporated and given equal rights.[88] Similarly, Wanger described the whole idea of the common humanity of a raceless world as '*Volk*-adverse and therefore nature-adverse and therefore also culture-adverse'.[89]

Such a polygenic notion of racial segregation and the proposition that 'colonial governance was principally a matter of solving the "race problem" was enough of a consensus issue by 1910'.[90] African linguist Carl Meinhof, who, despite his cosmopolitan image, shared with the conservatives the aversion to racial mixing, provides a good example of this line of thought. While, given his background in Protestant theology and his work with Protestant missionaries, he continued to rely on the monogenic idea behind the 'civilising mission', he firmly opposed any idea of racial mixing, especially in relation to the natives.[91] Meinhof even expressed concerns about Africans visiting, residing in, and being educated in Germany, for in his view no African could ever be a true German.[92]

[86] See Leon Poliakov, *The Aryan Myth: A History of Racist and Nationalistic Ideas in Europe* (New York: Barnes and Noble, 1996), 301–304.

[87] Josef Reimer, *Ein Pangermanisches Deutschland* (Berlin and Leipzig: Friedrich Luckhardt, 1905), 268, cited in von Joeden-Forgey, 438.

[88] Reimer, *Ein Pangermanisches Deutschland*, 130, cited in von Joeden-Forgey, 440.

[89] Klaus Wanger, *Krieg* (Jena: Costenoble, 1906), 67–68, cited in von Joeden-Forgey, 438–439.

[90] Von Joeden-Forgey, 'Nobody's People', 382. [91] *Ibid.*, 417.

[92] Carl Meinhof, *Deutschlands Pflichten in Afrika* (Hamburg: Deutsch-Evangelischen Laien-Missions-Bund, 1912), 12, cited in von Joeden-Forgey, 417.

Thus, the notion of the ethnic German 'self' is reflected in its relationship with the native 'other' as expressed in the campaign for settlement colonies; conversely, its polygenic, exclusionist framework for dealing with the 'other' is then reflected back on the image of the 'self' to make it even more racist and, hence, exclusionist, as the Nazi regime demonstrated later on. As a matter of fact, nearly two decades after the Herero–Nama genocide, Hitler himself became closely associated with a participant in that genocide – Franz von Epp, who had been a lieutenant during the war against the Herero and Nama.[93] Von Epp was not only a fervent advocate for German expansion at the expense of lower races but also one of the most influential figures in the establishment of the Nazi Party. And it is through von Epp that Hitler met many of the future elites of the party.[94] Although there may not be a causal relationship between the Herero–Nama genocide and the Holocaust under the Nazi rule, both events can be seen, as Olusoga and Erichsen argue, as the phenomenon of 'racial colonialism that viewed human history through the prism of a distorted form of social Darwinism, and regarded the earth as a racial battlefield on which the "weak" were destined to be vanquished'.[95]

In this sense, the nineteenth-century German understanding and execution of colonial policies, being informed by a conservative notion of the nation, sharply contrasted with the liberal vision of civilising the colonial 'other' through assimilation. As Meinhof asserted, German and French cultures were different in that Germans could not adopt 'foreign ways' without becoming a false people; this assertion reflects both 'the long-standing Romantic critique of the French universalism' and 'a more recent German colonial reformist critique of the supposedly assimilationist thrust of many French colonial policies'.[96] It is to this liberal version of colonialism that we turn in the following section.

The liberal approach to the colonial 'other' and international law

From assimilation to association: the case of the French civilising mission

The liberal notion of universalism distinctly dominated French colonialism in the late nineteenth century. Although from the very beginning,

[93] Olusoga and Erichsen, *Kaiser's Holocaust*, 12. [94] *Ibid.* [95] *Ibid.*, 361.

[96] Carl Meinhof, 'Suittlichkeit und Kreig', *Vortrage gehlaten im Hamburger Volksheim*, Nr. 10, 1914, cited in von Joeden-Forgey, 427.

France was involved in the colonial venture in Asia and Africa, French overseas expansion provoked little enthusiasm among the French people. One author thus commented that '[t]he French conquered an empire when their overseas trade was at a minimum and when their people were totally uninterested in the world beyond the seas'.[97] The Republican leader and premier, Jules Ferry, endeavoured to popularise the idea of French colonialism but mainly relied on strategic needs and patriotic duty, which in many ways echoed the official positions of other European countries.[98] For some other colonial proponents, national 'prestige' and not economic benefits was the strongest rationale for advancing French colonisation.[99] It was during the 1880s that the Republican politicians, along with businessmen, adventurers, and scholars, invoked the rhetoric of civilising mission (*mission civilisatrice*) to motivate the nation to acquire and invest in overseas possessions.[100]

The civilising mission, being premised upon the spirit of the French Revolution and the rational, secular ideals of the Enlightenment, was in fact a promise to advance humanity through education, abolish slavery, reform immoral cultural practices, stamp out superstition, improve the livelihoods of France's new colonial populations, and equip colonial societies with political and economic institutions and laws.[101] Putting the 'uncivilised' on the road to 'progress' was considered the primary goal of the French nation, and in this context, colonisation was conceived as something inseparable from the need to spread Republican ideals, culture, knowledge, and technology.[102] Given that the Enlightenment tone of the civilising mission matched the philosophy of the French nation, the appeal to civilisation appeared politically expedient in the 1880s in that 'it provided both a moral justification of and a patriotic motivation for expansionism'.[103] Yet, as Raymond Betts notes, the late-nineteenth-century French imperialists,

[97] Henri Brunschwig, *French Colonialism 1871–1914: Myths and Realities*, trans. William G Brown (London: Pall Mall Press, 1966 [1960]), 19.

[98] See Raymond F. Betts, *Assimilation and Association in French Colonial Theory, 1890–1914* (New York: Columbia University Press, 1961), 3. However, Ferry later claimed that France had a right to conquer 'inferior races' because it had a duty to civilise them. See James P. Daughton, *An Empire Divided: Religion, Republicanism, and the Making of French Colonialism, 1880–1914* (Oxford: Oxford University Press, 2006), 10–11.

[99] See Brunschwig, *French Colonialism*, 13–19.

[100] Daughton, *An Empire Divided*, 5.

[101] *Ibid.*, 5, 11.

[102] Alice Conklin, *A Mission to Civilise: The Republican Idea of Empire in France and West Africa, 1895–1930* (Stanford, California: Stanford University Press, 1997), 248–249.

[103] Daughton, *An Empire Divided*, 5, 10.

who were anxious to justify their stance to a traditionally anti-colonial nation, propagated the idea of a 'civilising mission' not only because such thoughts were appealing to the French but also because they helped to dispel fears about expenses and the possible absurdity of the new phase of overseas ventures.[104]

However, one obvious implication of the liberal, Enlightenment notion of colonialism was the assimilationist approach towards the native 'other' that stood in sharp contrast to that of the Germans. As a matter of fact, the notion of assimilation was always embedded in the French concept of liberal colonialism, despite intermittent and brief periods when it lost significance.[105] But it was during the early years of the Third Republic that assimilation became the guiding philosophy of the French colonial policy, realised by a series of laws and decrees that revived the natives' right to send elected representatives to the French parliament and declared that the French penal code would be applied everywhere.[106] The famous Cremieux Decree of 1870 allowed the Jewish population within Algeria to be naturalised; in the following year, Algeria received the right to elect deputies, and in 1875, senators. The decrees of *rattachement* of 1881, considered the core of the policy of assimilation, put various ministries in the metropolis in charge of services in Algeria.[107] Considering the historical salience of the idea of assimilation in French colonial policy, Betts thus notes, it can scarcely be surprising

[104] Betts, *Assimilation and Association in French Colonial Theory*, 30.

[105] During the drafting of the constitution of the Year III, François Antoine Boissy d'Anglas, a deputy keenly interested in constitutional matters and also in favour of a generous colonial policy, is reported to have declared: 'Attach the colonies to us by ties of common interest [. . .] so that they will be part of our indivisible republic and so that they will be protected and ruled by the same laws and the same government'; accordingly, the framers of the constitution affirmed in Article VI that 'The colonies are an integral part of the Republic and are subject to the same constitutional law'. Although the successful growth of the idea of assimilation during the Revolution was soon stunted with the advent of Napoleon, who despite being interested in colonial matters remained sceptical about assimilation, again in 1848 the new government vigorously translated the traditional French Republican ideas into legislation for the overseas regions. The Constitution of 4 November having declared that the colonies were to be an integral part of French territory, it was legislated that representatives from all the colonies would be elected to the French Parliament. But such efforts were largely destroyed with the change of the regime in France; the Constitution of 1852 declared anew a separate administration for the colonies. See Betts, 13, 17–19.

[106] *Ibid.*, 20.

[107] *Ibid.*, 20–21. For a detailed account of French colonial policies in Algeria, see, generally, David Prochaska, *Making Algeria French: Colonialism in Bone, 1870–1920* (Cambridge: Cambridge University Press, 1990).

that assimilation should have become the outstanding French colonial doctrine in the era of 'civilising mission' and Republican dominance. In his words: 'Even though the vast majority of Frenchmen never reflected on colonial theory, those who did established a line of thought which was consistent with Revolutionary philosophy and its subsequent development'.[108] Greatly stimulated by the Republican egalitarian spirit and nourished by the republic as a symbol of equality, the idea of assimilation never again ceased to play an important role in the French colonial policy and doctrine.[109]

The best expression of the liberal-assimilationist thrust of French colonialism was found in the language policies applied in the colonies. While the Germans followed measures in conformity with their overall exclusionist colonial policies to restrict the use of German by the natives, the French opted for just the opposite. The language policies that Meinhof proposed for the German colonies were informed mainly by a sense of colonial power and the proper direction of cultural flow. With his conviction that the only way to ensure the successful submission of the natives was the strict policing of the sharing of languages, he was wholehearted in his initiatives to educate colonialists, as much as possible, in colonial languages.[110] Although the Colonial Office and the Imperial governments in the colonies, in contrast, preferred to have the natives be taught in German, they did so with international political considerations of creating a token image of 'Germanisation' vis-à-vis the British and the French.[111] Meinhof, however, firmly believed that no matter what the pragmatic political benefits, Africans should not be allowed to learn German, for such an exchange was unnatural and constituted a form of 'cultural bastardisation'.[112]

Conversely, by the late 1890s, massive dissemination of the French language had become an essential aspect of French colonisation, in that French bureaucrats and colonists increasingly demanded the teaching of French in primary and secondary schools.[113] The issue of disseminating the French language, in fact, remained the focal point of the attack on Catholic missionary activities in the colonies by both the Freemasons and the Republicans in the metropolis. These groups often claimed, with

[108] Betts, *Assimilation and Association in French Colonial Theory*, 31. [109] See *ibid.*, 16.
[110] Von Joeden-Forgey, 'Nobody's People', 415.
[111] Hilke Meyer-Bahlberg and Ekkehard Wolff (eds.), *Afrikanische Sprachen in Forschung und Lehre: 75 Jahre Afrikanistik in Hamburg (1909–1984)* (Berlin: Dietrich Reimer, 1986), 19–28, cited in *ibid.*, 415.
[112] Von Joeden-Forgey, 416–417. [113] Daughton, *An Empire Divided*, 96.

certain exaggeration, that the Catholic priests taught their catechists Latin under the pretext that it was the liturgical language and never taught them French. Some argued that missionaries had no interest in teaching French because it would weaken their own domination by enabling their students to communicate with the 'French atheists'. The obvious conclusion, therefore, was that the missionaries felt no sense of duty to France and, hence, to the civilising mission.[114] Although the missionaries gradually bent to the assimilationist language policies, from the interior of West Cochinchina, one missionary, Mossard, questioned the value of teaching French to the Vietnamese peasants who, according to him, after learning French would no longer be peasants willing to work but would pose a serious threat to the stability of the French influence in the colony.[115]

Mossard's criticism went much beyond the language policy; in a sense, it could be seen as a reflection of a more deeply rooted tension between Republicanism and Catholicism in France. The Republicans labelled the clerics as 'anti-individual', 'anti-liberal', 'superstitious', and 'irrational' – characteristics that stood in sharp contrast to Republicanism. Having gained legislative power in the 1870s, Republicans devoted themselves to suppressing religious influence in every aspect of the national life, education being the most significant battleground.[116] The government not only forced religion teachers out of public schools but also expelled the Jesuits, more than 5,000 of them teachers, from France in the early 1880s.[117] However, paradoxically, the Republicans had to rely on Catholic missions to spread the message of the Enlightenment in the colonies, given the heavy cost of the project.[118]

Thus, the missionary involvement in the French colonial project was complicated by constant allegations from the Republican establishment and its allies in both the metropolis and the colonies that the missionaries' real dedication was to converting the native population to Christianity and not to civilising them.[119] James Daughton demonstrates how the Republicans' expectation of the clerics in the metropolis to uphold the liberal self-image of the French nation was quickly translated

[114] See *ibid.*, 95. [115] Cited in *ibid.*, 105. [116] *Ibid.*, 9.

[117] Ralph Gibson, *A Social History of French Catholicism, 1789–1914* (New York: Routledge, 1989), 128.

[118] Daughton, *An Empire Divided*, 5–6.

[119] *Ibid.*, 42–43. However, at a later stage, with the heightening of the Republican criticism, missionaries in fact took the defence, without much success, that Christianising is the first step towards civilisation.

into colonial policies that engendered direct confrontation with the missionaries and their work. For example, the formal separation of the church and the state in France following the Dreyfus affair severely impeded the functioning of missionaries in the remote areas of Indochina and created confrontation.[120] In return, Daughton continues, such confrontations between the missions and the administration in the colonies 'spurred republican politicians in Paris to call for policies to defeat the missions' both at home and in the colonies.[121] What appears from this interactive process is an account of how the liberal self-image was reflected in its relationship with the native 'other', and this experience of interaction with the colonies then reflected back on the discourse on the 'self' in the metropolis. In this context, it appears that the process advanced in line with the similar course that the conservative German nationalism undertook in its relationship with the natives, though the actual substance of German colonialism was quite different from that of the French.

However, the Republican vision of spreading the Enlightenment values by taking an assimilationist approach to the native 'other' met a more powerful force: the science of human evolution, which shook its very foundation during the late nineteenth century. While social Darwinism offered the ideology of race to the German nationalist project, its monogenic version allowed the liberal French nation to consider a hierarchical world order wherein some nations 'progressed' more than others. The theory of evolutionary progress strongly influenced French colonial thought, in that the difficulties of governing subject peoples could be explained by the differences among races and their socio-cultural attributes; the very idea of assimilation thus fell prey to this new idea.[122] For example, Commander Edmond Ferry argued that the Sudanese, who manifested the primitive state's most significant

[120] The Dreyfus affair was a political event in the 1890s and the early 1900s caused by the imprisonment of Captain Alfred Dreyfus, a Jewish officer in the French Army. Dreyfus was sentenced to life imprisonment in November 1894 on the charge of treason, which was proved baseless two years later. Dreyfus was exonerated and reinstated as a major in the French Army in 1906. The Dreyfus affair sharply divided the French society between Dreyfusards (Republicans) and anti-Dreyfusards (Catholic conservatives). This event facilitated anti-Semitic and right-wing campaigns, which in turn attracted more attacks on Catholicism inside France and also in the colonies. See *ibid.*, 86–97. For a detailed account of the Dreyfus event, see George R. Whyte, *The Dreyfus Affair – A Chronological History* (Hampshire: Palgrave Macmillan, 2005).

[121] Daughton, 16.

[122] Betts, *Assimilation and Association in French Colonial Theory*, 59.

characteristics, could reach the fortunes of civilisation in different stages, instead of by outright assimilation; the role of France in this evolutionary struggle was to aid the natives 'in this long and difficult climb toward the good and the beautiful'.[123]

The assimilationist thrust of the republic was opposed for practical considerations as well. French colonial administrators were accused of trying to transport their civilisation across the seas with the intention of bestowing it upon colonial people, while the British, it was argued, were guided only by the utilitarian goal of making colonies profitable.[124] Referring to the inherent tendency of the French colonial administration to replicate metropolitan ideologies instead of considering ground realities, Louis Brunel thus asserted: 'In order to govern her colonies England utilises the elements she finds on the spot while France imports hers from home'.[125] Jules Harmand's comparison of French colonial policies in Indochina with those of the British in India even led him to conclude that both India and Indochina were 'possessions', not 'colonies'. While 'colonies', according to him, were regions which were suitable for colonisation and where the Europeans find similar conditions to those of their country of origin, 'possessions' allowed the Europeans to assume only the role of director, of 'protector of the native races', without shouldering the expenses of governing them, something the British were successfully doing, unlike the French.[126] Against this backdrop, a new colonial policy – association – appeared on the scene to replace, at least theoretically, the long-standing assimilationist approach of the French colonial mission.

As a principle, the idea of association emphasised the importance of considering local needs; instead of universalism and centralisation, it focused on the variation in colonial practice depending on the colonies' geographic and ethnic composition as well as their level of socio-cultural development. Under this new system, all French efforts were to be directed towards developing the region through the association of the French and the natives wherein each would do what best suited its abilities and stage of development.[127] This shift from the idea of

[123] Edmond Ferry, *La France en Afrique* (Paris: Armand Colin, 1905), 228, 232, quoted in *ibid.*, 82–83.

[124] Betts, 43.

[125] Louis Brunel, *L'Etat et l'individu dans la colonization françoise moderne* (Paris: A. Fontemoing, 1898), 66–67, quoted in Betts, 45.

[126] Jules Harmand, 'Preface' in *L'Inde*, Sir John Strachey, trans. Jules Harmand (Paris: Bibliothèque générale de géographie, 1892), xxi, cited in Betts, 53–54.

[127] Betts, 106–107.

assimilation to that of association in a sense meant breaking with the Enlightenment philosophy of 'equality'. As Rene Maunier explained, the partnership between the metropolis and the colony went through three sequential phases: an expression of the idea and spirit of humanitarianism, then of equality, and finally of fraternity. Association developed in the first phase wherein 'there is no equality, but there is humanity and moderation. [. . .] there is collaboration and cooperation, but of superior and inferior'.[128]

Thus, 'association' prescribed the 'progress' of the colonies within the framework of native institutions, but the association was to occur with an underlying notion of inequality between the sides. To quote Betts:

> Germinated in the fertile soil of the Enlightenment, as were so many humanitarian ideas, and fed by the stream of thought emanating from the Quaker, association then implied mutual trust and friendly cooperation, but of two differently developed peoples whose relationship was described as one of teacher – or of 'governor' in the sense of protector – and pupil.[129]

With certain modifications, therefore, the French notion of the civilising mission remained alive; in place of an assimilationist approach driven by 'equality', now a hierarchical system would guide the process of native progress. However, given the omnipresence of moral concerns in the French colonial theory, it is argued, the ideas of assimilation and association often overlapped in practice; some of the imperialists even believed that association was a disguise for assimilation.[130]

International law and colonialism in the liberal tradition

The liberal model of colonialism, though presented here with specific reference to the French practice, demonstrates the fundamental tenets of the interaction between the European 'self' and the non-European 'other' within a liberal framework. Liberal writers had to find a principled position on colonialism and justify colonial people's deprivation of their own chosen way of life; thus, colonialism 'could not and did not remain an external historical phenomenon which liberals could comfortably ignore'.[131] In general, nineteenth-century liberal international

128 Rene Maunier, *The Sociology of Colonies*, ed. and trans. E. O. Lorimer, vol. I (London: Routledge and Kegan Paul, 1949), 297.

129 Betts, 108. Endnotes in original omitted. 130 *Ibid.*, 165–167.

131 Bhikhu Parekh, *Rethinking Multiculturalism: Cultural Diversity and Political Theory* (London: Macmillan, 2000), 34.

lawyers heavily relied on the notion of the standard of civilisation, for without such a standard it would have been impossible for them to rationalise massive colonisation of the non-European communities, and in the absence of any such specific 'standard' in practice, international lawyers came to focus on when these communities 'would have started to resemble the Europeans to the extent that they could be smoothly integrated into the European system'.[132]

For Westlake, as we saw in the preceding chapter, the defining feature of civilisation was the presence of appropriate Western-style institutions for the purpose of governance:

> No theorist on law who is pleased to imagine a state of nature independent of human institutions can introduce into his picture a difference between civilised and uncivilised man, because it is just in the presence or absence of certain institutions, or in their greater or less perfection, that that difference consists for the lawyer.[133]

In other words, for Westlake, it is neither the mental or moral characters nor domestic or social habits which distinguish the civilised from the uncivilised individual[134]; rather, he continues, natives must be able to provide necessary protection under a well-defined government to the people of the European race when the latter come into contact with the former.[135] By failing to do so, which was often the case with American or African tribes, he believed, these natives not only demonstrated their lower degree of civilisation but also provided the Western colonisers a justification for the establishment of a proper government under their auspices. For

> [t]he inflow of the white race cannot be stopped where there is land to cultivate, ore to be mined, commerce to be developed, sport to enjoy, curiosity to be satisfied. If any fanatical admirer of savage life argued that the whites ought to be kept out, he would only be driven to the same conclusion by another route, for a government on the spot would be necessary to keep them out.[136]

It is for this reason that, Westlake argues, international law has to treat such natives as uncivilised.[137]

[132] See Koskenniemi, *Gentle Civilizer of Nations*, 135. Cf. Antony Anghie, 'Finding the Peripheries: Sovereignty and Colonialism in Nineteenth-Century International Law', *Harvard International Law Journal* 40, no. 1 (1999), 22–25, 52–54.

[133] John Westlake, *Chapters on the Principles of International Law* (Cambridge: Cambridge University Press, 1894), 137.

[134] *Ibid.*, 141. [135] *Ibid.* [136] *Ibid.*, 142–143. [137] *Ibid.*, 143.

However, Westlake does not mean that such natives should be deprived of all rights. For him the question is more about the source of the rights and protections that might have to be made available to the natives. On this score, he held that the appreciation of such rights of natives should be left to the conscience of the civilised state within whose recognised territorial sovereignty natives are included.[138] Although the general rules of international law are meant for civilised nations, he continues, there is no restriction preventing such a state from enacting rules for the protection of those who fall outside the international society. But such rights of natives remain as moral rights and can scarcely be converted into legal rights: the treatment of the natives of the colonised territory is left to the conscience of the state to which the sovereignty of that territory is awarded.[139] In his words:

> Becoming subjects of the power which possesses the international title to the country in which they live, natives have on their governors more than the common claim of the governed, they have the claim of the ignorant and helpless on the enlightened and strong; and that claim is the more likely to receive justice, the freer is the position of the governors from insecurity and vexation.[140]

In this sense, nineteenth-century liberal international lawyers shared much with the naturalist jurists of the preceding centuries, despite their distinct positivist and naturalist approaches, respectively, to the structure of the interaction between the civilised Europeans and the uncivilised non-Europeans. As Anghie's oft-cited take on sixteenth-century Spanish theologist Francesco Vitoria demonstrates, Vitoria's justifications for Spanish colonisation of the American Indians depended, among many other factors, on the fact that the aborigines were almost completely unintelligent and, therefore, unfit to found or administer a lawful state up to the standard required by human and civil claims. Proof was abundant in his support: they were not capable of controlling their family affairs; they were without any literature or arts; and most importantly, they had neither proper laws nor magistrates.[141] As a consequence of such 'lack', according to Vitoria, it was natural that for the greater interest of the Indians, 'the sovereigns of Spain might undertake the

[138] *Ibid.*, 136. [139] *Ibid.*, 136, 140, 143. [140] *Ibid.*, 140.

[141] Francisco de Vitoria, *De Indis Reflection Prior*, trans. J. P. Bates (New York: Oceana Press, 1917 [1532]), 161. See also Anthony Anghie, 'Francisco De Vitoria and the Colonial Origins of International Law', *Social and Legal Studies* 5, no. 3 (1996), 321–336; A. Anghie, *Imperialism, Sovereignty and the Making of International Law* (Cambridge: Cambridge University Press, 2005), 13–31.

administration of their country, providing them with prefects and governors for their towns, and might even give them new lords, so long as this was clearly for their benefit'.[142] In Vitoria's writing, as Anghie observes, 'particular cultural practices of the Spanish assume the guise of universality as a result of appearing to derive from the sphere of natural law'.[143] These universal norms, constructed as a sophisticated manipulation of natural law theories, are then set as a standard on the basis of which peoples outside Europe were not only assigned an inferior image of 'barbarian' or 'uncivilised' in the succeeding centuries but also given a direction to follow to an enlightened universalist future. The colonial mission is then presented as a philanthropic project, the native being the main beneficiary:

> [T]his might be founded on the precept of charity, they being our neighbors and we being bound to look after their welfare. Let this, however, [. . .] be put forward without dogmatism and subject also to the limitation that any such interposition be for the welfare and in the interests of the Indians and not merely in the interest of the Spaniards. [. . .] And herein some help might be gotten from the consideration [. . .] that some are by nature slaves, for all the barbarians in question are of that type and so they may in part be governed as slaves are.[144]

The liberal rhetoric that the whole colonial project was advanced with a spirit of benevolence made Thomas Lawrence appreciate the philanthropic venture of the International Association of the Congo under the direction of the King Leopold II of Belgium, who spent his own resources for setting up 'civilised settlements in the vast area of the Congo basin, for the

[142] Vitoria, *De Indis Reflection Prior*, 161.

[143] Anghie, 'Francisco De Vitoria and the Colonial Origins of International Law', 326. See also Yasuaki Onuma, 'When Was the Law of International Society Born? An Inquiry of the History of International Law from an Intercivilisational Perspective', *Journal of the History of International Law* 2 (2000), 1–66. Vitoria's doctrinal position on Spaniard–Indian relations had profound influence on successive generations of international lawyers. Eighteenth-century German professor Christian Wolff, for example, similarly asserted that given their little care for intellectual virtues and neglect for perfecting the intellect, the barbarous nations followed the leadership of their natural inclinations and aversions in determining their actions, whereas cultured and civilised nations 'cultivate intellectual virtues', 'desire to perfect the intellect', 'develop the mind by training', and possess 'civilised usages or usages which conform to the standard of reason and politeness'. See Christian Wolff, *Jus Gentium Methodo Scientifica Pertractatum*, trans. Joseph H. Drake (New York: Oceana Press, 1964 [1749]), 33. Thus, he found it logical that the civilised would take the responsibility of training the barbarians so that the latter could join the civilised world (15–17).

[144] Vitoria, *De Indis Reflection Prior*, 161.

purpose of combating the slave-trade, and opening up the country to legitimate and peaceful commerce'.[145]

So the acts of colonisation were claimed as morally justified and were thus never seriously contested, let alone condemned, by liberal international lawyers. Koskenniemi offers a useful account of nineteenth-century French international lawyers in this regard. For example, although Louis Renault noted in his textbook published in 1879 that frequent misuse of power and imposition of unjust wars by the Europeans against the 'so-called barbarians' violated the most elementary rules of international law, his general criticism hardly counted as serious resistance to colonisation; in contrast, Renault expressed sympathy for the French consular jurisdiction in Turkey and China.[146] Likewise, Charles Solomon, despite stating in his harsh criticism of the civilising mission that '[n]o word is more vague and has permitted the commission of more crimes than that of civilisation' and that the language of civilisation was pure hypocrisy, in that it advanced only commercial interests, did not attack colonialism itself. Rather, he found the root of the problems in external issues such as egoism, greed, and vanity.[147] Koskenniemi traces similar criticism of colonial atrocities in the writings of Gaston Jeze (who condemned the destruction of native communities during the early European expansions) and Edouard Engelhardt (who insisted that territorial acquisition be connected with administrative duties). Nevertheless, Koskenniemi notes, these authors, like Solomon, did not protest colonialism itself but claimed that formal expansion of European sovereignty into colonial territories would be the only means to check the excesses of purely commercial colonisation.[148] Similarly, Swiss international lawyer Joseph Hornung, with all his humanitarianism, declared that colonialism – the moral mission towards world

[145] Thomas J. Lawrence, *The Principles of International Law* (London: Macmillan, 1895), 86. However, the later history of the Congo as a matter of fact stands in sharp contradiction with King Leopold's projected benevolence. It is to be noted on this score that when the King of Hitties – Suppiluliuma – conquered the country of Izuva in 1350 BC, he explained the conquest by the fact that the latter had belonged to the Hitties' kingdom for long, so he was seeking to *liberate*, and not *conquer*, people that were Izuva's subjects. In his words: '[T]he countries I had occupied I liberated, and their people remained in their places; the people I had made free returned to their folk'. See James B. Pritchard (ed.), *Ancient Near Eastern Texts Relating to the Old Testament*, 2nd edn (Princeton, New Jersey: Princeton University Press, 1955), 318, cited in Olga V. Butkevych, 'History of Ancient International Law: Challenges and Prospects', *Journal of the History of International Law* 5 (2003), 205.

[146] Koskenniemi, *Gentle Civilizer of Nations*, 105–106.

[147] See *ibid.*, 106.

[148] *Ibid.*, 107.

federation – was justified, albeit only if it was in the interests of the natives. Thus, in the late nineteenth century, in Koskenniemi's words, 'international legal history became a history of individual lawyers acting like so many chivalrous knights, defending the oppressed against the oppressors, peace against war, carrying the torch of civilization (from Greece and Rome) through dark ages to the present'.[149]

However, being developed within the Darwinist notion of cultural hierarchy, this inclusion in the federation did not encompass actual assimilation on the basis of equality. The European presence in colonies was devoted to, even if rhetorically, parenting its uncivilised children; there could be no question of equality in such an analogy. Thus, for Hornung, the European colonisers and the non-Europeans natives were not equal; instead, the natives were, to quote him, 'children, of course, but then let us treat them as one treats children, through gentleness and persuasion [. . .]. We accept the hegemony and trusteeship of the strong but only in the interests of the weak and in view of their full future emancipation'.[150] Having referred to the approving response to colonialism of nineteenth-century liberal international lawyers, Koskenniemi concludes that while their approaches were diverse, nineteenth-century international lawyers could nonetheless reconcile their apparently divergent positions by shifting their uses of exclusion and inclusion:

> [E]xclusion in terms of a cultural argument about the otherness of the non-European that made it possible to extend European rights to the native, inclusion in terms of the native's similarity with the European, the native's otherness having been erased by a universal humanitarianism under which international lawyers sought to replace native institutions by European sovereignty.[151]

This substantiates the theoretical proposition that the liberal approach to the 'other' envisaged the assimilation of the latter into high culture (here, civilisation) but, simultaneously, developing within the monogenic Darwinist notion of progress, kept the ethnic 'other' constantly at a distance – a pattern that appeared more sophisticated than (and in sharp contrast to) the German conservative notion of outright exclusion of the 'other'. As Partha Chattarjee argues, the British colonisation of India, on the one hand, held the promise of eradication of difference 'by bringing colonised people forward into the fold of progress and history' but, on the other hand, had to rely on the difference for its own survival, for 'once colonised "others" became modern subjects, colonial control

[149] *Ibid.*, 78. [150] Quoted in *ibid.*, 130. [151] *Ibid.*

would have lost its ideological foothold'.[152] Hence, the colonial power had to continue to underscore the difference between the coloniser and the colonised despite its promises of universal ideas and institutions.

Therefore, it is no surprise that although Mill believed that the ideally best form of government is representative government,[153] he nonetheless held that the colonisers and the colonised cannot live together under the same free institutions, for the absorption of the colonisers into the less advanced people would be an evil; therefore, the uncivilised natives must be governed as subjects.[154] For Mill, civilisation is an outcome of the quality of governance, and in this sense, the lack of civilisation in any community is the consequence of previous bad government that failed to demonstrate the usefulness of law and order. Therefore, Mill saw colonialism as a necessary corrective to the uncivilised social order and a means to foster national pride, self-confidence, a sense of greatness, lofty sentiments, and a high sense of moral purpose.[155]

Being a liberal, Mill believed that the habits of lawlessness hitherto present among the uncivilised communities may eventually be overcome with better governance, but as long as such habits exist, those societies cannot be governed with as little power exercised over them as over a people whose sympathies are on the side of the law.[156] Given that it is practically impossible for an uncivilised people to make any progress in civilisation until it has learnt to obey the rule and rulers, and hence, that the indispensable virtue of a government which establishes itself over a savage people lies in making itself obeyed, Mill argued that the constitution of such government 'must be nearly, or quite, despotic' to ensure this obedience takes root.[157] This is what Mill advocated as a policy for colonial administration.

Yet, not for all colonies! While colonies of the European race, for example, Canada and Australia, should enjoy, in both theory and practice, the fullest measure of internal self-government,[158] there is no

[152] Partha Chatterjee, *The Nation and Its Fragments: Colonial and Postcolonial Histories* (Princeton, New Jersey: Princeton University Press, 1993).

[153] By which he meant a government 'in which the sovereignty, or supreme controlling power in the last report, is vested in the entire aggregate of the community; every citizen not only having a voice in the exercise of that ultimate sovereignty, but being, at least occasionally, called on to take an actual part in the government, by the personal discharge of some public function, local or general'. See John Stuart Mill, 'Representative Government (1861)' in *Utilitarianism, Liberty, Representative Government* (London: Everyman's Library, 1964 [1910]), 207.

[154] *Ibid.*, 364. [155] Parekh, *Rethinking Multiculturalism*, 45.

[156] Mill, 'Representative Government', 179. [157] *Ibid.*, 197–198. [158] *Ibid.*, 378.

question of representative government for colonies such as India, which have failed to attain the desired level of civilisation. In his words: 'There are [. . .] conditions of society in which a vigorous despotism is in itself the best mode of government for training the people in what is specifically wanting to render them capable of higher civilisation. [. . .] Such is the ideal rule of a free people over a barbarous or semi-barbarous one'.[159]

This notion of cultural hierarchy as a precursor to the degree of civilisation, even among the non-self-governing communities, was also incorporated by liberal international lawyers in devising a system for recognising hitherto uncivilised nations as 'states' and hence new members of the international society. As liberal international lawyers argued, the treatment of new states desiring access to this society should not be uniform; instead, following liberal Darwinist principles, cases should be determined on the basis of the cultural progress of the nations seeking admission. James Lorimer, for example, held that civilised nations, as their right, may grant three stages of recognition: first, plenary political recognition for 'civilised humanity', that is, all the existing states of Europe with their colonial dependencies, *insofar as these are peopled by persons of European birth or descent* as well as the States of America; second, partial political recognition for 'barbarous humanity' comprising Turkey, China, Japan, and Siam; and finally, natural or mere human recognition for 'savage humanity', covering the rest of mankind.[160]

On the other hand, Lawrence differentiated between the admission of states hitherto barbarous (e.g., Turkey, Japan, and Persia) and the admission of states formed by civilised men in hitherto uncivilised states (e.g., the Transvaal, the Congo Free State, and Liberia). For the first category of states, he required that they should be, to some extent, civilised following the European model. Since the exact amount of civilisation required for this purpose could not be defined beforehand, Lawrence prescribed that each case must be judged on its own merits by the powers who dealt with it.[161] Although Lawrence did not provide any specific mechanism for admission of the states in the second category, it seemed obvious from this categorisation that these states had already attained a certain degree of civilisation. More specifically, these hitherto uncivilised states had transformed themselves with the help of civilised men who had taken the responsibility of civilising the uncivilised out of philanthropic zeal.

[159] *Ibid.*, 382.

[160] James Lorimer, *The Institutes of the Law of Nations: A Treatise of the Jural Relations of Separate Political Communities* (Edinburgh: Blackwood, 1883), 101–102.

[161] Lawrence, *The Principles*, 85.

Given that there was no defined standard of civilisation, the fate of states seeking admission to the international society remained at the mercy of the civilised European nations.

Conclusion

What I emphasise in the foregoing brief sketch of the German and French colonial policies is that the nineteenth-century colonial projects demonstrated a construction of the European 'self' and the non-European 'other' that was not defined by ethnicity alone. This narrative also explains how such a dynamic process of identity formation, presented through the lens of the conservative and liberal traditions of understanding the role of ethnicity, underscores the distinctiveness in the liberal and conservative perceptions of colonialism as well as their consequences. Far from being homogeneous, the story of colonialism, thus, tells us why the assimilationist thrust of liberal international lawyers, as expressed in the notion of 'civilising mission', remained very different from the conservative-exclusionist project of German colonialism as endorsed by international lawyers in the conservative Romantic camp.

The relationship between nineteenth-century colonial practices and legal approaches to managing twentieth-century ethnic conflicts has not been adequately recognised in the existing legal literature. My argument is that nineteenth-century nationalism and thinking about ethnicity had these two approaches, which need to be properly understood in order to appreciate subsequent developments of international law. For example, the force of nationalism having reached its peak on the eve of the Great War, the ethnic discourse on 'self' and 'other' came to shape the interwar international law in relation to the protection of the left-outs – the minorities – as the Eastern and Central European states were crafting their national self-images in the conservative sense. As we shall see in the following chapter, the very foundation of this interwar mechanism relied on how the liberal West portrayed the ethnic non-Western 'other' within Europe in contrast to its own image of the 'self' – a pattern that reappeared in the post–Cold War European mechanisms of minority protection. In this sense, international law, developed through the nineteenth-century discourse on the liberal and conservative streams of identity formation, demonstrates the ethnic dichotomy of 'self' and 'other' even in its present-day use.

3

Ethnicity in interwar international law

The minority protection regime in perspective

Introduction

The discourse on ethnicity and its salience, as understood in liberal and conservative traditions, for dealing with the colonial 'other' in the periphery and for the political organisation of metropolis nation-states continued long after the nineteenth century. The philosophical traditions vis-à-vis the treatment of ethnicity had profound impact on the way international law responded to the minority problem and managed ethnic tensions in the interwar period and beyond.

The idea of the protection of minorities in international law is marked by ambiguity. Although international law never offered any general recognition of group rights, minority groups enjoyed protection under a series of international treaties and conventions throughout history.[1] Among the first direct attempts at minority protection were measures to safeguard the religious minorities that appeared and grew in importance as a result of the Reformation.[2] With the emergence of nationalist ideology in the nineteenth century, which engendered new categories of minorities through the dichotomy of 'self' and 'other', the protection of national minorities once again became necessary.[3]

[1] Examples of pre-World War I treaties dealing with the issue of minority protection include the Peace of Augsburg (1555), the Pact of Warsaw (1573), the Edict of Nantes (1598), the Treaty of Vienna (1607), the Treaty of Westphalia (1648), the Treaty of Oliva (1660), the Treaty of Peace between France and Great Britain (1713), the Treaty of Paris between Great Britain and Spain (1763), the Treaty of Dresden between the King of Prussia and the Elector of Saxony (1745), the Congress of Vienna (1815), the Treaty of Berlin between Great Britain, Austria-Hungary, France, Germany, Italy, Russia and Turkey (1878), and the Convention of Constantinople between Austria-Hungary and Turkey (1879).

[2] *Ibid.*

[3] The Congress of Vienna (1815), for example, incorporated provisions protecting national minorities alongside religious minorities. Reflecting the dismemberment of the Polish state, Article I provides: 'The Poles, who are [...] subjects of Russia, Austria and Prussia, shall obtain a Representation and National Institutions, regulated according to the degree

Yet, despite the existence of a number of treaties protecting minorities at that time, no general system actually developed for the protection of minorities. Inis Claude provides a plausible explanation for such a failure: 'The system of minority protection based upon special treaties guaranteed by the great powers was condemned to failure by the inadequacy of its scope, the vagueness of substantive provisions, the rudimentary nature of its machinery and organisation, and the uncertainty, ineffectiveness and susceptibility to abuse of its sanctions'.[4] Given the repeated change of territorial borders due to the frequent outbreak of wars, these treaties were also *ad hoc*. It is generally agreed that it was only in the aftermath of the World War I that a *system* for the protection of minorities was established for the first time.

What I demonstrate in this chapter, however, is that the interwar mechanism for minority protection engendered a three-layer ethnic discourse that was expressed through the nineteenth century's liberal and conservative traditions. First, the interwar minority protection system came into being as a compromise between the liberal and conservative traditions vis-à-vis ethnicity and its role in the political organisation of nation-states. The idea of minority rights appeared as a fallback position where Wilson's proposition of the right to self-determination in conservative terms could not be realised, but liberal individualism as well as the assimilationist agenda always co-existed with the conservative ethnic notion of 'minority'. Secondly, a dichotomy between the liberal West and the conservative Eastern 'other' was evident in the imposition of special minority protection obligations on Eastern and Central European (ECE) states, while minorities within Western Europe remained outside any international protection. And finally, the inherent drawbacks of the system that became evident in its actual operation

of political consideration, that each of the Governments to which they belong shall judge expedient and proper to grant them'. See Michael Hurst (ed.), *Key Treaties for the Great Powers 1814–1914*, vol. I (Newton Abbot: David and Charles, 1971), 45. Various philosophies might have encouraged such protection of minorities. Goldsmith and Posner, taking an instrumentalist approach to international law, called such treaties '*symmetric* cooperative human rights law'. See Jack L. Goldsmith and Eric A. Posner, *The Limits of International Law* (New York: Oxford University Press, 2005), 113. In such treaties, according to them, 'each State contains a different ethnic and religious majority that cares about the well-being of coethnics or coreligionists who form a minority in the other State. The States enter a treaty that requires each State to grant rights to the minority living within its territory' (*ibid.*). They exemplified this thesis with the mechanism of the protection of religious minorities in the Treaty of Westphalia (1648).

4 Inis L. Claude, *National Minorities: An International Problem* (Cambridge, Massachusetts: Harvard University Press, 1955).

demonstrated another layer of the 'self–other' discourse in which, bypassing the international system, the agenda of mutual exclusion of the ethnic 'other' was brutally pursued in the process of constructing the ethnic self-image along conservative lines.

Minority rights as a compromise between the liberal and conservative traditions

The emergence of nationalism in the nineteenth century was closely associated with war. For nineteenth-century German thinkers, as we saw in Chapter 1, war was the necessary dialectic in the evolution of nations. Frequent outbreaks of war and the ensuing re-drawing of state territories gave birth to fresh minority problems in Europe. States pursued the goal of establishing nation-states, but in reality, what they ended up with were multi-nation states and, in the same process, a number of nations, such as the Germans, turned into multi-state nations. The Paris Peace Conference following the Great War aggravated the minority issue by drastically redrawing the frontiers in Eastern and Central Europe after the collapse of the old empires. In the aftermath of the war, international law had to respond to this minority 'problem' against the backdrop of the most influential notion of the time – self-determination.

In his famous Fourteen Points, Wilson enshrined the notion of self-determination, without actually using the term, as one of the key guiding principles of the post-war international order.[5] In the aftermath of the war, his first draft of the League covenant categorically mentioned in Article III the principle of self-determination, which, along with the provision of certain territorial adjustments, was to qualify the mutual guarantee of political independence and territorial integrity among the contracting powers.[6]

However, the Wilsonian proposition of self-determination, being premised on the centrality of ethnicity in the political organisation of nation-states, faced criticism from even other American delegates as it transpired that the territorial adjustments made at the Paris Peace Conference were unlikely to satisfy all nationalist claims and, therefore, unlikely to prevent ethnic tensions from erupting. David Miller – an American jurist and one of the draftsmen of the League of Nations covenant – asserted in his

[5] For the full text of Wilson's address to the Congress, see Gregory R. Suriano (ed.), *Great American Speeches* (New York: Gramercy Books, 1993), 143–146.

[6] See Miller, *The Drafting of the Covenant*, vol. II (New York: G. P. Putnam's Sons, 1928), 70.

comment on Wilson's draft that such a general provision of self-determination 'will make that dissatisfaction permanent, will compel every Power to engage in propaganda and will legalize irredentist agitation in at least all of Eastern Europe'.[7]

Miller was not alone in criticising Wilson's proposition. It is evident from US Secretary of State Robert Lansing's personal narrative of the peace negotiations in Paris that he was extremely critical of the idea of self-determination as a general principle, let alone as a *right*.[8] Although, when faced with vehement opposition from other statesmen, Wilson dropped the idea of self-determination in his fourth draft and also in the covenant, Lansing found it regrettable that Wilson nevertheless did not openly disavow the principle as the standard for the determination of sovereign authority; hence, the phrase remained one of the general bases for peace negotiation.[9]

Perhaps Wilson himself was aware of the limitations of his policy of self-determination expressed along the conservative line, and for this reason he may have had to deviate from this principle on a number of occasions. In a note written on 30 December 1918, Lansing claims that in the actual application of the principle Wilson rather relied on a number of exceptions to his own creation: millions of ethnic Germans were denied the right to self-determination and transferred to the new states of Poland and Czechoslovakia under the Treaty of Versailles; Austrian Tyrol was ceded to the Kingdom of Italy under the Treaty of Saint-Germain against the will of the vast majority of the entire population of that region; Austria was denied the right to form a political union with Germany; and the peoples of Estonia, Latvia, Lithuania, Ukraine, Georgia, and Azerbaijan were left to the mercy of Great Russia despite their distinct identities and their aspirations to become independent states.[10]

Such deviations from the principle of self-determination, so far as the German minorities were concerned, were quite obvious, for the application of the principle of self-determination otherwise could have meant the unification of Germany.[11] In fact, following the collapse of the Habsburg Empire in October 1918, the pre-war representatives of the German territories of Austria-Hungary passed a draft constitution,

[7] *Ibid.*, 71.

[8] Robert Lansing, *The Peace Negotiations: A Personal Narrative* (Boston, Massachusetts: Houghton Mifflin Company, 1921), 95

[9] *Ibid.* [10] *Ibid.*, 98–100.

[11] See Mark Mazower, *Hitler's Empire – Nazi Rule in Occupied Europe* (London: Penguin Books, 2008), 31–33.

which declared that 'Germany-Austria is a component part of the German Republic'.[12] It was difficult for the victors of the war to see Germany pocket the benefit of their victory; 'the Entente Powers had not really fought for four years merely to preside over the expansion of Germany'.[13] Thus, deviating from the principle of self-determination, the Treaty of Versailles insisted on the establishment of an independent Austria, wherein ethnic Germans were a majority. Later, in an Advisory Opinion, the Permanent Court declared the customs union between Austria and Germany a violation of Article 88 of the Treaty of Saint-Germain and Protocol No. 1 signed at Geneva on 4 October 1922, which stipulated the continuation of Austria as an independent state.[14] Additionally, Germany had to cede territories inhabited by ethnic Germans. The Versailles arrangement handed over 1.2 million Germans to Poland; 3.5 million to Czechoslovakia; 550,000 to Hungary; 250,000 to Italy; 800,000 to Romania; 700,000 to Yugoslavia; and 220,000 to the Baltic states; it turned Germans into the largest minority population in Europe.[15]

However, during the peace negotiations, efforts were made to reconcile the classical notion of sovereignty and the conservative notion of self-determination. As Miller asserted, since the principle of self-determination could not be generally applied,

> [i]t is submitted that the contrary principle should prevail; as the drawing of boundaries according to racial or social conditions is in many cases an impossibility, protection of the rights of minorities and *acceptance of such protection by the minorities* constitute the only basis of enduring peace.[16]

Thus, instead of Wilson's initial proposal of incorporating self-determination as a general principle, on the one hand, an unqualified

[12] *Ibid.*, 31–32. [13] *Ibid.*, 33.

[14] *Customs Régime between Germany and Austria*, PCIJ Report (1931), Ser. A/B, No. 41. However, in the dissenting opinion, Judges M. Adatci, M. Kellogg, Baron Rolin-Jaequemyns, Sir Cecil Hurst, M. Schücking, Jonkheer van Eysinga, and M. Wang held the view that the numerous restrictions were imposed on Austria's liberty of action in the Treaty of Saint-Germain; such was also the case with the 1922 Protocols Nos. II and III signed at the time of the Austrian Reconstruction scheme. 'They affected Austria in matters military, financial or economic, which touch most closely on the national sovereignty. None of them were reciprocal in character. Yet they were all regarded as compatible with Austria's sovereignty and independence. *A fortiori* it seems to follow that a customs regime, such as that proposed in the Vienna Protocol, organised on a basis of parity and reciprocity, does not prejudice the independence of Austria' (86/53).

[15] Mazower, *Hitler's Empire*, 33–34.

[16] Miller, *The Drafting of the Covenant*, vol. II, 71. Italics in original.

guarantee of political independence and territorial integrity of all state members of the League of Nations was stipulated, and, on the other hand, the nationalities within the new states that were not granted the right to self-determination for pragmatic or strategic reasons were put under an international mechanism of minority protection. In other words, the notion of the protection of minorities appeared as a fallback position where the principle of self-determination in the conservative sense could not be applied.

However, it was not easy for the liberal West to design a mechanism for the protection of Eastern minorities, who not only were the product of the conservative Eastern tradition of relying on ethnicity for the political organisation of nation-states but also desired to maintain their ethnic features.[17] This resulted in a reconciliation of the two traditions. It is, therefore, a significant characteristic of the interwar minority protection mechanism that while producing a number of legal experimentations to 'manage' nationalist passions,[18] it actually avoided any general recognition of minority rights. Instead of any provision for minority protection in the League covenant, as Wilson initially proposed, a series of minority treaties was concluded to put certain ECE states under the treaty obligation of protecting minorities within their territories, with the guarantee mechanism being entrusted to the League.[19] As Thornberry notes:

[17] This aspect of the interwar minority protection mechanism will be detailed in the following section.

[18] See, generally, Nathaniel Berman, 'A Perilous Ambivalence: Nationalist Desire, Legal Autonomy, and the Limits of Interwar Framework', *Harvard International Law Journal* 33, no. 2 (1992); also, N. Berman, 'But the Alternative Is Despair: European Nationalism and the Modernist Renewal of International Law', *Harvard Law Review* 106 (1993), 1792–1904.

[19] In Article 12 of the Polish Minority Treaty, which served as a model minority treaty, Poland agreed that 'the stipulation in the Foregoing Articles, so far as they affect persons belonging to racial, religious or linguistic minorities, constitute obligations of international concern and shall be placed under the guarantee of the League of Nations'. This guarantee clause stipulated that 'any Member of the Council of the League of Nations shall have the right to bring to the attention of the Council any infraction of any of these obligations, and that the Council may thereupon take such action and give such direction as it may deem proper and effective in the circumstances'. Poland further agreed in this article that any difference of opinion as to questions of law or fact arising out of these articles between the Polish government and any one of the Principal Allied and Associated Powers or any other power, a member of the Council of the League, would be held to be a dispute of an international character under Article 14 of the Covenant of the League; that is, a dispute that could be heard and decided by the Permanent Court of International Justice (PCIJ). The Polish government thereby consented that any such dispute would, if the other party thereto demanded, be referred to the PCIJ. Similar guarantee clauses were found in other minority treaties as well. Thus, unlike the minority

> [T]he Wilson clauses were more than rules against discrimination – they would have required the relevant States to act in a positive manner toward their 'racial or national' minorities. They included collective rights. As a general formula, this approach, interposing minorities as collectivities with special claims on the State, provoked general resistance.[20]

However, the fact remains that Wilson himself had something else in mind. During the session of the Supreme Council on 23 June 1919, in a brief exchange with Headlam-Morley (a member of the British delegation) about the use of minority language as a medium of instruction in schools in Poland, Wilson is reported to have expressed the view that the American model of cultural assimilation should also be applicable to Eastern and Central Europe. When he was reminded that the German population was long established in the territories to be ceded and in some Polish towns even constituted the majority, he replied: 'Yes, but their properties will become part of Poland and it is not our wish that they remain German forever'.[21]

Nevertheless, it needs to be noted that throughout the peace conference, Wilson had to advance his pro-minority ideas against immense pressure from his counterparts in Europe and even his own deputies. Regarding the Jewish population in the ECE states, at a session of the Council of Four on 1 May 1919, the US president indeed drew the attention of the Supreme Council to the anti-Semitic pogroms in Poland and Romania and read out the Jewish draft treaty of 29 April, but he had to agree with the other members in their unanimous rejection of demands for a 'group autonomy' for Jews.[22] Lloyd George adopted the same assimilationist approach towards the Jewish minorities in Poland: '[E]very effort ought to be made for the Jews of Poland to merge in Polish nationality, just as the Jews in Great Britain or France became merged in British and French nationality'.[23] He was particularly concerned about

treaties of the pre-WWI era, the minority treaties under the League provided a guarantee mechanism, both internal and external. Most importantly, this time, a neutral international organisation took charge of securing implementation, while in the early days, it was only at the discretion of the big powers.

20 Patrick Thornberry, *International Law and the Rights of Minorities* (Oxford: Clarendon Press, 1991), 39.

21 Paul Mantoux, *Délibérations du Conseil des Quatres. Notes de L'Officier Interprete*, vol. II (Paris: 1955), 489, cited in Christian Raitz von Frenz, *A Lesson Forgotten – Minority Protection under the League of Nations. The Case of the German Minority in Poland, 1920–1934* (New York: St. Martin's Press, 1999), 66.

22 Mantoux, *Délibérations du Conseil des Quatres*, vol. I, 440, cited in Frenz, *A Lesson Forgotten*, 59.

23 FRUS, *The Paris Peace Conference*, vol. VI, 626.

the risk of 'the creation of a state within a state' associated with the claim of autonomy for the minorities.[24]

Ultimately, while defining the protected minorities in the Polish Minority Treaty, the phrase 'persons belonging to linguistic, racial and religious minorities' rather than 'national minorities' was used in order to avoid recognition of them as a separate legal corporation within the state.[25] Given the liberal underpinning of the French understanding of nationalism, France even initially refused to endorse any objective criteria, such as ethnicity, language, or religion, as the basis for the application of the right to self-determination; instead, it proposed the principle of plebiscite, which would guarantee the primacy of individual choice in conformity with the French liberal ideology.[26] Although the provision for a plebiscite was not extended to most of the transferred territories, the transferred population had the essential right to decide on their political allegiance, which again demonstrated the tendency to reduce the collectivism in the notion of minority to individualism.[27]

Thus, to what extent the *raison d'être* of the minority protection regime was the 'protection' of minorities at all remains an open question. The Report of de Mello-Franco revealed that the architects of the minority protection system in no way envisioned the minorities as groups of inhabitants who would regard themselves as permanently foreign to the general organisation of the country; instead, they intended for the minorities a certain legal protection which might gradually prepare the way for the conditions necessary for the establishment of a complete 'national unity' within an environment of mutual respect.[28] Joseph Roucek noted that the minority treaties never intended to mitigate the differences of groups within a state; on the contrary, the treaties expressed a desire to promote the consolidation of the states, which would then give the minorities certain rights, thereby protecting them from ultra-nationalism and, in this way, contain ethnic tensions leading to international conflict.[29]

[24] Mantoux, 440, cited in Frenz, 59. [25] See Article 12 of the Polish Minority Treaty.

[26] French government note of 15 November 1918 sent to the US government. See FRUS, *The Paris Peace Conference*, vol. I, 349.

[27] See Article 91 (3) of the Versailles Treaty of 28 June 1919, which stipulated: 'Within a period of two years after the coming into force of the present Treaty, German nationals over 18 years of age habitually resident in any of the territories recognised as forming part of Poland will be entitled to opt for German nationality'.

[28] Report of Afranio de Mello-Franco, 'Council Meeting of 9 December 1925', *League of Nations Official Journal* 7, no. 2 (February, 1926), 142.

[29] Joseph S. Roucek, *The Working of the Minorities System under the League of Nations* (Prague: Orbis Publishing, 1929), 74.

A legal advisor to the American Peace Commission to Paris, Manley Hudson, wrote in 1921 that in the troubled situation of world affairs, the first and foremost responsibility of the peace conference was to establish a stable peace and that, in this connection, it was mandatory to anticipate new instances of irredentism, which might call for future vindication.[30] In this context, Dorothy Jones questions the very intention of the League behind protecting minority rights:

> [T]he original intent was not so much minority protection as border protection. The thinking went like this: Peace in the future would depend on the stability and acceptance of the borders newly drawn by the peacemakers across much of Europe. Dissatisfied minorities within those borders had the potential to be, at best, centres of unrest and, at worst, invitations for intervention. Protect the minorities, make their protection a part of fundamental law that could not be changed without permission of the League, and you protect the settlements on which peace will depend.[31]

In that sense, the idea of minority protection came on board when it was more or less ascertained that the conservative right to self-determination could not be applied to all nationalities, a fact that had the necessary potential for destabilising the peace that the Paris Conference was expected to bring forth.

The minority regime, created as a safety valve, also served the power-politic interest of the Allied Powers advanced through the 'self–other' dichotomy, in that they extended their control into the domestic political sphere of certain ECE states. The minority rights regime also secured strategic interests of the Allied Powers, in that these treaties apparently demonstrated the promise of stabilising the newly established political frontiers by 'reconciling disaffected ethnic groups with their non-dominant status under governments, which in most cases intended to establish homogeneous nation states'.[32] As Berman rightly puts it, '[i]nternational [m]inority protection is the permanent embroidering of sovereigns into the international legal community'.[33] This, together with the official and unofficial inclination of the key peacemakers towards assimilationist policies,

[30] Manley O. Hudson, 'The Protection of Minorities and Natives in the Transferred Territories' in *What Really Happened at Paris? The Story of the Peace Conference, 1918–1919 by American Delegates*, ed. Edward Mandell House (New York: Charles Scribner's Sons, 1921), 208.

[31] Dorothy V. Jones, 'The League of Nations' Experiment in International Protection', *Ethics and International Affairs* 8 (1994), 88.

[32] Frenz, *A Lesson Forgotten*, 71. [33] Berman, 'But the Alternative Is Despair', 1874.

underscores the fact that no real significance was attributed to the protection of the ethnic phenomenon of the 'minority' itself.

However, it would be less than fair to portray the interwar minority protection regime as a purely assimilationist mission. Instead, efforts were made to reconcile the victors' liberal ideology with the conservative ethnic-nationalism of the East, which ultimately gave the minority treaties a hybrid character and the whole regime a transitory nature. The Polish Minority Treaty, which served as a model for other similar minority treaties, is an archetypical example of such an effort of reconciliation. On the one hand, Poland guaranteed equality before the law and undertook to assure full and complete protection of life and liberty as well as the free exercise of religion and language to *all inhabitants* of Poland without any distinction of birth, nationality, language, race, or religion[34]; on the other hand, Poland had to guarantee that the minorities within its territory would enjoy the same treatment and security as other Polish nationals and also an 'equal right to establish, manage and control at their expense charitable, religious and social institutions, schools and other educational establishments, with the right to use their own language and to exercise their religion freely therein'.[35] Therefore, the Polish Minority Treaty adopted a hybrid character incorporating both liberal individualism and the conservative ethnic group phenomenon. As Thornberry notes, the two classes of rights, 'dealing with the rights of all inhabitants and nationals, reflect the preoccupations of Western statesmen, who were convinced that whatever rights minorities should have would be served best in a liberal setting'.[36]

The hybridity of the minority rights regime under the League is precisely shown in the advisory opinion of the Permanent Court in the *Minority Schools in Albania* case, wherein the court declared:

> The idea underlying the treaties for the protection of minorities is to secure for certain elements incorporated in a State, the population of which differs from them in race, language or religion, the possibility of living peacefully alongside that population and co-operating amicably with it, while at the same time preserving the characteristics which distinguish them from the majority, and satisfying the ensuing special needs.[37]

[34] Articles 2 and 7 of the Polish Minority Treaty.

[35] Article 8 of the Polish Minority Treaty. Also Article 9 of the same treaty relating to the use of minority language in schools located in minority-populated areas.

[36] Thornberry, *International Law and the Rights of Minorities*, 43.

[37] PCIJ Report (1935), Ser. A/B, No. 64, 17.

Thus, to attain this object, the court continued, it was necessary to ensure that not only were minorities treated equally to the other nationals of the state but also that suitable means for the preservation of their racial peculiarities, their traditions, and their national characteristics were made available.[38]

With reference to the modernist experimentation, however, Berman argues that such an understanding of 'equality' in substantive terms by the court in the *Minority Schools in Albania* case, as opposed to the Albanians' reliance on formal equality, was in fact a double deviation from the statist approach to international law. First, in interpreting the Albanian Declaration of Minority Rights in question, the court, with its deference to nationalism, relied on the minorities' view of what was 'essential' to them. Second, in doing so, the court paved the way for international experimentation as well as the expansion of international authority.[39] But what is more significant for our purpose is the observation that in this case the court attempted to deviate through judicial activism from the assimilationist approach of the peacemakers to the minorities.[40] Conversely, the dissenting opinion reveals that a simultaneous counter-effort was made to underscore the assimilationist goal of the minority rights regime with the argument that the interpretation of the declaration in question must not deviate from the actual will of the state parties.[41]

Earlier, in the *German Settlers Case*, the Permanent Court in its Advisory Opinion held the view that the Polish action of evicting certain German settlers from their land under the law of 14 July 1920 was undoubtedly a virtual annulment of the civil rights of the settlers acquired under their contracts with the Prussian government as part of Prussia's Germanisation programme. The court then observed that the Polish activities in question were contrary to the principle of equality, in that it subjected the settlers to a discriminating and injurious treatment to which other citizens holding contracts of sale or lease were not subjected. And since Poland, in its minority treaty signed with the Allied Powers, guaranteed equal treatment for all Polish citizens, such action was a violation of the minority treaty provisions.[42] However, the court's opinion is significant for its own ambivalence. While underscoring the primacy of the private rights of individual settlers, and thereby extending

38 *Ibid.* 39 Berman, 'A Perilous Ambivalence', 370–372. 40 See *ibid.*

41 PCIJ Report (1935), Ser. A/B, No. 64, 27.

42 *Questions Relating to Settlers of German Origin in Poland Case*, PCIJ Report (1925), Ser. B, No. 6, 36–37.

protection to the members of the ethnic German community under Polish repression, the court bypassed the political aspects of the whole issue of Germanisation – a product of the conservative German nationalist thrust – declaring that the political purpose behind the colonisation scheme could not affect the private rights acquired under the German Civil Code.[43] At the same time, though, the court refuted in this particular context the Polish claim to be constructing and consolidating their national 'self' through the process of de-Germanisation.[44] In another case, such Polish efforts at de-Germanisation in Upper Silesia as liquidating the factory owned by Germans at Chorzow as well as liquidating certain rural estates were also declared a violation of the Geneva Convention (1922) between Germany and Poland concerning Upper Silesia.[45]

Likewise, in the *Rights of Minorities in Upper Silesia (Minority School)* case, the Permanent Court, on the one hand, decided in favour of the individual choice of the parents (or legally responsible persons) in the matter of sending their children to a German minority school and upheld that any verification or dispute by the educational authorities in such a decision was a violation of the Geneva Convention concerning Upper Silesia (1922). On the other hand, the court indicated that the right to choose the language was not an unrestricted right, in that such choice had to reflect the children's true use of language. In this way, the court attempted to balance the Polish claim of objectivity, founded in nationalism, with an individualist approach, one that advanced the unusual and paradoxical German claim of subjectivity, premised on the strategic aim of re-Germanisation.[46] The Permanent Court's attitude towards ethnicity located against the backdrop of liberalism – the ideology that had been juxtaposed with conservative Romanticism throughout the nineteenth century and now emerged victorious – symbolised the interwar minority protection mechanism in the most significant way.

[43] *Ibid.*, 33. [44] *Ibid.*, 37.

[45] *Case Concerning Certain German Interests in Polish Upper Silesia*, PCIJ Report (1926), Ser. A, No. 7. See also *the Case Concerning the Factory at Chorzow*, PCIJ Report (1925), Ser. B, No. 3; PCIJ Report (1928), Ser. A, No. 17.

[46] PCIJ Report (1928), Ser. A, No. 15. However, in his dissenting opinion, Judge M. Nyholm called the court's decision contradictory, for '[a] declaration *which cannot be disputed or verified* is entirely unimpeachable. Such a declaration cannot be limited by rules of law. The requirement according to which the declaration must correspond exactly to the facts is only a pious wish and any limitations as regards its sincerity come solely within a *moral* sphere. Since the declaration cannot be examined and since all objections or disputes in regard to it are excluded, the declarer is not subject to a legal obligation and the declaration must be taken as it stands. Consequently, the maker of the declaration may of his own free will make a declaration without considering whether it corresponds to the actual state of affairs' (63).

A similar compromising attitude was also demonstrated in the fact that although minority groups were recognised as separate entities in practice, formally the League repeatedly denied any international standing to minority groups. The League was rather comfortable with the understanding that the arrangements were between the treaty states and the League, the latter being the guarantor of the promises made by the former. The negotiations during the Paris Conference revealed that although the British Delegation initially proposed allowing individual members of the minority groups to draw the attention of the League Council or the Permanent Court or both to the violations of minority rights, they later submitted to the French proposition to keep the international guarantee to a minimum level.[47] James Headlam-Morley, who initially proposed to allow persons belonging to minority groups, along with League members, to have recourse to the council, later changed his position because of his apprehension that his plan might have encouraged minorities within Western Europe to claim the right to appeal to the League Council.[48] However, the issue was finally referred to the Supreme Council of the Peace Conference, which ultimately decided to restrict the

[47] In a memorandum of 16 May 1919, James Headlam-Morley – a Cambridge classicist who had served in the Political Intelligence Department of the Foreign Office since April 1918 – wrote in preparation for a Supreme Council meeting on the following day that although it might be acceptable to allow both League members and injured persons themselves to draw the attention of the League Council to violations of minority rights, it would be most undesirable as well as most dangerous to permit the inhabitants or citizens of any state to directly approach the League except through their own government. See James W. Headlam-Morley, *A Memoir of the Paris Peace Conference*, ed. Agnes Headlam-Moreley et al. (York: Methuen Young Books, 1972), 109. Another member of the British delegation, Philip Noel Baker, in contrast, adopted a purely legal approach to the issue, in that he was in favour of allowing individual members of the minorities to file complaints directly to the Permanent Court after exhausting all local remedies (Philip Noel Baker to Headlam-Morley, Memorandum of 19 May 1919. See League of Nations Secretariat, *Registry Files, 1919–1946* [41.681.681]). During a session of the committee on 19 May 1919, Cecil proposed a dual system comprising the provision for recourse both to the council by the members of the League Council and to the PCIJ by individuals. See David Hunter Miller, *My Diary at the Conference at Paris*, vol. XIII (New York: Appeal Press, 1924), 96. On the other hand, Berthelot, a member of the French delegation, categorically rejected various British proposals and proposed a 'three guarantees' mechanism: first, both individuals and communities shall have the right to bring the matter to the notice of a member of the council of the League of Nations. Under the second guarantee, the council could examine the complaint, either reject it or refer it to the PCIJ, whose final decision constituted the third guarantee. See Miller, *My Diary*, vol. XIII, 103–105.

[48] Headlam-Morley, *A Memoir*, 139. These two key European powers then strongly opposed the United States and Italy, who suggested that all member states of the League should have the right to have recourse to the council of any violation of the minority provisions.

right to appeal to members of the League Council alone.[49] And in this way, the 'minority' itself was denied direct access to the mechanism supposedly designed for its protection and its members thereby pushed to the periphery in the discourse on the protection of their rights. As Roucek approvingly wrote in a publication of 1929, the minority treaties did not constitute the minorities as new special subjects of international law; the protection of minorities was, thus, given internationally but within the state.[50]

Thus, the interwar minority protection regime demonstrated an inherent tension between the conservative ethnic notion of minority protection and the liberal assimilationist agenda of the victors of the war. Various actors, the Permanent Court being the most prominent, attempted to mitigate this tension. However, these efforts were marked with a clear message that ethnic primitiveness was undesirable – a fact that characterised the whole minority protection regime in a number of ways.

The liberal West and its conservative 'other' within Europe

In Article VI of the Supplementary Agreements to the second draft of the covenant, Wilson prescribed a minority article that read:

> The League of Nations shall require *all new States* to bind themselves as a condition precedent to their recognition as independent or autonomous States, to accord to all racial and national minorities within their several jurisdictions exactly the same treatment and security, both in law and in fact, that is accorded to the racial or national majority of their people.[51]

In the following draft, the proposed article widened its scope by extending this stipulation to *all states* – old and new – seeking admission to the League.[52] A similar safeguard was also enumerated specifically for religious minorities.[53] However, these proposed draft articles were not finally included in the covenant, again to avoid any general recognition of minority rights; instead, the Allied and Associated Powers concluded a series of treaties, all of them with ECE states, giving the latter special legal obligations to protect minorities within their territories.[54]

[49] FRUS, *The Paris Peace Conference*, vol. VI, 514.

[50] Roucek, *The Working of the Minorities System*, 75.

[51] See Miller, *The Drafting of the Covenant*, vol. II, 91. Emphasis added.

[52] *Ibid.*, 105.

[53] *Ibid.*

[54] There were five minorities treaties concluded between the Allied and Associated Powers and the following new or enlarged states: with Poland, signed at Versailles on 28 June 1919; with Czechoslovakia, signed at St. Germain on 10 September 1919; with

Subjecting some ECE states to international scrutiny regarding minority protection under the League, instead of creating a universal system of minority protection, naturally engendered controversy during the Paris Peace Conference. At the plenary meeting of the conference on 31 May 1919, the representatives of some of these countries, led by Romanian Prime Minister M. Bratianu, stated that they would accept such obligations of minority protection if all the state members of the League accepted similar obligations.[55] Noting that a clause in the draft imposing general recognition of religious toleration on all League members had in fact been rejected by the Great Powers, the representatives made it clear that they were not prepared to admit any interference by foreign governments. Such interference would not only infringe the cardinal principle of state sovereignty but, being confined to only certain ECE states, would also violate the principle of sovereign equality.[56] In a memorandum submitted to the Peace Conference, the Polish delegation underscored the double standard, referring to the fact that while Poland was asked to accept specific obligations concerning the protection

the Kingdom of the Serbs, Croats, and Slovenes (Yugoslavia), signed at St. Germain on 10 September 1919; with Romania, signed at Paris on 9 December 1919; and with Greece, signed at Sevres on 10 August 1920. Reciprocity dictated that similar minority protection clauses be included in the Peace Treaties concluded with four of the defeated states: Austria (signed at St. Germain-en-Laye on 10 September 1919), Bulgaria (signed at Neuilly-sur-Seine on 27 November 1919), Hungary (signed at Trianon on 4 June 1920), and Turkey (signed at Lausanne on 24 July 1923). Several other states made unilateral declarations, assuming similar obligations upon being admitted to the League of Nations: Albania on 2 October 1921; Lithuania on 12 May 1922 (including the application of the declaration to the Territory of the Memel, which was placed under Lithuanian sovereignty as an autonomous region by the Convention of 8 May 1924 between the Allied and Associated Powers and Lithuania); Latvia on 7 July 1923; Estonia on 7 September 1923; and Iraq on 30 May 1932. The minority system also applied to special situations such as the Aaland Islands pursuant to the declaration by Finland to the League on 27 June 1921 and the German–Polish Geneva Convention concerning Upper Silesia of 15 May 1922. See, generally, League of Nations Information Section, *The League of Nations and the Protection of Minorities of Race, Language, and Religion* (Geneva: League of Nations Secretariat, 1927), 5–19; Frank Koszorus, Jr., 'The Forgotten Legacy of the League of Nations Minority Protection System' in *Essays on the World War I: Total War and Peacemaking – A Case Study on Trianon*, ed. B. K. Kiraly (New York: Atlantic Research and Publications, 1982).

55 See League of Nations, *The League of Nations and the Protection of Minorities*, 17. See also FRUS, *The Paris Peace Conference*, vol. VI, 88; FRUS, *The Paris Peace Conference*, vol. III, 400; Harold William Vezeille Temperley (ed.), *A History of the Peace Conference of Paris*, vol. V (London: Henry Frowde and Hodder and Stoughton, 1921), 129. The meeting took place in an environment of confidentiality; the press was excluded, and the proceedings were regarded as confidential.

56 *Ibid.*

of German minorities in Poland, the Treaty of Versailles contained no such stipulations concerning the protection of the Polish and other minorities within Germany.[57] Czechoslovakian and Yugoslavian delegates insisted on amending the objectionable clauses.[58]

The urge to generalise the system of minority protection, instead of imposing special obligations on only certain countries, lived long beyond the Paris Conference, though without much success. Upon his return to Warsaw from the conference at the end of July, the then Polish Prime Minister Ignacy Jan Paderewski expressed the need for securing reciprocity, addressing the Ratification Commission of the Constitutional Assembly in the following words:

> Great injustice was done in the peace pact in allowing language and cultural rights to Germans living in Poland, while such rights are not guaranteed to Polish people living in Germany. It will be necessary for the constitutional convention to demand such rights for the Poles in Germany when Germany is taken into the League of Nations.[59]

In the Sixth Committee of the Third Session of the Assembly of the League in 1922, the representatives of Latvia and Finland proposed a general mechanism for minority protection. Three years later, at the Sixth Session of the Assembly (meeting of 14 September 1925), the Lithuanian delegation proposed that the Sixth Assembly of the League should set up a special committee to prepare a draft convention that would include all the state members of the League, setting forth their common rights and duties with regard to minorities. The proposal was vehemently opposed by the majority of the speakers and was finally withdrawn.[60]

While responding to such oppositions, the Western great powers attempted to locate the special obligations for the ECE states in a historical continuum – obligations to which new entrants to international society must commit. As Georges Clemenceau wrote in a letter to Paderewski referring to Poland's position against any special obligation of minority protection under the Polish Minority Treaty:

> [T]his Treaty does not constitute any fresh departure. It has for long been the established procedure of the public law of Europe that when a State is

[57] League of Nations, *The League of Nations and the Protection of Minorities*, 17. See also FRUS, *The Paris Peace Conference*, vol. VI, 539–540.
[58] Hudson, 'The Protection of Minorities', 213.
[59] Unknown, 'Poland as a Free Nation' in *Current History* 10, part 2, no. 3 (1919), 492.
[60] League of Nations, *The League of Nations and the Protection of Minorities*, 17–18.

> created, or even when large accessions of territory are made to an established State, the joint and formal recognition by the Great Powers should be accompanied by the requirement that such State should, in the form of a binding international convention, undertake to comply with certain principles of government. This principle, for which there are numerous other precedents, received the most explicit sanction when, at the last great assembly of European Powers, the Congress of Berlin, the sovereignty and independence of Serbia, Montenegro, and Roumania were recognised.[61]

Referring to the statements made by the British, French, Italian, and German plenipotentiaries in support of imposing special obligations on the new states of Serbia, Montenegro, and Romania in the Congress of Berlin, as recorded in the Protocol of 28 June 1878, Clemenceau continued that the Principal Allied and Associated Powers would be irresponsible if they departed from this established tradition of stipulating additional obligations for new states.[62] Evidently, for Clemenceau, the legitimacy of such a supervisory role emanated from a realist argument: Poland was indebted to the military might of the great powers for its very re-emergence as an independent, sovereign state.[63]

Clemenceau's effort to historicise the imposition of special obligations on new states was later substantiated by a number of publicists. For example, Hudson shared the view that there were sufficient precedents before the peacemakers in Paris for imposing additional obligations on the new states and on states to which large accessions of territory were to be made.[64] In a publication of 1928, Lucy Mair recorded the earliest

[61] Letter addressed to Polish President I. Paderewski by the president of the conference and the French premier, G. Clemenceau, transmitting to him the treaty to be signed by Poland under Article 93 of the Treaty of Peace with Germany (Paris: 24 June 1919). See FRUS, *The Paris Peace Conference*, vol. VI, 629–634; Temperley, *A History of the Peace Conference of Paris*, vol. V (Appendix IV), 433.

[62] *Ibid.*

[63] Wilson adopted the same power-politic approach while responding to the opposition of Romania's premier to discriminatory minority protection obligations on 31 May 1919. To quote Wilson: 'I beg him to observe that he is overlooking the fact that he is asking the sanction of the allied and associated powers for great additions of territory which come to Rumania by the common victory of arms, and that, therefore, we are entitled to say: "If we agree to these additions of territory we have the right to insist upon certain guarantees of peace"'. See FRUS, *The Paris Peace Conference*, vol. III, 407–409.

[64] Hudson noted that the Conference of London in 1832 prescribed a form of government to Greece on the occasion of its admission to the family of nations; recognition of the acquisition of the Ionian Islands by Greece in 1864 was made subject to the guarantee of religious freedom. The Congress of Berlin in 1878 that Clemenceau specifically mentioned was another example he had in mind. He, thus, concluded that for almost

precedent: the Congress of Vienna of 1814 stipulated clear provisions of minority protection while creating the United Netherlands.[65] The most detailed account of such precedents is found in Temperley's edited volume, *A History of the Peace Conference of Paris*, published in 1921. However, his conclusion, which followed an apparently linear narrative of imposing special minority protection obligations on new states, threw light on a rather different aspect of the issue. It would be, therefore, worthwhile to quote his conclusion in full:

> Summing up, we may say then that by this time it had become a recognized principle of European international custom that in *Eastern Europe* the establishment of new States was a matter of general interest, which required the formal recognition of the Great Powers, who, in fact, though not in law, were, acting as the Concert of Europe, the final court and authority for dealing with all matters of general European concern. It was also established that at least in the East of Europe such recognition should only be given on certain conditions. *In fact, the right was assumed of imposing upon these States certain principles of government which had come to hold the position of fundamental principles to which all civilised States conformed.*
>
> It is perhaps equally necessary to note that this action was confined to the East of Europe; the territorial changes which culminated in the formation of the Kingdom of Italy were not made the subject of a European Conference, still less were those by which the German Empire was built up, and in neither of these two cases was the suggestion even made that conditions should be attached to the recognition of the fait accompli. *This distinction between the East and the West of Europe, based as it is on a real difference between the characters of the peoples and the political situation, is of great importance, and was [. . .] followed at Paris.*[66]

What appears, therefore, is that underlying the general claim of continuity of a tradition of imposing special minority protection obligations on new states or states to which territories had been ceded, there was a dichotomy of 'West' and 'East'. Throughout the nineteenth century, it was generally the non-Western states in Europe that had to consent to such obligations.

a century, it had been an established practice, if not a principle of the public law of Europe, that guarantees to religious minorities should be included among the provisions dealing with the transfer of territory inhabited by heterogeneous peoples. See Hudson, 'The Protection of Minorities', 209.

65 Lucy P. Mair, *The Protection of Minorities – The Workings and Scope of the Minorities Treaties under the League of Nations* (London: Christophers, 1928), 30.

66 Temperley, *A History of the Peace Conference of Paris*, 116–117. Emphasis added.

Berman argues that the very idea of nationalism was at the heart of this East–West dichotomy. According to him, although the term 'national' was not ultimately used in the definition of protected minorities in the final version of the treaty, the dichotomy between Eastern and Western Europe often centred on the implications of the word 'national' to describe the 'minority group', and '[t]he 1919 debate about the "nationalness" of minorities was understood not only as opposing states to minorities generally but also as opposing two different cultural conceptions of group identity – those of Western and Eastern Europe'.[67]

Berman's reference to 'nationalness' here needs to be understood in the nineteenth century's conservative Romantic sense of ethnicity as the foundation of the nation, in contrast to the liberal version that characterises the Western 'self'. The liberal construction of Eastern Europe was premised for the purpose of a special minority rights regime upon the notion that Eastern Europe was the 'home' of the conservative tradition of understanding the 'self' in ethnic terms. And it is in this process that the East becomes the 'ethnic other' of the liberal West, for which ethnicity has no real relevance. In other words, the minority problem was seen as the result of the conservative Eastern tradition of relying on the centrality of ethnicity in nation-building. And because of the instrumentalist intuition of this liberal construction, the ethnic character of the East is a source of conflict that needs to be managed through the minority protection mechanism.

It is, therefore, no surprise that in its Advisory Opinion in the *Greco-Bulgarian Communities* case, the Permanent Court found the ethnic elements, such as 'sentiment of solidarity' and the salience of collective identity, to be attributes of 'Eastern Countries'. With reference to the mutual emigration of the Greco-Bulgarian communities, the court interpreted the concept of a 'community', which appeared in later use as analogous to 'minority', in the following words:

> The criterion to be applied to determine what is a community within the meaning of the articles of the Convention [. . .] is the existence of a group or persons living in a given country or locality, having a race, religion, language and traditions of their own, and united by the identity of such race, religion, language and traditions in a sentiment of solidarity, with a view to preserving their traditions, maintaining their form of worship, securing the instruction and upbringing of their children in accordance

[67] Nathaniel Berman, 'International Law of Nationalism: Group Identity and Legal History' in *International Law and Ethnic Conflict*, ed. David Wippman (Ithaca, New York: Cornell University Press, 1998), 40–42.

with the spirit and traditions of their race and mutually assisting one another.[68]

The objective features of the community that unite it – same race, religion, and language and traditions of their own – and the subjective factor, that is, the willingness to maintain these features, formed the core of a 'community' in the court's perception. Having so defined the notion of 'community', the court then attributed the ethnic character of the 'community' specifically to Eastern countries. In the court's view, the very structure of the Greco-Bulgarian Convention of 27 November 1919 that provided for the population transfer was designed to ensure that the individuals forming the communities could respectively make their homes permanently among their own race, those with 'the very mentality of the population concerned'.[69] Such an arrangement had its justification in the century-old (conservative) tradition of the Eastern countries, which the court thought was necessary to take into account in dealing with the case before it.

However, in his analysis of the case, Berman disputes the perspective that the court's reference to the 'East' in its definition of 'communities' is an extraordinary deference accorded to the traditions of the 'primitive' Balkans. Instead, he highlights the modernist schema that the court adopted, by both referring to the 'East' in registering its respect for 'primitiveness' and 'real nationalism' and bypassing the dichotomy of nationalist and internationalist stances by portraying the 'East' 'as the very birthplace of advanced international experimentation with the legal regulation of nationalist disputes'.[70] Berman, nonetheless, endorses the view that it was indeed 'the court's recognition of the extraordinary importance of ethnic "solidarity" and the kin-states in the Convention that makes its augmentation of *international* authority and discretion in this case so striking'.[71] In a later publication, he interpreted the court's opinion essentially within the framework of cultural differences between the East and the West. The court declared that the existence of the protected Balkan 'communities' was rooted in their members' 'sentiment of solidarity' rather than in the law of the territorial sovereign; Berman concluded that thus internationalism prevailed over the state law 'through the projection of a collectivist "Eastern Tradition", which could only be safeguarded internationally'.[72]

[68] Advisory Opinion, PCIJ Report (1930), Ser. B, No. 17, 33. [69] *Ibid.*, 21.
[70] Berman, 'But the Alternative Is Despair', 1858–1859.
[71] *Ibid.*, 1859. Italics in original. [72] Berman, 'International Law of Nationalism', 40.

As a matter of fact, the protection of the League was not extended to any minority within the Western states. Although German minorities suffered in a number of states both under and outside League jurisdiction, Germany itself adopted brutal policies towards the minorities within its borders, and the League had no means to stop that. Yet, in response to the criticism of the Paris Conference that it did not include defeated Germany in the minority protection obligation, Temperley relied on the scope of the provisions that these obligations were meant for completely new states or states to which very extensive territories were assigned.[73] He, thus, argued that it would have been inappropriate to bring Germany under such a minority protection mechanism, in that it was neither newly emerged nor had gained any territory following the war.[74] Temperley then warned that the inclusion of Germany could have jeopardised the interests of other great powers, who also had significant minorities within their territories, by engendering a universal system of minority protection and thereby bringing them under international scrutiny.[75] It is implied that only non-Western states should be under such international supervision.

Thus, France and Italy, despite receiving extensive territories populated by minorities, similarly remained conspicuous exceptions to the League's scope of minority protection. France was not even asked to guarantee the protection of German minorities in Alsace-Lorraine; it was generally regarded as a case of annexation, hence no question of special obligation was raised.[76] France later deported 200,000 German speakers from Alsace-Lorraine with impunity.[77] Similarly, despite receiving South Tyrol with 0.25 million ethnic Germans and 480,000 Yugoslavs, Italy was also exempted from any minority protection obligation. In the case of Trentito, unlike in Alsace-Lorraine, there was a suggestion made that Italy provide guarantees for the protection of German minorities. However, the Italian delegation held that any such suggestion was entirely inconsistent with its position as a Principal Power.[78] Italy therefore remained outside the scope of the minority protection mechanism. Hudson offered a rationale for such privileges that goes beyond the official Italian position: 'Even if Italy's position as a Principal Power had not seemed to her representatives to preclude it, perhaps her record

[73] Temperley, 141. [74] *Ibid.* [75] *Ibid.*, 142.
[76] Hudson, 'The Protection of Minorities', 212. [77] Mazower, *Hitler's Empire*, 39.
[78] Comments made by Hudson in an interview. See Hudson, 'The Protection of Minorities', 474.

of religious toleration and political equality would have seemed a sufficient reason for not binding her with a separate minorities treaty'.[79]

However, the fact remains that a determined anti-German policy was advanced in Trentino, South Tyrol, with the enthusiastic support of the local Italian population and, later, with the full approval of the Fascist government. In January 1923, by a Decree of the Prefect, a number of German schools were closed, and all German children were required to attend Italian schools, wherein teaching in German was prohibited. By another decree of 15 October 1925, both written and oral forms of any language other than Italian were prohibited in all the proceedings of the courts.[80] In an interview with a Paris newspaper in February 1926, Signor Mussolini spelled out his plan to Italianise the acquired territory in a candid manner:

> Now in all the schools of this province the teaching of the Italian language is obligatory, all post and railway officials are Italians, and we are just now about to settle there a large number of Italian families. One thousand families of ex-combatants will be sent to South Tyrol with a view to promoting the amelioration of the soil. [. . .] In this way we shall succeed in Italianising the country [. . .].[81]

Thus, the dichotomy of West and East within Europe is demonstrated in two ways: first, the problem of minorities is articulated as a concern for Eastern Europe alone, both because the different characters of these people mean that these states have 'special needs', to use Temperley's words, and because of the conservative tradition of emphasising the centrality of ethnicity in the nation-building process. Secondly, in dealing with these minorities, the political independence of East European states was restricted by international minority protection treaties and, thereby, 'internationalising' the minority issue, to use Berman's term. While the prerogative of sovereignty of these countries was made subject to the protection of their minorities, the Allies continued to defer to Western European sovereignty in refusing to extend international scrutiny to all League members.[82] No such restriction was imposed even on Belgium's sovereignty; instead, it enjoyed an unqualified right to self-determination despite its heterogeneous demographic composition.[83]

[79] *Ibid.*, 212.
[80] For a detailed account of oppressive policies against German and Yugoslav minorities in Italy, see Mair, *The Protection of Minorities*, 207–214.
[81] Quoted in *ibid.*, 209. [82] *Ibid.*, 49.
[83] Number seven of Wilson's fourteen points states that 'Belgium, the whole world will agree, must be evacuated and restored, without any attempt to limit the sovereignty which

Within this dichotomy of the liberal West and conservative East, wherein the West was determining the fate of its Eastern 'other', there was an obvious incentive for the 'other' to define its 'self' along the lines of liberal cultural attributes of the West. Thus, in a memorandum presented to the Peace Conference, the representatives of Armenia endeavoured to make their case for self-determination by referring clearly to Western elements of their civilisation. The complementary note to the memorandum included the following:

> [The Armenians] are an Aryan and Christian people, almost submerged in a sea of Turko-Moslems. By origin and in his outlook of life, the Armenian is a westerner, but he lives in contact with the Turks and the Tartars, who are the most backward peoples of the Orient. [...] Is it, therefore, to be wondered at that Armenia aspires with all the force of her soul to be closely connected with the western world, and to have an immediate and quick means of contact with the west?[84]

Having located Armenia within the Western cultural sphere, the argument then relied on a 'standard of civilisation' very much in conformity with the nineteenth century's liberal notion of colonialism in relation to the 'other' within the Armenian territory: the Armenians were the only element in Armenia capable of setting up a civilised and free state, and the rest were secondary either in number or in importance; the others were semi-civilised races which had no arts, no literature, no recorded history, and, which, in the course of their existence, had not made any contribution to the development of the Armenian civilisation. Yet, the representatives expressed colonial benevolence by offering these half-civilised peoples the fruits of modern civilisation under Armenian rule.[85] Such efforts from a group in the ethnic 'periphery' to portray its self-image as a reflection of the liberal civilisation must undoubtedly be seen in a historical continuum.

An interesting link between the special obligation for the ECE states and the nineteenth century's colonial idea of civilising the 'other' is evident in a work by Roucek. While offering a legal justification for

she enjoys in common with all other free nations. No other single act will serve as this will serve to restore confidence among the nations in the laws which they have themselves set and determined for the government of their relations with one another. Without this healing act the whole structure and validity of international law is forever impaired'.

[84] The Armenian National Delegation, *The Armenian Question Before the Peace Conference*, A Memorandum Presented Officially by the Representatives of Armenia to the Peace Conference at Versailles on 26 February 1919 (Appendix), 19.

[85] *Ibid.*, 6, 28.

discriminatory interwar minority protection treaties, he approvingly referred to the nineteenth century's international legal doctrines on recognition as they related to the inclusion of the uncivilised, non-European 'other' in the family of civilised nations. He then continues that

> [s]ince recognition once given is practically final, the conditions that have been attached at the time of the collective recognition are more in the nature of restrictions upon subsequent conduct, qualifying, though without sanction, the rights of full membership in the international community. The Minorities Treaties constitute a case of conditional recognition. The states before admitting to the family of nations a newly organised state can surely demand that it be so constituted that its internal organisation guarantee a peaceful development in international life and not endanger the peace of the international community.[86]

After all, what the Western powers asked from these ECE states regarding the protection of minorities, he argued, was not different from the normal conduct to be expected of a 'civilised' state; hence, such provisions did not constitute any violation of the sovereignty of these states.[87] And even if some states were in fact compelled to sign the minority treaties (Romania could be a relevant case to remember), Roucek considered such acts of compulsion a 'necessity' for securing world peace – 'the price to be paid for all social progress'.[88]

To refute the claim of equality by the ECE states, he further asserted that the notion of equality of states was a myth developed by the naturalists of the seventeenth and eighteenth centuries. He was, however, convinced that with the emergence of positivism in the nineteenth century, the myth had been dispelled; from then on it was generally true that small powers were equal before international law in the same sense that the inhabitants of a colony were equally subject to the same colonial law.[89] The colonial legacy of interwar minority protection appeared even more clearly in his work: he linked the special responsibility of the Western great powers in world affairs to instances in the nineteenth century when the leading powers of Europe undertook to address concrete problems before them by mutually setting forth certain principles of inter-state relations; the Berlin Africa Conference of 1884–1885 came as an obvious example in this connection.[90]

Thus, what the preceding discussion reveals is that the interwar minority protection mechanism demonstrated the ethnic dichotomy of 'self'

[86] Roucek, *The Working of the Minorities System*, 60. Footnote in the original omitted.
[87] *Ibid.*, 65. [88] *Ibid.*, 66. [89] *Ibid.*, 68. [90] *Ibid.*, 69.

and 'other', which was expressed in the liberal West's construction of the conservative East. Instead of prescribing any universal minority protection norms that could have brought all states under international scrutiny, the minority protection mechanism targeted only certain ECE states, on the grounds that a special mechanism was necessary to address the potential for violence that ethnic primitiveness engenders. The ethnic character of the people in the East as well as their conservative tradition of perceiving the national self-image in ethnic terms exemplified this ethnic primitiveness.

This East–West dichotomy within Europe can be perceived as a continuation of the historical role that ethnicity played in the nineteenth-century colonial encounters between the European 'self' and its non-European 'other'. However, the ethnic discourse on the 'self' and the 'other' in the interwar minority protection mechanism was not confined to the dichotomy of liberalism and conservatism alone. As the following discussion reveals, the tripartite interactions among minorities, their host-states, and their kin-states – all in the process of defining the 'self' within the conservative Romantic framework – exposed the practical drawbacks of the interwar minority protection mechanism.

The ethnic 'other' within the ethnic 'self': a case of reciprocal exclusion

While re-creating Poland as a sovereign state, the Versailles Treaty unmistakably envisaged the Polish state along the conservative ethnic line. Article 91 of the Treaty allowed Poland to deny citizenship to certain ethnic German residents in Poland.[91] Simultaneously, the same article provided for the inclusion of certain Poles within the Polish state who usually resided outside the territory of the new state.[92] As Berman notes: 'These provisions link ethnic and state nationality in a manner that seems to be informed by the notion that the right to political ties should be

[91] Article 91 in part reads: 'German nationals, however, or their descendants who became resident in these territories after 1 January 1908, will not acquire Polish nationality without a special authorisation from the Polish State'.

[92] Clause 4 of Article 91 of the Versailles Treaty stipulates that 'Poles who are German nationals over 18 years of age and habitually resident in Germany will have a similar right to opt for Polish nationality'. Clause 9 of the article mentions that '[...] Poles who are German nationals and are in a foreign country will be entitled, in the absence of any provisions to the contrary in the foreign law, and if they have not acquired the foreign nationality, to obtain Polish nationality and to lose their German nationality by complying with the requirements laid down by the Polish State'.

based on individuals' membership in the ethnic nation, rather than on presence in a territory defined by state boundaries'.[93]

It was then Poland's turn to undo the Germanisation project advanced under Prussian rule. Having enshrined ethnicity in the concept of the Polish nation, the Western powers at the same time reinforced the ethnic character of Eastern Europe on the basis of which the interwar minority protection mechanism was constructed. Nevertheless, in the actual implementation of this conservative nationalist project, the matter became much more complicated, given that as a precondition to the re-acquisition of sovereignty, Poland had to extend Polish citizenship to certain ethnic Germans who were born in Poland of 'parents habitually resident there, even if at the date of the coming into force of the present Treaty, they were not themselves habitually resident there'.[94] When the Polish government refused to extend Polish nationality to former German nationals if their parents were not habitually resident in Poland both on the date of birth of the persons concerned and on the date of the enforcement of the treaty, the Permanent Court in an Advisory Opinion held that such an interpretation by Poland amounted to a breach of international treaty obligations.[95]

However, the council failed to bring forth any concrete agreement concerning this issue following the decision of the court; instead, direct negotiations opened between Poland and Germany under the presidency of a neutral chairman. The negotiation resulted in an agreement that for the purpose of Polish citizenship, continuous residence of those ethnic Germans in Poland was not necessary, but their continuous possession of a domicile was.[96] Following the negotiation, the Convention of January 1925 spelled out the provisions concerning the expulsion of the optants for German nationality. The first group of German optants, numbering 20,000, had to leave Poland on 1 August 1925. While Germany had insisted on a postponement to this date, it had made little

[93] Berman, 'But the Alternative Is Despair', 1831.

[94] See Article 4 of the Polish Minority Treaty. According to Article 91 (1), 'German nationals habitually resident in territories recognised as forming part of Poland will acquire Polish nationality *ipso facto* and will lose their German nationality'. Article 91 (3) stipulated that within a period of two years after the coming into force of the present Treaty, German nationals over eighteen years of age habitually resident in any of the territories recognised as forming part of Poland will be entitled to opt for German nationality.

[95] *The Question Concerning the Acquisition of Polish Nationality Case*, PCIJ Report (1923), Ser. B, No. 7.

[96] See Mair, *The Protection of Minorities*, 88–90. See also Roucek, *The Working of the Minorities System*, 102–107.

preparation to receive them. The terrible situation in the camps wherein the returned Germans stayed drew media attention and triggered anti-Polish agitation amongst the nationalists within Germany, who then demanded the retaliatory action of the forcible expulsion of the Poles from Germany to make 'space' for the returning Germans.[97]

In contrast, with the drastic defeat in the war and with no immediate hope of altering the Versailles settlement, German officials were forced to send, at least officially, the state's nineteenth-century notion of ethnic nationalism into hibernation – for an interim period that lasted only a little more than a decade. Although there existed an ultra-nationalist urge for confrontational policies towards Poland and other Eastern European states, where a significant number of ethnic Germans faced discriminatory treatment, the official position in the 1920s held that a 'correct relation' had to be maintained with these countries.[98] The German foreign minister, Gustav Stresemann, was the proponent of such a policy; his strategic argument was that if there were no Germans in Eastern European countries, it would be difficult for Germany to advance its revisionist agenda. Stresemann thus adopted a policy of internationalising the plight of German minorities by having Germany join the League and position itself as the 'Protector of Minorities' in the continent.[99] Being a conservative nationalist, Stresemann located the minority issue within the broad nationalist agenda of creating, in his words, 'a state the political borders of which encompass all the German peoples living within the contiguous area of German settlement in central Europe and who wish to be connected with the Reich'.[100] As a part of the same project, Stresemann advocated for a liberal minority school within Germany with a view to rationalising the claim of more extensive rights for the overseas German minorities. As a matter of fact, even in the face of severe opposition from conservative nationalists as well as the authorities in East Prussia, in 1928 the Prussian cabinet did adopt a decree that guaranteed the creation of minority language schools with government funding.[101]

In the meantime, generous support was extended to a number of organisations, such as the European Nationalities Congress, to voice the rights of minorities, especially German minorities. Protecting the *Kultur* of the ethnic Germans in the ceded territories was also a great concern, which demanded government aid to German newspapers as

[97] Mair, 90–91. [98] Mazower, *Hitler's Empire*, 35. [99] *Ibid.*, 38.
[100] Quoted in *ibid.*, 38. [101] Frenz, *A Lesson Forgotten*, 160.

well as to boarding schools and clubhouses.[102] Yet, in another strategic move, Germany avoided any direct official involvement with minority organisations in the ceded territories; instead, it adopted a policy of supporting German minorities through a number of covert organisations. Nineteenth-century pan-German organisations such as the Association for Germans Abroad (VDA), founded in 1881, and the General German Associations, established in 1890, became active again.[103] New organisations, such as the German Foreign Institute (DAI) and the German Defense League, were also established to regenerate a German cultural self-consciousness among the German minorities.[104] In 1920, two major intermediary institutions were set up in Germany to channel funds secretly from various government agencies to minority organisations: one specially designed to support all German newspapers abroad and the other to facilitate and subsidise primary schools, various charities, clubs, libraries, theatres, and all remaining minority institutions.[105] In 1925, a 'privately owned' institute was established in The Hague – *Hollandsche Buitenland-Bank* – which received more than eight million marks from the German government to be distributed as credits to German farmers in Poland.[106]

However, German politics on the minority issue drastically changed with the Nazis' seizure of power in 1933. Nazi legal theorists asserted the primacy of each state's self-interest and race in the realm of international relations, as we shall see soon. As a matter of fact, Nazi international law, having its foundation in the racial theory of law and the state, was dedicated to dismantling the idea of international law itself. Being premised on the nineteenth-century concepts of Romanticism and cultural specificity as well as polygenic social Darwinism, the racial theory of law proposed that each of the various races and peoples had its own law which was inseparably bound up with that specific race or people; law was so specific to the cultural understanding that it could be neither replaced by the law of another people nor transferred to another race.

Under such a construction of law, the obvious question was whether any idea of international law could be compatible with the Nazi ideology. In fact, shortly after Hitler's seizure of power, Nazi international lawyer Ludwig Schecher, in a publication of 1933, reduced the whole idea of international law to 'an *emblem* of rules belonging exclusively to the German order of law'

[102] *Ibid.*, 143.
[103] Anthony Komjathy and Rebecca Stockwell, *German Minorities and the Third Reich* (New York: Holmes and Meier Publishers, 1980), 2.
[104] *Ibid.*, 2–3. [105] Frenz, *A Lesson Forgotten*, 144. [106] *Ibid.*, 144–145.

with the assertion that, for Germany, international law was nothing but the rules concerning its external relations, which had been recognised and accordingly incorporated in its municipal law and which remained valid as long as this recognition lasted, for 'the competence of the national state cannot be limited by any norm binding its sovereign will'.[107]

Nevertheless, such an approach to international law was pragmatically and strategically difficult to advance, given Germany's weak military and economic position at the time. What followed was a series of reconciliatory approaches to international law. However, the extent of reconciliation that Nazi international lawyers were willing to afford largely corresponded to Germany's shifting foreign policies, which again depended on the economic and military might of the Third Reich. Hence, the approaches to international law varied: from the liberal claim for sovereign equality premised upon natural law jurisprudence and principles of justice, to a soft take on the racialist notion of international law – in which racially delimited groups would accept each other in an international system – to the realist argument that international law was not the end in itself but was created in the service of the interests of the states.[108]

For example, Karl Georg Bruns claimed that the true basis for a genuine legal community of coordination is the 'concept of equality' as expressed in the duty of respecting the 'existence' and 'independence' of other members of the international community. Meanwhile, some other international lawyers, such as Carl Bilfinger and Ammann Schweizer, argued that the idea of 'equality' was relative to the concrete value, meaning the natural superiority or inferiority, of the race represented by each state.[109] Simultaneously, publicists such as Otto Koellreutter and Herbert Kraus propagated the view that given the political character of international law, it was destined to be superseded by state interests.[110]

107 Ludwig Schecher, *Deutsches Aussenstaatsrecht* (1933), cited in John H. Herz, 'The National Socialist Doctrine of International Law and the Problems of International Organisation', *Political Science Quarterly* 54, no. 4 (1939), 539. However, Schecher's view was rejected by Kraus. See Herbert Kraus, 'Das zwischenstaatliche Weltbild des Nationalsozialismus', *Juristische Wochenschrift* 44 (1933), cited in Heiko Meiertöns, 'An International Lawyer in Democracy and Dictatorship – Re-Introducing Herbert Kraus', *European Journal of International Law* 25, no. 1 (2014), 269.

108 Cf. Lawrence Preuss, 'National Socialist Conceptions of International Law', *American Political Science Review* 29, no. 4 (1935), 594–609, with Herz, 'The National Socialist Doctrine of International Law', 536–554.

109 See Herz, 541–544; also, Preuss, 603–604.

110 See Preuss, 598. Also, Herz, 545. Cf. Meiertöns, 'An International Lawyer in Democracy and Dictatorship – Re-Introducing Herbert Kraus', 255–286.

Other reconciliatory approaches attempted to devise a system of international law structured on the basis of race, yet simultaneously tended to minimise the role of international law in international relations. Carl Schmitt's is the most significant of these, not only because he was the most renowned international lawyer in the Nazi regime but also because his works are today considered relevant as a criticism of neo-liberal imperialism.[111] In an article published by the National Socialist Party in 1934, Schmitt explicitly presented the subjective dimension of international law, which he believed had its foundation in the *volkische* character of states.[112] This dimension entailed a criticism of the liberal world view of universalism – an idea propagated by the Jews who never had any specific territory of their own – which inherently denied cultural specificity as the foundation of the state as well as of law, both national and international.[113] For him, the idea of law, *Nomos*, supposed a concrete order and a concrete community that stood above individuals.[114] This idea of specificity premised upon the interplay of land and race found expression in the famous (or infamous) theory of *Grossraum* (Grand Space) that he published just before World War II.

In line with the American Monroe Doctrine, within Schmitt's *Grossraum*, the hegemonic power would have the right to interfere in the international matters of subordinate states within the 'Grand Space' so as to bring them into harmony with the grand design, and external states would have no right to interfere in the conduct of affairs within the *Grossraum*. Thus, the international community would be a collection of *Grossraums* – each constructed on the basis of a specific culture, and it

[111] For this argument, see Anthony Carty, 'Carl Schmitt's Critique of Liberal International Legal Order Between 1933 and 1945', *Leiden Journal of International Law* 14 (2001), 25–75. For a counter-argument, see Andrea Gattinni, 'Sense and Quasisense of Schmitt's Grossraum Theory in International Law – A Rejoinder to Carty's "Carl Schmitt's Critique of Liberal International Legal Order Between 1933 and 1945", *Leiden Journal of International Law* 15 (2002), 53–68.

[112] Carty, 'Carl Schmitt's Critique', 31. [113] *Ibid.*, 32–33, 36, 38.

[114] A detailed criticism of individualism and liberal imperialism through the use of international law as a tool by the Anglo-American liberals appeared in his work, *The Nomos of the Earth*. See Carl Schmitt, *The Nomos of the Earth in the International Law of the Jus Publicum Europaeum* (New York: Telos Press, 2003 [1950]). Although published in 1950, this volume was completed just before World War II ended. Given that by that time the fate of Germany was more or less decided, many of his racial ideas did not directly appear in *The Nomos of the Earth*; rather, the book warns about the dominance of the Anglo-American ideologies and their potential disastrous consequences for the post–World War II world order.

was the Reich that would protect the *Grossraum*.[115] However, the distinctiveness of the doctrine appeared in the fact that, being a loyal Nazi ideologist, Schmitt declared that through the Reich the ultimate responsibility to protect the grand cultural space would shift to the Fuhrer, whose acts supposedly conferred 'political reality, historical truth and a great international future' on the German Reich.[116]

However, within the top Nazi official circle, Schmitt's theory of *Grossraum* was translated, in denial of his intellectual contribution, into the theory of *Lebensraum* (Living Space), which entitled Germany as a racially superior state to expand geographically as far as its biological needs carried it and in whatever manner was deemed necessary for this purpose.[117] As Mazower puts it, the uniqueness of this Nazi philosophy was that

> Germany's organisation of Europe would differ from France's in that no single set of norms would be imposed; each 'worthy' racial group would be allowed to develop independently and enjoy its own *Lebensraum*. The solution to the problem of European nationalism was thus a continent of nations, each in its own space, working together under the rule of the region's 'natural' leader, Germany.[118]

However, Andrea Gattinni argues that under such a hierarchical construction, there could be no question of 'international law' at least among the constituent members of the *Grossraum*; no other power could even interfere in their relations within that space.[119] Nothing could be a better normative foundation for Germany's imperial expansion towards the East.

Yet, in spite of his commitment to the Nazi ideology of racial superiority and ensuing anti-Semitism, and despite the Nazis' incorporation of some of his ideas, Schmitt's theory of international law was to prove 'less than sufficient' to reach Hitler's ever-increasing imperialist goal. Thus, within the regime he was attacked by the extremists for his reliance on an international legal order of *Grossraum* instead of a *volkische* order. Ironically, it was even argued that his theory of *Grossraum* would create a predicament when Germany intervened in another *Grossraum*.[120]

115 Detlev F. Vagts, 'International Law in the Third Reich', *American Journal of International Law* 84 (1990), 687–690; Carty, 'Carl Schmitt's Critique', 34–47; Gattinni, 'Sense and Quasisense', 57–62.

116 See Carty, 'Carl Schmitt's Critique', 42.

117 Vagts, 'International Law in the Third Reich', 687–690; Carty, 'Carl Schmitt's Critique', 74.

118 Mazower, *Hitler's Empire*, 247.

119 Gattinni, 'Sense and Quasisense', 61.

120 For an account of the criticism of Schmitt by the Nazi regime, see Carty, 'Carl Schmitt's Critique', 71–73.

By that time, it had been decided that if any international law could be in conformity with Hitler's interventionist agenda, it must offer the flexibility to legitimise any arbitrary expansion of the *Lebensraum*.

Thus, while Detlev Vagts puts Schmitt in the category of the 'opportunist' Nazi international lawyers, in the 'fanatic' category he finds Theodro Maunz and Norbert Gurke, who glorified the racial and anti-Semitic theories and also rationalised the use of violence.[121] In this way, the collaborating Nazi international lawyers coped with the changing requirements of the regime. In the face of attacks on his *Grossraum* theory, Schmitt himself brought a number of modifications to satisfy his Nazi bosses, although without any result.[122] John Herz succinctly identified this pattern in 1939 as follows:

> The doctrine of the 'law of nature' belonged to the years when Germany's 'equal rights' had still to be assured. The system of the 'realists' corresponds to the stage of national unification of 'Greater Germany'. Once this goal of 'racial satiation' is attained there will be no difficulty in preserving only the realistic parts of the theory based on the dogma of the 'eternal struggle of races'. Then, and only then, we shall have a doctrine consistent both within itself and with general National Socialist *Weltanschauung*.[123]

Against this politico-legal backdrop, the Nazi lawyers thus claimed that treaties were binding as long as they did not jeopardise the racial health of a people; war, not law, was the ultimate arbiter of international order.[124] With such a perception of international order, Nazi Germany became more explicitly and directly involved in the minority affairs of other states. Given the racial foundation of the regime, such external involvements were often

[121] Vagts' assessment of the role of individual German international lawyers under Nazi rule can be categorised along the lines of protestors against the regime (such as Helmuth von Moltke, Karl Strupp, and Rudolfe von Laun), opportunists, and fanatics. For details, see Vagts, 'International Law in the Third Reich', 681–686. On the other hand, Arthur Kaufmann claims that most international lawyers under Nazi rule advocated the National Socialist cause out of conviction, even if opportunism and ambition occasionally played a role. See Arthur Kaufmann, 'National Socialism and German Jurisprudence from 1933 to 1945', *Cardozo Law Review* 9 (1987–1988), 1629–1649. However, many of the collaborating Nazi lawyers later changed their position and remained influential in the post-war German legal arena, though not in international law per se. For an account of their post-war careers, see Mathias Reimann, 'National Socialist in Jurisprudence and Academic Continuity: A Comment on Professor Kaufmann's Article', *Cardozo Law Review* 9 (1987–1988), 1651–1662.

[122] Carty, 'Carl Schmitt's Critique', 73.

[123] Herz, 'The National Socialist Doctrine of International Law', 553–554.

[124] For details, see Vagts, 'International Law in the Third Reich', 692–693; also, Mazower, 44–45.

propagated along the lines of ethnic affiliation with the minorities. Thus, while the minority protection mechanism under the League categorically denied kin-states the role of protectors of their co-ethnics, in a debate in the League Assembly in 1933, the German delegate defended interventions by the kin-states with this argument:

> [T]he individual these days feels himself bound to his ethnic nationality and to the culture with which he is associated by ties much more close than that of former times. We call this tendency the avowal of the link of the *Volkstum* – that is to say, the ethnic nationality. This avowal expresses the unity of feeling in all those who are bound by common blood or by a common language, and who enjoy the same civilization and customs.[125]

Juxtaposing the ethnic phenomenon of minorities with the individualist framework of the minority protection mechanism under the League, Schmitt similarly argued that Germany must be assigned a special role in the minority protection system to protect the 'Eastern space' from the ideological hegemony of liberalism; there had to be a defence of the national peculiarity of each ethnic group against Western assimilation, and it had to be by Germany.[126]

Nazi Germany under Hitler and his notorious aides, including Himmler, was committed to its long-standing agenda of Germanising Eastern Europe. However, such a vision of Germanisation was different in character to previous efforts, in that it was set to advance the nineteenth-century German philosophy of historicism and race on a previously unforeseen scale. The Nazis' invasion policy was marked by their conviction that the Eastern territories had been occupied by the Teutonic knights many centuries ago.[127] But to match the racial underpinnings of the regime, such re-occupation of the 'ancient territories' necessitated the elimination of anything non-German. Such an idea was also rationalised by the social Darwinist notion of the 'survival of the fittest'. In his classic work, *Behemoth*, Franz Neumann explains how the Nazi idealists had recourse to the works of the nineteenth-century polygenist Gobineau, which were later reworked by Houston Stewart Chamberlain and Richard Wagner. They, along with conservative nationalist Friedrich List, offered the Nazis the necessary ideological foundation for advancing imperialism on the basis of race.[128] List, in support of his acceptance of racial theories, wrote in 1846 that

[125] Mello-Franco, *League of Nations Official Journal*, sp. supp. 120 (1933), 23.
[126] See Carty, 'Carl Schmitt's Critique', 40. [127] Mazower, 181.
[128] Franz Neumann, *Behemoth: The Structure and Practice of National Socialism 1933–1944* (New York: Harper and Row, 1966 [1942]), 98–111.

> [t]here is hardly any doubt that the Germanic race has, by virtue of its nature and character, been preferentially selected by Providence for the solution of the great task – to lead the affairs of the world, to civilize the wild barbaric countries, to populate those still uninhabited, for none of the others has the capacity to emigrate *en masse* and to found more perfect communities in foreign lands [. . .] and to keep free of the influences of barbaric and semi-barbaric aborigines.[129]

As Neumann claims, List, in this sense, was the first to develop a racial theory of imperialism that Hitler not only spelled out in *Mein Kampf* but also put in practice through the National Socialist foreign policy of Eastern expansion.[130] Wagner was in agreement with List in asserting that the German culture, as created by the Germanic race, is superior to all others. It is, therefore, no surprise that he interpreted the German victory in the Franco-Prussian war of 1870 in biological terms: Germany was destined to win this war simply because the Gallic race of France was biologically inferior to the Germanic.[131] Wagner had significant influence on his son-in-law, Chamberlain, who also believed that the Teutonic race comprises those who genuinely shape 'the destinies of mankind, whether as builders of the state or as discoverers of new thoughts and of original art [. . .]. Our whole civilisation and culture today is the work of one definite race of men, the Teutonic'.[132]

Very much in line with these influential nineteenth-century proponents of racial imperialism, Nazi idealist Ernest Krieck repeatedly emphasised that politics was a struggle for existence. In an address to students in 1933, shortly after the Nazis seized power, Krieck asserted: 'The purpose of our political faith is the salvation of the German by leading him to his victory over the inferior races exemplified by the Jew, through reconciliation to the Fuhrer'.[133] Himmler is reported to have said with reference to his predecessors' mild approach to Germanisation: 'Our mission is not to Germanise the East in the old sense – bringing the German language and laws to those living there, but rather to ensure that in the East dwell only men with truly German, Germanic blood'.[134] That was an open agenda for complete extermination of the 'other', which of course was later to

[129] Friedrich List, 'Über den Wert und die Bedingungen einer Allianz zwischen Grossbritannien und Deutschland (1846)' in Friedrich List, *Schriften, Reden, Briefe*, vol. III (Berlin: Hobbing, 1931), 267–98. Quoted in *ibid.*, 105.

[130] Neumann, *Behemoth*, 106. [131] *Ibid.* [132] Quoted in *ibid.*, 107.

[133] Quoted in Uriel Tal, '"Political Faith" of Nazism Prior to the Holocaust (1978)' in *Religion, Politics and Ideology in the Third Reich – Selected Essays of Uriel Tal* (London: Routledge, 2004), 20.

[134] Quoted in Mazower, *Hitler's Empire*, 181.

materialise. Again, for Himmler such massacres were part of the 'necessary ethnic separation of races and peoples in the European New Order as well as in the interest of the security and purity of the German Reich'.[135]

However, before such an exclusionist mission could be realised, the Nazi regime directed its minority policy towards transforming the international mechanism of minority protection under the supervision of the League into a bilateral issue, thereby facilitating its involvement as a kin-state. Sidelining the British and the French, Germany started negotiating in bilateral terms with the states hosting German minorities. In this context, Schmitt argued that in concluding a series of bilateral treaties for the protection of German minorities, the Reich had firmly rejected the Versailles Treaty for minority protection.[136] While Schmitt perceived such a disavowal of the Versailles system as an essential step towards the creation of *Grossraum*, other Nazi jurists too generally conceived of bilateralism as a necessary attempt to minimise international law to contractual relations among individual states.[137]

Given that Poland was also unhappy about the Versailles arrangements (their special obligations regarding minority protection), by signing a ten-year non-aggression pact on 26 January 1934, the Nazi regime offered Poland an incentive to violate its international treaty obligations. The pact allowed Germany considerable time for rearmament but simultaneously offered Poland an opportunity to re-Polonise the Prussianised Poles as well as to 'clear up' the border regions by displacing the disloyal German elements.[138] So, induced by the German politics on the minority issue, Poland increasingly deviated from the treaty obligations and in November 1937 signed the Minority Declaration jointly with Germany, formally declaring the question of minority protection a bilateral issue between them and thereby accepting Germany as an advocate for German minorities.[139] As a principle, it was clearly contrary

135 Quoted in *ibid.*, 247. See also Michael Burleigh, *The Third Reich – A New Story* (London: Pan Books, 2001 [2000]).

136 See Carty, 'Carl Schmitt's Critique', 43.

137 For the details of this argument, see Herz, 'The National Socialist Doctrine of International Law', 547.

138 Komjathy and Stockwell, *German Minorities and The Third Reich*, 71, 73.

139 *Ibid.*, 85. The Polish motive behind the declaration was to gain commitment from Germany regarding the non-violation of Polish rights in Danzig. Poland also had the hope that such a declaration would ameliorate the condition of 1,300,000 Poles inside Germany who were outside any special minority protection mechanism. Hitler, on the other hand, had the purpose of neutralising Poland before taking over Austria and invading Czechoslovakia.

to the Versailles understanding that kin-states would be kept out of minority affairs. Having gained a recognised position in minority affairs inside Poland, Germany was now better equipped to manoeuvre the minority issue internally and internationally, and set premises for its revisionist claims.

Ironically, the Nazi minority policies, being submerged in strategic calculations, could not ameliorate the condition of the already troubled German minorities in Poland. Sometimes Berlin's outcry for the protection of minorities appeared to be merely rhetorical and strategic, in that on a number of occasions Germany traded minority interests for diplomatic convenience, as was the case with the Non-Aggression Pact and the Minority Declaration. At the same time, Poland relied on de-Germanisation in the process of constructing her own ethnic identity, which the Great Powers moderately authenticated at Versailles. Even after the declaration, 'untrustworthy' German families were relocated or expelled from strategically important areas under the Frontier Zone Decree of 22 January 1927.[140] The overall number of German minority schools and the percentage of German pupils declined despite high demand for such schools. Whereas in the school year 1921–1922, there were 1,250 German-language elementary schools in Pomerelia and Posen, the number dropped to a meagre 160 in 1937–1938 due to a number of laws restricting the operation of private minority schools.[141] In Polish Upper Silesia, enrolment in German minority schools was made conditional upon passing a rigorous language test before an all-Polish panel, and many German teachers were transferred to the Polish schools away from the border provinces.[142]

Yet, that was not the worst. Although 'land reform' had been a key policy of de-Germanisation since the beginning, the situation of the German minorities deteriorated significantly during this time. The area of German land redistributed, almost exclusively to Poles, under the land reforms stood at 8,444 hectares in 1936; increased to 20,325 hectares in 1937; to 22,254 hectares in 1938; and to 22,732 hectares in 1939.[143] In the western provinces, the amount of land distributed between 1937 and 1939 (99,230 hectares) almost matched that in the entire decade from 1926 to 1936 (101,206 hectares).[144] These land 'reforms' caused severe unemployment among the Germans, who were then compelled to emigrate to Germany. It was reported in 1938 that in Upper Silesia the

[140] *Ibid.*, 86–87. [141] Frenz, *A Lesson Forgotten*, 226. [142] *Ibid.*, 249.
[143] Komjathy and Stockwell, *German Minorities and the Third Reich*, 87. [144] *Ibid.*, 87.

unemployment rate amounted to 62 percent among German trade union members and approached 80 percent in other German organisations, while the general rate in Upper Silesia was just 16 percent.[145] During the same period, a number of German cultural organisations were dissolved and their valuable properties were also confiscated.[146]

The foregoing account of the treatment of minorities under pre–World War II Germany and Poland, thus, demonstrates how the task of mutual exclusion of the ethnic 'other' was advanced in the process of constructing their ethnic self-image along the line of the conservative tradition of the nineteenth century. Although the extents of the brutality employed in the process are in no way comparable, the ethnic dichotomy of 'self' and 'other' continued to inform the whole structure of the campaign that took its final shape in the midst of the war.

Conclusion

The interwar international law of minority protection relates to the nineteenth century's ethnic dichotomy of the European 'self' and the non-European 'other' as expressed in colonialism, in that the same ethnic discourse on 'self' and 'other' was translated through the liberal and conservative traditions into the dichotomy of the liberal Western 'self' and the conservative non-Western 'other' within Europe. The regime also witnessed the exclusionist response to the ethnic 'other' – minorities – in the process of constructing the ethnic self-image. At the same time, the interwar minority protection mechanism demonstrated a tension that resulted from the efforts to reconcile the liberal assimilationism of the West with the ethnic underpinning of conservative minorities and their host states in Eastern Europe.

Nazism collapsed, as did the minority protection mechanism with its guarantor, the League. But the liberal–conservative dichotomy within Europe as well as the tension that emanated from the response of liberal individualism to the ethnic phenomenon attributed to the concept of 'minority' survived much longer than the interwar international law. The international protection of minorities in the aftermath of World War II, especially in the post–Cold War context, continued to demonstrate this dichotomy and this tension, as we shall see in the following chapter. In this sense, the interwar minority protection mechanism could be understood as an important link between the nineteenth-century idea

[145] Frenz, 248. [146] See Komjathy and Stockwell, 89–90.

of colonialism and the post–World War II regime of minority protection, in each of which the ethnic dichotomy of 'self' and 'other', expressed through the liberal and conservative streams, provides the necessary analytical framework for a better understanding of international law as it was applied to these systems and also constructed in the process.

4

Ethnicity in the era of liberalism

Human rights, minority protection, and the post–Cold War paradigm shifts

Introduction

While in the interwar period the notion of self-determination was closely associated with the minority protection regime (in that where the Wilsonian concept of self-determination could not be applied, minority protection was adopted as a fallback position), in the aftermath of World War II the idea of self-determination was primarily expressed through decolonisation. In fact, as Rosalyn Higgins argues, before the claim for decolonisation gained prominence in the discourse on self-determination, the mention of self-determination in the UN Charter simply meant equal rights of all states to non-interference in their internal affairs.[1] It was only through the activism of the new states of Asia and Africa in the General Assembly that the concept of self-determination turned into the moral and legal force behind decolonisation.[2] However, at the same time, these new states were aware of the potential danger of fragmentation that came with an ethnicity-defined version of self-determination; hence, they preferred to rely on the principle of *uti possidetis*, which facilitated a peaceful decolonisation process in Latin America between the late eighteenth century and the early nineteenth

[1] Rosalyn Higgins, *Problems and Process: International Law and How We Use It* (Oxford: Oxford University Press, 1994), 111–114.

[2] See United Nations General Assembly, *Declaration on the Granting of Independence to the Colonial Countries and Peoples*, Res. 1514 (XV), 947th Plenary Meeting, 14 December 1960; General Assembly, *Principles which should Guide Members in Determining whether or not an Obligation Exists to Transmit the Information Called for under Article 73e of the Charter*, Res. 1541 (XV), 948th Plenary Meeting, 15 December 1960; General Assembly, *Declaration on Principles of International Law concerning Friendly Relations and Cooperation among States in accordance with the Charter of the United Nations*, Res. 2625 (XXV), 25th Session, 24 October 1970. See also Thomas D. Musgrave, *Self-Determination and National Minorities* (Oxford: Clarendon Press, 1997), 69–77, 91–96.

century.[3] The Colonial Declaration of 1960 thus not only reinforced the colonial borders in Asia and Africa but also indicated the manner in which postcolonial states would be shaped by the notion of fundamental human rights.[4] Subsequent General Assembly resolutions as well as decisions of the International Court of Justice also unequivocally declared the primacy of territorial integrity of states over ethnic claims for self-determination.[5]

Thomas Franck sees this pattern as a reconciliatory move; in his words: 'The disintegration of Spanish imperialism in America produced the norm of *uti possidetis*. The end of the German, Austrian, and Ottoman empires [in the interwar period] gave rise to self-determination. In the post-1945 era *uti possidetis* and self-determination were redefined and synthesised into a doctrine of decolonisation'.[6] While the conservative notion of self-determination in the Paris Peace Conference attempted to undo established borders in order to create states along ethnic lines, the principle of *uti possidetis* cemented the territorial borders arbitrarily drawn by the colonial powers[7] and endorsed the multi-ethnic composition of the postcolonial states.[8] It is in the context of this drastic ideological shift from the conservative 'ethnic' to the liberal 'territorial' notion of statehood in post–World War II international law that I explain the issue of minority protection in this chapter.

The interwar arrangement of minority protection was already in decline some years prior to the outbreak of World War II and there was no enthusiasm for its continuation.[9] Given the discriminatory

[3] See Musgrave, *Self-Determination and National Minorities*, 91–96.

[4] *Declaration on the Granting of Independence to the Colonial Countries and Peoples*, Articles 1, 7.

[5] See *Declaration on Principles of International Law concerning Friendly Relations and Cooperation among States in accordance with the Charter of the United Nations*, 1970. See also *Legal Consequences for States of the Continued Presence of South Africa in Namibia* (South West Africa), Advisory Opinion, ICJ Reports (1971), para. 52; *Frontier Dispute* (Burkina Faso and Mali) Case, ICJ Reports (1986), para. 25.

[6] Thomas M. Franck, *Fairness in International Law and Institutions* (Oxford: Oxford University Press, 1995), 147.

[7] However, the option of changing territorial borders by voluntarily joining another state or by remaining in a constitutional relationship with the former colonial power remained open. See General Assembly, *Principles which should Guide Members in Determining whether or not an Obligation Exists to Transmit the Information Called for under Article 73e of the Charter*, principles VI–IX.

[8] Franck, *Fairness in International Law*, 149.

[9] A number of factors, according to Kunz, contributed to this shift: first, not only was the new law restricted to Europe but it was not even general in Europe. It was a strictly particular international law, binding only on certain states, not on all where there were

character of the minority protection regime as well as the political manoeuvring of the minority issue by Nazi Germany, the idea of the protection of minorities under the League became an easy victim of widespread criticism following the war. However, John Humphrey notes that there were deeper reasons for the change in attitude towards minorities: first, the shift in political power and influence from Europe to the United States, which itself was a country of immigration, and, second, the emergence of the new countries in Africa and Asia, which demonstrated a preoccupation with nation-building and consequently with assimilationist projects.[10]

The post–World War II phase of international law was indeed set to reaffirm faith in and promote certain crucial values: fundamental human rights, the dignity and worth of individuals, and equal rights of men and women and of nations large and small, among others.[11] In this new era, however, 'progress' equated to liberal values, and universalism simply meant the imposition of these values on a global scale. Thus, since the inception of the United Nations, an individualist notion of human rights had become the dominant vocabulary through which the concept of 'minority' was expressed. While the minority protection regime under the League was of a hybrid nature – incorporating both collective and individual rights – under the new arrangement after World War II, the minority protection system was replaced with a human rights regime exclusively centred on the universal protection of individual rights.

The rationale for this shift is given in a study by the United Nations Secretariat in 1950 that concludes

> If the problem is regarded as a whole, there can be no doubt that the whole minorities protection regime was in 1919 an integral part of the system established to regulate the outcome of the First World War and create an international organisation, the League of Nations. One principle of that system was that certain States and certain States only (chiefly States that had been newly reconstituted or considerably enlarged) should be subject to obligations and international control in the matter of minorities. But

minorities. Second, there was the procedural inefficiency of the League of Nations. Third, even early on, opinions unfavourable to this new law were voiced. Fourth, again even early on, there were attempts to get rid of the whole problem of minorities by way of population transfers and exchanges. See Joseph L. Kunz, 'The Present Status of the International Law for the Protection of Minorities', *American Journal of International Law* 48 (1954), 284.

10 John P. Humphrey, 'The United Nations Sub-Commission on the Prevention of Discrimination and the Protection of Minorities', *American Journal of International Law* 62 (1968), 870.

11 See the Preamble of the Charter of the United Nations.

> this whole system was overthrown by the Second World War. All the international decisions reached since 1944 have been inspired by a different philosophy. The idea of general and universal protection of human rights and fundamental freedoms is emerging. It is therefore no longer only the minorities in certain countries which receive protection, but all human beings in all countries who receive a certain measure of international protection.[12]

The then US undersecretary of state, Sumner Welles, in an address delivered at the commencement exercises at the College of Negroes, Durham, on 31 May 1943, justified this move towards the human rights regime by raising an 'ethical' question:

> [I]n the kind of world for which we fight, there must cease to exist any need for the use of that accursed term 'racial or religious minority'. [. . .] is it conceivable that the peoples of the United Nations can consent to the reestablishment of any system where human beings will still be regarded as belonging to such 'minorities'?[13]

This ideological shift was well sketched by Joseph Kunz in 1954 when he wrote about the changing pattern of international law:

> He who dedicates his life to the study of international law in these troubled times is sometimes struck by the appearance as if there were fashions in international law just as neckties. At the end of the First World War, 'international protection of minorities' was the great fashion [. . .]. Recently this fashion has become nearly obsolete. Today the well-dressed international lawyer wears 'human rights'.[14]

Unlike the short-lived regime of minority rights, this new era of individualist human rights, however, looked permanent, at least until the end of the Cold War.

Against this backdrop, this chapter explores how the notion of ethnicity, expressed in the liberal and conservative traditions, shapes the liberal perception of the minority and of minority protection in three different ways. I argue that in the internal context, wherein a minority is juxtaposed with the majority within a given polity, the minority is defined as an ethnic phenomenon along the line of the conservative tradition and, therefore, perceived as the primitive 'other'. On the other hand, the liberal individualist response to minority *protection* endeavours to remove this conservative

[12] United Nations, *Study of the Legal Validity of the Undertakings Concerning Minorities* (1950), UN Doc. E/CN4/367.

[13] US Department of State, *US Department of State Bulletin*, VIII, no. 206 (5 June 1943), 482.

[14] Kunz, 'The Present Status of the International Law for the Protection of Minorities', 282.

notion of 'ethnicity' from 'minority'. And finally, in the post–Cold War European context, it is again the contrast between the liberal and conservative traditions vis-à-vis the role of ethnicity in the political organisation of nation-states that explains the reasons behind a differentiated minority protection mechanism within Europe. The following is an account of the complicated roles that ethnicity plays in relation to international protection of minorities in these three different contexts.

Understanding the 'minority' as an ethnic phenomenon

Any study on minorities necessarily refers to the complexities involved in defining the term.[15] Francesco Capotorti, in his seminal report on minorities, asserts that '[t]he preparation of a definition [of minority] capable of being universally accepted has always proved a task of such difficulty and complexity that neither the experts in this field nor the organs of the international agencies have been able to accomplish it to date'; hence, there is no generally accepted definition of the term 'minority' despite the fact that numerous references to minorities are found in international legal instruments of all kinds.[16] Even a couple of decades after the Capotorti Report, the 1993 Steering Committee on Human Rights to the Council of Minorities concluded that no agreement on a definition of 'minority' was possible.[17] No general understanding could be achieved at the European level either, so far as the definition of 'national minority' was concerned. Thus, given the impossibility of formulating a definition of 'national minority' that could be approved by all the member states of the Council of Europe, the Framework Convention for the Protection of National Minorities adopts a pragmatic approach.[18]

[15] See Kristin Henrard, *Devising an Adequate System of Minority Protection* (The Hague: Martinus Nijhoff, 2000); Thornberry, *International Law and the Rights of Minorities*; Capotorti Report (1977); Natan Lerner, *Group Rights and Discrimination in International Law*, 2nd edn (The Hague: Martinus Nijhoff, 2003); John Packer, 'Problems in Defining minorities' in *Minority and Group Rights in the New Millennium*, ed. Deirdre Fottrell and Bill Bowring (Leiden: Brill Academic Publishers, 1999); John Packer, 'On the Definition of Minorities' in *The Protection of Ethnic and Linguistic Minorities in Europe*, ed. J. Packer and K. Myntti (Abo/Turku: Abo Akademi University Press, 1993).

[16] Capotorti Report, 5.

[17] CDHH (93) 22, Strasbourg, 8 September 1993, feddh 93.22, 7–9. See Henrard, *Devising an Adequate System*, 27.

[18] Council of Europe, *Explanatory Report to the Framework Convention for the Protection of National Minorities* (1995), ETS No. 157, paragraph 12.

This difficulty in defining a minority within the liberal framework is obvious, in that the effort to define the minority represents an endeavour to define the indefinable, rationalising the irrational. Formulating a general definition of a group that is identified by the centrality of ethnic affiliation essentially contradicts the liberal proposition that ethnicity has no real value and is relevant, if at all, only for instrumental purposes.[19] Yet, as the liberal instrumentalist intuition dictates, the minority, having its foundation in the conservative ethnic tradition, is a source of conflict[20]; hence, some form of definition of a minority is necessary to ascertain with whom to deal. As a result, a series of context-specific definitions of 'minority' emerged, each highlighting the definitional debate as well as the need for some sort of working definition.

However, the need for defining a minority goes beyond the mere substantive and procedural specificity that effective protection of the groups in question arguably requires. Rather, this need is related to a process in which some groups are attributed certain distinct characteristics and, thereby, identified as the conservative 'other' vis-à-vis liberal progressiveness. This conservative ethnic notion of the minority then reflects back on the distinctiveness of the majority, or vice versa. Almost all the definitions of the minority incorporated in various post–World War II international and regional human rights instruments include this phenomenon of identifying a minority as the ethnic 'other'.

For example, in 1950 the UN Sub-Commission on Prevention of Discrimination and Protection of Minorities formulated guidelines for a definition of 'minority', one of which conceives of minorities as those non-dominant groups in a given population that 'possess and wish to preserve stable ethnic, religious or linguistic traditions or characteristics markedly different from those of the rest of the population'.[21] Consequently, the sub-commission's definition of minorities appeared in 1954 as 'those non-dominant groups in a population which possess and *wish to preserve* ethnic, religious or linguistic traditions or characteristics markedly different from those of the rest of the

[19] As we saw in Chapter 1.

[20] See, for example, Franck, *Fairness in International Law and Institutions*, 140–169. See also T. Franck, 'Postmodern Tribalism and the Right to Secession' in *Peoples and Minorities in International Law*, ed. Catherine Brölmann, René Lefeber, and Marjoleine Zieck (Dordrecht: Martinus Nijhoff, 1993), 3–27; Rosalyn Higgins, 'Postmodern Tribalism and the Right to Secession: Comments' in *Peoples and Minorities in International Law*, 29–35. The following chapter details the liberal international lawyers' response to ethnicity in ethnic conflicts.

[21] UN Doc. E/CN4/358. See Henrard, *Devising an Adequate System*, 20.

population'.[22] Thus, the concept of 'otherness' in the sub-commission's understanding of the minority is translated into the subordinate position of the minority in a given society compared to the majority. At the same time, by wishing to preserve its distinctive characteristics as the insignia of its identity, the minority appears as a symbol of the nineteenth century's conservative tradition of defining the 'self' in ethnic terms, which makes it different from the liberal understanding of the 'self' as a non-ethnic or post-ethnic notion. In other words, this process of defining a minority can be seen as an ambiguous pronouncement: in one direction it speaks of the 'otherness' of the minority understood in terms of its ethnic differentiation from the majority; the converse of its 'otherness' is the affirmation of the ethnic homogeneity of the majority. In another direction it may speak to the liberal tradition by emphasising the contrast between those who are committed to speaking the language of ethnicity in their self-identification and the majority who have dispensed with such a condition.

A similar approach to the 'minority' was also adopted by the Special Rapporteurs on minorities in their seminal works. Considering different complexities involved in the term, the Capotorti Report defines the minority, in the context of Article 27 of the International Covenant on Civil and Political Rights (ICCPR), as

> a group which is numerically inferior to the rest of the population of a State and in a non-dominant position, whose members possess ethnic, religious or linguistic characteristics which differ from those of the rest of the population and who, if only implicitly, maintain *a sense of solidarity*, directed towards preserving their culture, traditions, religion or language.[23]

Another Special Rapporteur, Jules Deschenes, in the text transmitted to the Human Rights Commission in 1985, defines the minority as

> a group of citizens of a state, constituting a numerical minority and in a non-dominant position in that state, endowed with ethnic, religious or linguistic characteristics which differ from those of the majority of the population, having *a sense of solidarity* with one another, motivated, if only implicitly, by *a collective will* to survive and whose aim is to achieve equality with the majority in fact and in law.[24]

[22] UN Doc. E/2573 (1954), 48–49. See Lerner, *Group Rights and Discrimination*, 9. Emphasis added.

[23] For a detailed discussion on the definition of 'minority', see Capotorti Report, 5–15. Emphasis added.

[24] Jules Deschenes, *Proposals Concerning a definition of the Term 'Minority'* (1985), UN Doc. E/CN4/Sub.2/1985/31, Sec. 181. Emphasis added.

	Size	Power		
	Dominant Group			
Group A	+	+	Majority Group	
Group B	–	+	Elite	
	Subordinate Group			AD and BC = typical inter-group configuration
Group C	+	–	Mass Subjects	
Group D	–	–	Minority Group	

Figure 4.1 Inferiority of minority in power and demography
Source: Schermerhorn (1996).

With the exception that Deschenes specifically mentions achieving equality as an aim of the minority, these two definitions appear identical in all respects.

The mention of 'a sense of solidarity' in these definitions demands particular attention. It is this sense of solidarity and collective will that makes a minority, as a group, different from a group of individuals formed for everyday purposes in rational terms. Here remains the fundamental contrast between the liberal and conservative attitudes towards the way in which identity of the 'self' is perceived. Besides, in both the definitions, the minority is depicted as a group identified by primordial characteristics which are not only distinct from the rest of the population (or majority) but also meant to be preserved as distinct. The 'minority' defined in this way is assigned a specific position in the 'self' and 'other' discourse.

The hierarchy of this relationship is, furthermore, informed by a sense of inferiority attached to the definition of 'minority': the minority is a group that is inferior in number or size as well as power to the majority. Inferiority in both the categories of demography and power is crucial, for a small group can well be in the dominant position. The reverse is also true: numerically larger groups can be in a subordinate position. Therefore, an image of the minority essentially captures a condition of inferiority in relation to both demography and power. Richard Schermerhorn[25] puts it lucidly in the figure above.

[25] Richard Schermerhorn, 'Ethnicity and Minority Groups' in *Ethnicity*, ed. John Hutchinson and Anthony D. Smith (Oxford: Oxford University Press, 1996), 17.

The phenomenon of 'otherness' in the minority was also emphasised by the state parties commenting on the provisional interpretation of the term 'minority' provided by the Special Rapporteur, Capotorti. The Finnish government held the view that any ethnic, religious, or linguistic group different from the majority of a given society constituted a minority.[26] Likewise, the Greek government's position on 'minority' was that the characteristic features of a minority group should be sufficiently distinctive to be clearly distinguishable from the majority.[27] In the same vein, the Dutch government maintained that the 'difference between a minority and the rest of the population should not only be sufficiently distinct but also sufficiently big, beyond gradual transitions and minor gradations'.[28] Clearly, efforts were made to draw a line between the 'other' with certain primordial characteristics and the 'self'.

In the more recent international and European instruments too, adopted following devastating ethnic conflicts in the aftermath of the fall of the Soviet Union and the breakup of the former Yugoslavia, the minority is conceived in the same fashion. The text of the Declaration on Persons Belonging to Minorities (1992) and the document issued by the CSCE Meeting of Experts on National Minorities (1991) both perceive minorities as bearers of 'ethnic, cultural, linguistic and religious identity'.[29] The Steering Committee on Human Rights to the Council of Europe, on the other hand, could not agree on a definition of the minority but, in the end, formulated a list of criteria to identify 'persons belonging to national minorities'; the possession of primordial features, the distinctiveness of these features from the rest of the population, and the collective wish to preserve their distinctive identity remain at the core of this list.[30] Similarly, the Parliamentary Assembly of the Council of Europe defines a national minority as a group of persons in a state who, among other attributes, display distinctive ethnic, cultural, religious, or linguistic characteristics and are motivated by a concern to preserve together that which constitutes their common identity, including their culture, their traditions, their religion, or their language.[31]

[26] See Capotorti Report, 7 [27] *Ibid.* [28] *Ibid.*

[29] See Lerner, *Group Rights and Discrimination*, 22.

[30] CDHH (93) 22, Strasbourg, 8 September 1993, feddh 93.22, 7–9. See Henrard, *Devising an Adequate System*, 27.

[31] Parliamentary Assembly of the Council of Europe, 'On an additional protocol on the rights of national minorities to the European Convention on Human Rights' (1993), Recommendation No. 1201, Doc. 6742, *Official Journal* 10 (1995). In 1990 the Parliamentary Assembly gave a first indication of its understanding of the meaning of 'national minority' in Recommendation 1134: 'separate or distinct groups, well defined and established on the territory of a state, the members of which are nationals of the state

Although there is no general definition of national minorities at the level of the Organisation for Security and Co-operation in Europe (OSCE), Kristin Henrard claims that 'there is a silent, practical consensus in the OSCE that the concept "minority" concerns a non-dominant, distinct, numerical minorities within a state'.[32] Thus, in the mandate for the High Commissioner on National Minorities, it is suggested that a national minority would typically fulfil two conditions: 'First of all, a minority is a group with linguistic, ethnic, or cultural characteristics, which distinguish it from the majority. Secondly, a minority is a group which usually not only seeks to maintain its identity but also tries to give stronger expression to that identity'.[33]

The Framework Convention for the Protection of National Minorities (FCNM, 1994) avoids any formal legal definition of minorities, and the Explanatory Report rationalises this evasion in strategic terms: '[I]t is impossible to arrive at a definition capable of mustering general support of all Council of Europe member States'.[34] However, a number of state parties offered their version of a definition of 'minority' while ratifying or acceding to the convention, and in most cases, the categories of distinctiveness of ethnic characteristics and the desire to maintain these characteristics remained omnipresent along with the claim that minorities must be the citizens of the concerned state party. For example, Estonia declared that minorities are Estonian citizens who

> reside on the territory of Estonia; maintain longstanding, firm and lasting ties with Estonia; are distinct from Estonians on the basis of their ethnic, cultural, religious or linguistic characteristics; are motivated by a concern to preserve together their cultural traditions, their religion or their language, which constitute the basis of their common identity.[35]

and have a certain religious, linguistic or other characteristics which distinguish them from the majority of the population'.

[32] Henrard, *Devising an Adequate System*, 30.

[33] Conference for Security and Co-operation in Europe, *CSCE Helsinki Document 1992: Challenges of Change* (9–10 July 1993). Available at: www.osce.org.

[34] *The Framework Convention for the Protection of National Minorities*, Explanatory Report, para. 12.

[35] See, for example, the declaration by Estonia on 6 January 1997 at: www.conventions.coe .int. Regarding this requirement for citizenship in defining the minority, it would be interesting to note that the Human Rights Committee in its General Comment on Article 27 adopted the position that the article applies to everyone belonging to one of the named categories of minorities and present within a country, including migrant workers and even visitors. See HRC, General Comment No. 23, UN Doc. CCPR/C/21/Rev.1/Add.5 (1995), para. 5.2. This is, of course, a deviation from the intention of the state parties formulating the article, and, as one commentator asserts, this is 'perhaps best interpreted

Like FCNM, the now-defunct UN Working Group on National Minorities, after an early unsuccessful attempt to adopt a definition of 'minority', refrained from any further attempt.[36]

Taken together, what is common in all these definitions and ways of understanding the term 'minority' is the image of a group in a subordinate position, which has at its core certain ethnic features that the members of the group not only share but also intend to preserve as an insignia of their identity. This very desire to preserve these features makes minorities the symbol of the conservative passion. In this sense, the minority is not only the 'other' of the majority within a given polity because of its distinctive ethnic features but also the 'other' of liberal universalism due to its tendency to portray the self-image in ethnic terms. Therefore, instead of being understood as an isolated object with certain distinctive features, the minority needs to be perceived in relational terms – it is in this uneven relationship with the majority (in the realm of power and in terms of demographic composition) and liberalism (at the ideological level) that the 'minority' is consistently defined and understood as distinct as well as primitive.

However, while it is generally accepted that the objectively recognisable fact of having ethnic, religious, and linguistic characteristics differing from those of the rest of the population should be the starting point of every effort to formulate a definition of the minority,[37] John Packer's approach to the concept of a minority sheds light on a different aspect. Claiming that arguments to determine fixed features of minorities fail to take into account the capacity of human beings to shape and change themselves according to their aspirations and talents, he concludes that

as representing the personal views of committee members rather than an authoritative interpretation of the text of the Covenant'. See Hurst Hannum, 'New Minority Rights for the Twenty-First Century' in *The Universal Declaration of Human Rights: Fifty Years and Beyond*, ed. Yael Danieli, Elsa Stamatopoulou, and Clarence J. Dias (Amityville, New York: Baywood Publishing, 1999), 169. See also H. Hannum, 'The Concept and Definition of Minorities' in *Universal Minority Rights*, ed. Marc Weller (Oxford: Oxford University Press, 2007), 60–61. Pentassuglia also argues that this expansive approach by the HRC has not been adopted by state parties in their response to the committee. See, generally, Gaetano Pentassuglia, *Defining 'Minority' in International Law: A Critical Appraisal*, 2nd rev edn (Rovaniemi: Lapland University Press, 2000), 18–36.

[36] The first chairman of the Working Group, Asbjørn Eide, outlined this approach in 'Report on the Possible Ways and Means of Facilitating the Peaceful and Constructive Solution of Problems Involving Minorities'. UN Doc. E/CN4/Sub.2/AC.5/2005/2 (2005). See also Hannum, 'The Concept and Definition of Minorities', 63–64.

[37] See Henrard, *Devising an Adequate System*, 31.

such arguments are fundamentally flawed.[38] Packer, therefore, defines a minority as 'a group of people who freely associate for an established purpose where their shared desire differs from that expressed by the majority rule'.[39] This perception of the minority, within the paradigm of the human rights philosophy and law, as a free association of individuals whose desires vary at different times and in different contexts, represents what is always at the centre of the liberal imaginary. Thus, in Packer's contractualist approach, the inherent positive value to be protected and promoted is not culture per se but rather the individual's desire as well as freedom to associate with the culture as a part of his or her identity which is valuable and, because of that, requires protection.[40]

Within Packer's theoretical approach to a minority as an association, it is the 'free desires of individuals' that determine the nature of such an association – classified as a positive association, which is formed by the voluntary choices of the constituent members, or a negative association, constructed by the majority or other external forces such as the state.[41] Although in one place Packer locates an individual in the context of his or her social life and surroundings as opposed to an 'American extreme of the isolated individual', he nevertheless understands a minority group as 'individuals in community'.[42] And therefore, any claims of '"collective rights" in the sense of rights to be enjoyed by entities themselves' or 'the rights of minority cultures', as opposed to the 'cultural rights of minorities' are perceived by Packer as illiberal in nature, as they appear to justify actions which could violate human rights.[43] In this way, the reduction of a minority group to individuals is justified, as it allows no question of protecting any particular culture.

In the following chapter, we shall discuss some of the inherent problems of such an approach in relation to ethnic conflicts. For now, it is to be noted that although Packer's liberal definition of the minority stands in contrast to the definitions of 'minority' as conservative ethnic phenomenon, adopted at different institutional levels,[44] it is essentially this liberal approach that is in place to address the issue of minority

[38] Packer, 'Problems in Defining Minorities', 247.

[39] Packer, 'On the Definition of Minorities', 45.

[40] Packer, 'Problems in Defining Minorities', 247.

[41] See *ibid.*, 254–260. Packer asserts that it is common for a negative association to experience dynamics that lead it to develop the attributes of a positive association, a phenomenon which Packer terms 'dynamic transformations'.

[42] *Ibid.*, 244. [43] *Ibid.*, 242–243.

[44] Besides institutions, authors on the minority issue also took the same approach. For example, in Fawcett's book he adopts a working definition of the 'minority' as 'a group in

protection, as we shall see in the following section. Yet, this contrast between the approaches taken by Packer and various international instruments remains useful, in that it brings to the fore the idea that these instruments themselves are not explicitly liberal, although they may be interpreted that way. There are two ways of seeing this differentiation: one which turns upon the essentially instrumental value of the references to ethnicity and the other which affirms, through the numerical inferiority of the minority, the distinctive ethnicity of the majority. The problem with Packer's position, of course, is that he fails to engage with what he, like many liberals, explicitly understands to be the problem – the link between ethnicity and violence – and assumes a position that tends to hide ethnicity by excluding it from the discourse, by not talking about it.[45] The problem with the alternative position that Packer is alert to is that if there is this link between ethnicity and violence, then reinforcing it in regimes for minority protection may just end up affirming its value and importance.

Dismantling ethnicity in minority 'protection'

The liberal disavowal of the protection of minorities in the conservative sense was explicit from the outset of the post–World War II international legal order. The issue of the protection of the constitutive elements of minorities as well as their sense of solidarity (hereinafter, minority protection) was carefully avoided during the San Francisco Conference, though few references to minorities were actually made.[46] In the Charter

a country which possesses and has common will – however conditioned – to preserve certain habits and patterns of life and behaviour which may be ethnic, cultural, linguistic or religious, or a combination of them, and which characterise it as a group. Further such a minority may be politically dominant or non-dominant'. See James Fawcett, *The International Protection of Minorities* (London: Minority Rights Group, 1979), 4. Kristin Henrard's working definition of the 'minority' is as follows: 'a "minority" is a group numerically smaller than the rest of the population of a state. The members of this non-dominant group have ethnic, religious or linguistic characteristics different from those of the rest of the population and show, even implicitly, a sense of mutual solidarity focused on the preservation of their culture, traditions, religion or language'. This working definition, Henrard admits, is a slightly adapted version of Capotorti's definition. Its most remarkable divergence with Capotorti's definition is the absence of any nationality requirement for the members of a minority. See Henrard, *Devising an Adequate System*, 48.

45 Cf. Franck, *Fairness in International Law and Institutions*, 140–169; Franck, 'Postmodern Tribalism and the Right to Secession', 3–27.

46 The representative of France remarked that international intervention to prevent abuse of minorities might sometimes be necessary to maintain the peace. In a later discussion, the

of the United Nations, discrimination on the basis of sex, race, language, religion, and birth place has been explicitly prohibited in a number of places,[47] and for the framers of the charter, the reliance on 'non-discrimination' was the appropriate way of addressing the issue of minority rights.[48]

The omission of minority protection provisions in the charter was compensated by the creation of the United Nations Sub-Commission on Prevention of Discrimination and the Protection of Minorities – a subordinate body of the then United Nations Commission on Human Rights. Initially, two sub-commissions were proposed: one for the 'prevention of discrimination' and the other for the 'protection of minorities'. But the Commission on Human Rights in its first meeting decided to form one sub-commission tasked with both prevention and protection.[49] This move, Humphrey notes, allowed the UN to easily 'dodge responsibility for the protection of minorities'.[50]

As a matter of fact, the sub-commission's work towards the protection of minorities made little progress, in that the member states of the commission had almost no interest in the protection issue; rather, they wanted the sub-commission to concentrate on the issue of non-discrimination.[51] To quote Humphrey: 'In the higher bodies of the UN, there has never been any serious intention of doing anything about minorities'.[52] Accordingly, the sub-commission decided to focus on the prevention of discrimination and to defer a further study of the problem of the special protection of minorities pending the issuing of a specific directive on the subject by the commission.[53] However, the sub-

representative of Belgium said of the Economic and Social Council that 'minority questions fall properly within its province, but under another name and, though on a wider territorial basis, without the special guarantees which in this connection would result from the system of the League of Nations'. See Thornberry, *International Law and the Rights of Minorities*, 118. For a chronological account of minority protection in international law, see also Jennifer J. Preece, 'Minority Rights in Europe: From Westphalia to Helsinki', *Review of International Studies* 23, no. 1 (1997), 75–92. Different historical approaches to minorities are briefly discussed in J. Preece, 'National Minorities and International System', *Politics* 18, no. 1 (1998), 17–23.

47 Articles 1(3), 13, 55, and 76 of the Charter.

48 Thornberry is of the opinion that 'the Charter *does* have a view on minorities to be read by necessary implication, that the issue is now part of human rights'. See Thornberry, *International Law and the Rights of Minorities*, 119.

49 For details, see United Nations, UN Doc. A/CONF32/6, 1947, paras. 114–115.

50 Humphrey, 'The United Nations Sub-Commission', 870.

51 For an evaluation of the sub-commission's work on minority protection, see *ibid.*, 869–888.

52 *Ibid.*, 872.

53 United Nations, UN Doc. E/CN4/711.

commission complained on a number of occasions that its reports were being neglected by the Commission on Human Rights and that its proposals were rejected either by the Economic and Social Council or by the General Assembly.[54] As Kunz noted in 1954, '[t]here is a feeling in the Sub-Commission as if the United Nations were reluctant to do something about the protection of minorities'.[55]

This attitude of avoiding the issue of minority protection within the UN system can be seen in the successive efforts to change the name of the sub-commission to remove the word 'minority': in 1965, it was proposed that the name of the sub-commission should be changed to the Permanent Committee of Experts of the Commission on Human Rights;[56] again in 1979, the sub-commission recommended that its name be changed to the Sub-Commission on Human Rights.[57] Success finally came in 1999 when the Sub-Commission on Prevention of Discrimination and the Protection of Minorities was renamed the Sub-Commission on Promotion and Protection of Human Rights; the latter, however, ceased to exist in 2006 when all its mandates and activities were assumed by the Human Rights Council's Advisory Committee.[58]

In the Universal Declaration of Human Rights (UDHR), too, as in the charter, the principle of non-discrimination prevails without any reference to minorities, although in a General Assembly Resolution in 1948, it was mentioned that the UN could not remain indifferent to the fate of minorities.[59] During the drafting of the declaration, the sub-commission proposed a draft article to the commission covering various aspects of the protection of minority rights.[60] However, the majority of members in the commission and the General Assembly opposed any such inclusion of the minority protection provision. It was argued that the liberal universal and individual human rights contained in the declaration would, in

54 See Kunz, 'The Present Status of the International Law', 285–286. 55 *Ibid.*, 286.

56 United Nations, *ECOSOC Official Records* (1965), 41st Session, Supp. No. 8, 119.

57 United Nations, Sub-Commission on Human Rights Resolution 9A (XXXII) (1979), UN Doc. E/CN4/Sub.2/435.

58 See United Nations, General Assembly Resolution 60/251, 10 March 2006.

59 United Nations, *Fate of Minorities* (1948), General Assembly Resolution 217c (III), 10 December 1948.

60 The draft article read: 'In States inhabited by well-defined ethnic, linguistic or other groups which are clearly distinguished from the rest of the population, and which want to be accorded differential treatment, persons belonging to such groups shall have the right, as far as is compatible with public order and security, to establish and maintain their own schools and cultural or religious institutions, and to use their own language and script in the press, in public assembly and before the courts and other authorities of the State, if they so choose'. See United Nations, UN Doc. E/CN4/21, Annex A 23.

themselves, provide the necessary protection for minorities through the principle that everyone, without discrimination, was entitled to every right contained in the declaration.[61] It was the dominant thought at that time.[62] The US representative, Eleanor Roosevelt, explicitly declared that there should be no minority provision in the declaration and asserted that 'the best solution of the problem of minorities was to encourage respect for human rights'.[63] The General Assembly, consequently, adopted the UDHR without any provision for minority protection; instead, it requested the council to ask the Commission on Human Rights and the sub-commission to make a thorough study of the problem of the minorities.[64] Once again, the issue of minority protection was compromised, and the omission was compensated with a toothless measure.

Thus, in dealing with minorities under the UN, the paradigm shifted from the conservative notion of 'minority protection', as was the case under the League, to the liberal agenda of 'prevention of discrimination'. The liberal regime of human rights, which was equipped with the individualist principles of equality and non-discrimination, was designed to respond to the problems of members belonging to minority groups without addressing the *group per se*. However, the sub commission understood the concept of 'minority protection' in a way that required the state agencies to take positive action to protect the culture, language, and religion of minority groups. Therefore, at its first session in 1947, the sub-commission suggested that the prevention of discrimination means the 'prevention of any action which denies to individuals or groups of people equal treatment which they may wish', while the protection of minorities is the 'protection of non-dominant groups which, while wishing in general for equality of treatment with the majority, wish for

[61] United Nations, UN Doc A/C3/SR161, 720.

[62] However, some states, such as the USSR, Denmark, and Yugoslavia, proposed provisions for minority protection. The Yugoslav representative gave the following rationale behind their proposal to insert a specific provision for minorities: 'In order to secure the protection of individuals who formed a community, that community must first of all be recognised and protected. Thus the principle of the recognition and protection of national minorities as communities must appear in the Declaration of Human Rights. The cultural and ethnical roots of all persons belonging to a national minority [...] depended upon the recognition of the minority itself as an ethnic group. Individual human rights were dependent on the position which the community enjoyed in the State in which it lived'. See *ibid.*

[63] United Nations, UN Doc. A/C.3/SR.161, 726.

[64] See United Nations General Assembly, 3rd Session, *Official Records*, Part I, Resolutions, 77.

a measure of differential treatment in order to preserve basic characteristics which they possess and which distinguish them from the majority of the population'.[65] Nevertheless, at the following session, the commission approved the text concerning the prevention of discrimination but postponed a study of the text concerning the protection of minorities.[66]

As a matter of fact, the idea of protecting minorities in the conservative sense violates the fundamental tenets of liberalism. As Kunz notes, although the prevention of discrimination is due to all minorities, it is only a part of 'human rights', a matter of equality, and not a part of the international law for the protection of minorities, for the latter must give specific minority rights, special privileges, and services. It must go beyond mere equality and prevention of discrimination.[67] Such a perception of minority protection contradicts the liberal idea of non-discrimination, which assumes that differential treatment on the grounds of ethnicity is fundamentally irrational. This proposition completely undercuts the idea that groups should be protected on the basis of their ethnic features and solidarity. Hence, the issue of 'minority protection' was to be addressed through the liberal individualist principle of 'non-discrimination'.

Efforts were also made to reconcile the concepts of prohibition of discrimination and minority protection by highlighting the artificiality of the distinction between them and then locating them within the broader framework of human rights. Capotorti, for example, takes the view that these two concepts are 'merely two aspects of the same problem: that of defending fundamental human rights'.[68] The same opinion is held by Warwick McKean, who asserts that these 'concepts are not unrelated or contradictory, but are complementary methods of attaining equality of treatment for all persons'.[69] Vierdag criticises any perception of a distinction between prevention of discrimination and protection of minorities and asserts that no references to the protection of minorities need be made, for minority protection can be realised through the granting of human rights in combination with the principle of non-discrimination.[70]

[65] United Nations, UN Doc. E/CN4/52, sec V. [66] See Capotorti Report, 40.

[67] Kunz, 'The Present Status of the International Law', 286. [68] Capotorti Report, 41.

[69] Quoted in Francesco Capotorti, *Monograph 23 Prepared towards the Study on the Rights of Persons Belonging to Ethnic, Religious and Linguistic Minorities*, UN Doc. E/CN4/Sub. 2/384/Add5, para. 24, UN Sales No. E78 XIV, I.

[70] E. W. Vierdag, *The Concept of Discrimination in International Law – With Special Reference to Human Rights* (The Hague: Martinus Nijhoff, 1973), 158.

However, reliance on only the principles of equality and non-discrimination within an individualist framework to address the protection of minorities can be technically problematic for two reasons: first, it has the potential to ignore the *raison d'être* of the discrimination and, thereby, to overlook its character. When an individual faces discrimination on the grounds of ethnicity, the discrimination actually arises because of his or her affiliation with a particular ethnic group. Therefore, considering the act of discrimination as something merely done against an individual and perceiving such discrimination as a violation of his or her individual rights outside the realm of group identity, would be misleading. In a number of cases before the European Court of Human Rights (ECtHR), individual members of the Roma community alleged ethnicity-based discrimination (which is a violation of Article 14 of the European Convention) in relation to the enjoyment of their individual right to life, right to dignity, and freedom from torture and other inhuman and degrading treatment. In some of these cases, the court found these incidents of discrimination to be rooted in the ethnic-Roma origin of the victims. For example, in the case of *Moldovan and others* v. *Romania*, the court noted that the attacks were directed against the applicants because of their Roma origin, and the applicants' Roma ethnicity appeared to have been decisive for the length and the result of the domestic proceedings; hence, the court concluded that Article 14 was violated.[71]

Secondly, given that the idea of the prevention of discrimination is set to ensure 'equality' among individuals of different ethno-cultural affiliations and therefore is transitory in nature, in the long run it has the potential to encourage assimilation of the minority groups into the dominant cultures in a given polity in the absence of any specific guarantee of rights for minority groups. However, as Thornberry argues, the protection of minorities is supposed to be permanent, provided that the minority remains a minority in need of special protection, unless the composition of a population or the balance of

[71] ECHR (2005), Application Nos. 41138/1998 and 64320/2001. Nevertheless, the standard of the proof that the court set in *Velikova* v. *Bulgaria* for a successful Article 14 claim, that is, the proof must be beyond a reasonable doubt, is quite high, and hence a debacle in itself. See ECHR (2000), Application No. 41488/1998. In a subsequent case, Judge Bonello, in a dissenting opinion, argued for a lowered burden of proof stating that '[n]o more effective tool could be devised to ensure that the protection against racial discrimination becomes illusory and inoperative than requiring from a victim a standard of proof that, in other civil law disputes, is required of no one else'. See *Anguelova* v. *Bulgaria*, *ECHR* (2002), Application Nos. 43577/1998 and 43579/1998.

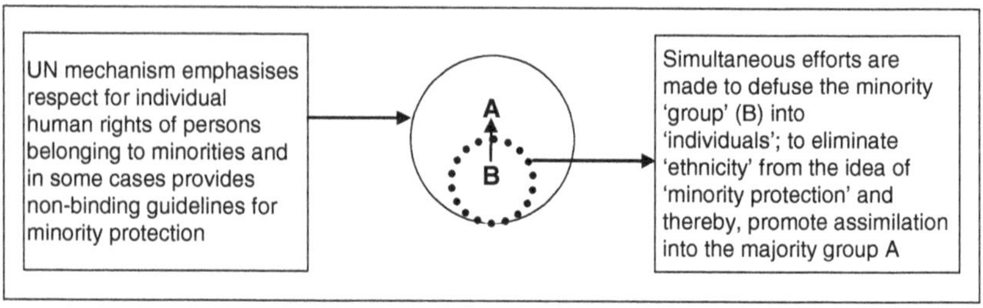

Figure 4.2 Dismantling ethnicity in minority protection

political power changes.[72] Thus, the transitory as well as the individualist notions of equality and non-discrimination are bound to be insufficient so far as the protection of the minority is concerned. Instead, the possibility remains that they might be used as the *modus operandi* of assimilation and the extinction of group identity – the ways of removing ethnicity from the notion of minority (Figure 4.2).

From the liberal standpoint, this is nothing short of desired, in that the protection of minorities in the liberal sense can at its best be perceived as the protection of minorities from the very constitutive elements of their identity – ethnicity. Given that ethnicity, expressed in the conservative tradition of perceiving the self-image, turns the minority into the victim of oppression by the majority and also undermines the individual rights of the minority group members, the liberal way of minority protection would thus logically mean the suppression of ethnicity through the individualist principles of equality and non-discrimination. In other words, the liberal version of minority protection appears as an emancipatory project: the liberal not only constructs minorities as a symbol of conservative traditions but also protects them from the curse of ethnicity – the very constitutive element of minorities. The conservative notion of minority protection, meaning the promotion of ethnic features and solidarity, is therefore incompatible with liberalism. Yet, in the real world, the continued existence of minorities keeps the underlying ethnic phenomenon alive and thereby poses a constant challenge to this liberal imaginary. The liberal way of dealing with this pragmatic challenge reveals its hesitancy at and reconciliatory approach to the idea of actively promoting ethnic identities, as the following discussion demonstrates.

Shortly after the Paris Peace Conference of 1946, Kunz wrote in an editorial comment:

[72] Thornberry, *International Law and the Rights of Minorities*, 126.

> The Potsdam Agreement and the attitude taken by the United States and the United Kingdom at the Paris Peace Conference of 1946, an attitude in favour of assimilation rather than of perpetuation of racial minorities, is certainly very different from the attitude taken by the Paris Peace Conference of 1919. The new idea of international protection of 'human rights' is a different idea which does not include specific minority rights, *although the problem of the protection of minorities is bound to come up again within this new framework.*[73]

Kunz's prediction materialised vividly in the incorporation of Article 27 in the ICCPR, which endeavoured to address the issue of the minority within the individualist framework of the covenant.[74] This article is often cited for its image as a pro-minority provision. Rights guaranteed to members of minorities to enjoy their own culture, to profess and practise their religion, or to use their own language in community with other members of their group are certainly of a unique character given the silence on the minority issue in the previous UN human rights instruments. The phrase 'in community with the other members of their group' surely envisages the right-bearer in the context of a group. Nevertheless, the right-bearers are definitely the individual members of the groups, not the group as such, very much in conformity with the then dominant philosophy – liberal individualism.[75] This formulation was necessary, according to Capotorti, for three reasons: historical continuity, maintaining coherence with the overall individualist tone of the covenant, and, lastly and perhaps most importantly, mitigating the threat to territorial integrity and political independence of existing states as well as upholding the individual freedom of voluntary assimilation.[76]

The *travaux preparatoires* of the covenant exhibits the state parties' reluctance towards any general recognition of rights for minority groups. The initial draft of the article in fact tended to address the issue of

[73] Joseph Kunz, 'The Italo-Austria Agreement on the Austrian South Tyrol', *American Journal of International Law* 41 (1947), 443. Emphasis added.

[74] Article 27 stipulates: 'In those States in which ethnic, religious or linguistic minorities exist, persons belonging to such minorities shall not be denied the right, in community with the other members of their group, to enjoy their own culture, to profess and practice their religion, or to use their own language'.

[75] As Jones explains, when individual members of a group hold rights as separate individuals, their several individual rights, though they lead to a collectivity, do not add up to a group right. A right is a group right only if it is borne by the group *qua* group; '[w]hat distinguishes a right as a group right is its subject rather than its object – who it is that holds the right rather than what the right is a right to'. See Peter Jones, 'Human Rights, Group Rights and Peoples' Rights', *Human Rights Quarterly* 21 (1999), 82–83.

[76] Capotorti Report, 35.

minority protection in conservative terms in the following words: 'Ethnic, religious and linguistic minorities shall not be denied the right to enjoy their own culture, to profess and practise their own religion, or to use their own language'.[77] However, in the final text, 'persons belonging to such minorities', not the minorities themselves, appear as the subject of this right. The difference between these two phrases – rights of minorities and rights of the persons belonging to minorities – is significantly wide, and it unequivocally demonstrates the intention of the framers of Article 27 categorically to exclude the minority as a conservative, corporate connotation. The tension between individualism and minority rights, as highlighted by Thornberry in the following comment, indicates what might be seen as a century-old tension between the liberal and conservative philosophical traditions:

> The balance between 'minority rights' and 'individual rights' is an aspect of a larger question, but it is resolved in the Covenant in favour of individual rights. The minority's 'claim' on individuals, even in the case of a minority in difficulties of self-preservation, has only a secondary or subordinate importance. The minority does not mediate between the individual and the State; it has no rights as such to preserve its identity. The individualistic and libertarian focus of human rights law is evident here [. . .].[78]

The liberal tone of Article 27 is substantiated when read with Article 5(1) of the covenant, which stipulates that nothing in the covenant will be interpreted in a way that would jeopardise the individual rights and freedoms guaranteed in other provisions of the covenant.[79] As a matter of fact, invariably every international declaration and convention that mentions the need for minority protection also emphasises that such protection operates within the limits of the human rights regime and, in this sense, is subject to the enjoyment of rights and freedoms of individual members.[80] This primacy of individualism is also reinforced in the

[77] United Nations, UN Doc. E/CN4/Sub.2/112.

[78] Thornberry, *International Law and the Rights of Minorities*, 176–177.

[79] Article 5(1) provides: 'Nothing in the present Covenant may be interpreted as implying for any State, group or person any right to engage in any activity or perform any act aimed at the destruction of any of the rights and freedoms recognised herein or at their limitation to a greater extent than is provided for in the present Covenant'.

[80] For example, the UNESCO declaration on cultural diversity states that '[n]o one may invoke cultural diversity to infringe upon human rights guaranteed by international law, nor to limit their scope' (Art. 4). The UN declaration on minority rights states that any rights or duties recognised in the declaration 'shall not prejudice the enjoyment of all persons of universally recognised human rights and fundamental freedoms' (Art. 8:2).

Optional Protocol to the ICCPR, which recognises the competence of the Human Rights Committee established under Article 28 of the covenant 'to receive and consider communications from individuals subject to its jurisdiction who claim to be victims of a violation by that State Party of any of the rights set forth in the Covenant'.[81]

Thus, in the cases of *Lansman et al.* v. *Finland I and II* as well as *O. Sara et al.* v. *Finland*, although the group rights of the Sami indigenous communities of Finland were threatened by the mining, logging, road construction, and other related activities, the complainants brought the issue under Article 27 and not under Article 1 of the same covenant, the article that guarantees a people's right to self-determination. Given that the established case law of the Human Rights Committee (HRC) and the General Comment on Article 27 provide that Article 1 does not fall under the monitoring competence of the committee, as it confers a right on 'peoples' and not to individuals, Article 27 was a strategic choice for these communities.[82] In the *Bernard Ominayak, Chief of the Lubicon Lake Band* v. *Canada* case, the committee took a similar view regarding Article 1.[83] In the case of *Kitok* v. *Sweden*,[84] Ivan Kitok, a member of a Sami Family, claimed violations – caused by the Swedish law that divided the Sami people into two groups on the basis of their continuous, or not, engagement in reindeer herding – of his rights to breed reindeer and to land and water in the Sorkaitum Sami Village under both Article 1 and Article 27 of the covenant. The committee decided that the claim under Article 1 was inadmissible under the Optional Protocol. However, the communication was declared admissible under Article 27, since 'the author had made a reasonable effort to substantiate his allegations that he was the victim of a violation of his [individual] right to enjoy the same rights enjoyed by other members of the Sami community'.[85] In more recent cases, for example, in *J. G. A Diergaardt et al.* v. *Namibia*[86] and *Gillot* v. *France*,[87] the committee held that Article 1 is nevertheless

Similarly, the Framework Convention on National Minorities adopted by the Council of Europe stipulates that the convention must be interpreted in a way that complies with the European Convention on Human Rights (Art. 23).

[81] Article 1 of the Optional Protocol to ICCPR, 1966.

[82] Annelies Verstichel, 'Recent Development in the UN Human Rights Committee's Approach to Minorities, with a Focus on Effective Participation', *International Journal on Minority and Group Rights* 12 (2005), 31.

[83] HRC (1990) No. 167/1984, CCPR/C/38/D/167/1984.

[84] HRC (1988) No. 197/1985, CCPR/C/33/D/197/1985. [85] Paras. 5.1, 5.2, 5.3, and 5.4.

[86] HRC (2000) No. 760/1996, CCPR/C/69/D/760/1996, para. 10.3.

[87] HRC (2002) No. 932/2000, CCPR/C/75/D/932/2000, para. 13.4.

relevant in the interpretation of other rights protected by the covenant, in particular Articles 25, 26, and 27.[88]

This, in any event, endorses the individualistic character of the rights enshrined in Article 27. This individualistic nature is perhaps best demonstrated in the *Lovelace* v. *Canada* case, wherein the committee rightly found that the Indian Act violated Sandra Lovelace's individual rights by denying her membership in the Tobique band because she married a non-Indian.[89] Under the Canadian legislation, Indians who ceased to be members of an Indian band (in this case due to marriage with a non-Indian) lost certain privileges, including the right to reside on a reserve.[90] Thus, the committee's preference for Lovelace's individual right to enjoy her cultural membership is a classic example of a liberal conception of band membership being substituted for a conservative one, in that Lovelace did not have the right to be a member of the band under its own criteria, which the committee regarded as discriminatory.

Yet, at the same time, the HRC does not ignore the relevance of minority protection in the conservative sense. Though in the *Lovelace* case the committee decided in favour of Lovelace's individual right to enjoy her culture in community with other members along the line of Article 27, it nonetheless underscores the significance of the Indian Act for the protection of Indian communities. In this case the committee set the *ratio decidendi* that 'a restriction upon the right of an individual member of a minority must be shown to have a reasonable and objective justification and to be necessary for the continued viability and welfare of the minority as a whole', which later on guided the committee's decision in the *Kitok* case.[91] Therefore, in the latter case, the committee found the discrimination against Ivan Kitok justified for the sake of the preservation and well-being of the Sami minority.[92] In the General Comment on

[88] Alexander H. E. Morawa, 'The United Nations Treaty Monitoring Bodies and Minority Rights, with particular Emphasis on the Human Rights Committee' in *Mechanisms for the Implementation of Minority Rights*, ed. M. Weller and A. H. E. Morawa (Strasbourg: Council of Europe Publishing, 2004), 39.

[89] HRC (1981) No. 24/1977, A/36/40. [90] See *ibid.* [91] Para. 9.8.

[92] However, in more recent cases, Henrard notes, it appears that the committee gives 'a lot weight and even precedence to the State's interests and views in its evaluation of facts to determine whether or not there has been a violation of the article'. See Henrard, *Devising an Adequate System*, 184. The *Lansman et al.* v. *Finland I* and *II* cases would be pertinent examples in this context. The committee's pro-state approach in these cases is significant for one more reason: these cases deal with the conflict of interest between minority and the state in contrast to an individual versus group issue as in the *Lovelace* case or *Kitok* case.

Article 27, too, the committee observes that the enjoyment of the rights under the article may require positive legal measures of protection and measures to ensure the effective participation of the members of minority communities in decisions which affect them.[93]

The issue of the protection of minorities within the liberal framework appeared in a number of other international human rights instruments, and necessarily, non-discrimination was regarded as the applicable principle. For example, the International Convention on the Elimination of All Forms of Racial Discrimination (1965) authorises special measures necessary to secure adequate advancement of certain racial or ethnic groups, namely, steps involving preferential treatment for the members of groups that suffer discrimination; however, such affirmative measures shall not be continued after the objectives have been achieved.[94] This view was endorsed later by the Committee on Elimination of Racial Discrimination in its General Recommendation No. 32 on the provision of special measures under Articles 1(4) and 2(2) of the convention, although the committee understood the time limitations in essentially functional terms.[95] Nevertheless, the specific mention of the 'transitory' character of these affirmative measures clearly envisages assimilation as the ultimate fate of the minorities. The aim of the special measures is to

> restore the balance between the respective positions of the various groups, including minority groups, but the ultimate objective of the convention is the uniform treatment of individuals to whatever group they belong. The fear of providing an excuse for a policy of separation prevailed over the awareness of the need for the members of different groups, especially minority groups, to live in perpetuity under different regimes, based on their special characteristics.[96]

The UNESCO Convention on the Elimination of Discrimination in Education obliges the contracting states to allow members of national minorities to establish and maintain, in certain circumstances and under certain conditions, their own educational institutions, but neither

93 United Nations, *United Nations Human Rights Committee General Comment on Article 27 of the ICCPR* (1994), 50th session, no. 23, Sec. 7. See UN Doc. CCPR/C/21/ Rev. 1/ Add.5.

94 Article 2, Clause 2 of the Convention. See *United Nations General Assembly Resolution 2106 (XX)* (21 December 1965). Available at: www.unhchr.ch.

95 See CERD, General Recommendation No. 32, *The Meaning and Scope of Special Measures in the International Convention on the Elimination of Racial Discrimination*, UN Doc. CERF/C/GC/32, 24 September 2009, para. 27.

96 Francesco Capotorti, 'Protection of Minorities under Multinational Agreements on Human Rights', *Italian Yearbook of International Law* (1976), 9.

provision generates specific financial and other related responsibilities for the latter. Conversely, it is expressly stipulated that national sovereignty should not be prejudiced by the exercise of this right.[97]

Other non-binding international declarations also attempted to address the minority issue, albeit indirectly. The UNESCO Declaration on Race and Racial Prejudice (1978) affirms that all individuals and groups have the right to be different, to consider themselves to be different, and to be regarded as such.[98] However, it is argued that attributing rights to all groups – whether dominant or not – could amount to the confirmation and perpetuation of the *de facto* dominance of one or more groups.[99] The UN Declaration against Intolerance and Discrimination Based on Religion and Belief (1981) grants certain rights that can only be exercised in groups, although the declaration does not devolve any group rights to religious minorities.[100]

Henrard stresses that since the concept of 'minority identity', in line with the minority phenomenon itself, has strong group connotations, an important factor in gauging the potential contribution of a certain mechanism to adequate minority protection is the extent to which that mechanism implies the recognition and protection of this group dimension.[101] As the preceding discussion demonstrates, under the UN regime, the issue of 'minority' – understood as a group constructed along the line of the conservative tradition of relying on the centrality of ethnicity in identity formation – was either avoided or addressed through the individualist framework. Despite a gradual shift from the complete omission of the minority issue, as in the charter and the UDHR, to recognition of the rights of individual members of these minorities to maintain their ethno-cultural identity, as in Article 27, no effective provision for the 'protection of minorities' actually came to light during this period.

[97] Article 5, Clause 1(c) of the convention.

[98] Article 1, Clause 2 of the declaration. See UNESCO General Conference, *UNESCO Declaration on Race and Racial Prejudice* (1978), UN Doc. E/CN 4/Sub. 2/1982/2/Add.1/annex V. Available at: www.unesco.org.

[99] See Henrard, *Devising an Adequate System*, 203.

[100] UN General Assembly, *Declaration on the Elimination of All Forms of Intolerance and of Discrimination Based on Religion or Belief* (1981), A/RES/36/55. Available at: www.un.org/documents. See also Henrard, *Devising an Adequate System*, 203.

[101] Kristin Henrard, 'The Protection of Minorities through the Equality Provisions of UN Human Rights Treaties: The UN Treaty Bodies', *International Journal on Minority and Group Rights* 14 (2007), 145.

Instead, in the face of repeated emphasis on the individualist human rights, including limited rights of individuals to cultural identity in the absence of any positive measure for the maintenance of these cultures, the issue of the 'protection' of minorities sank into theoretical insignificance. Such a prevailing order, from the perspective of ethnic minorities, readily permits the subordination of minorities to the majority culture under the veil of liberal principles of non-discrimination, equality, and so on.[102] Within the liberal individualist framework, it is not even considered necessary to 'protect' the very constitutive ethnic elements of the groups, such as culture, per se.[103] Thus, the international machinery invested energy in taking out the conservative notion of ethnicity from the 'minority' and reducing the latter to individuals who would share a common national (and also international) liberal culture.

However, the pragmatic necessity of minority protection remained alive, a fact that is substantiated by the gradual paradigmatic shift in the functioning of the UN vis-à-vis minorities. The pressing need to restore ethnicity in 'minority protection' emerged at the end of the Cold War with the eruption of a series of ethnic conflicts, which could not be wished away. This provided a fresh impetus for minority protection in international law. Most of the literature on minority rights covering this period suggests a causal relationship between violent ethnic conflicts and the resurgence of the claim for group rights for minorities. Some relate the absence of minority group rights directly to the eruption of ethnic conflicts.[104] It is also quite plausible to suggest that even if there were extensive provisions protecting ethnic minorities, those might themselves have been condemned for keeping the spirit of ethnicity alive. Nevertheless, in the aftermath of the Cold War, the protection of minorities in conservative terms once again gained attention as a viable pragmatic response to ethnic tension. Thus, while in the preceding regime ethnicity was conceived as a political void and minority protection was understood in purely liberal-individualist terms, in the post–Cold War phase, ethnicity came to push the agenda of minority protection towards the conservative line. This made the liberal hesitancy

[102] See Anthony Anghie, 'Human Rights and Cultural Identity: New Hope for Ethnic Peace?' *Harvard International Law Journal* 33, no. 2 (1992), 345.

[103] See, generally, Packer, 'Problems in Defining Minorities'. Also, Brian Barry, *Culture and Equality* (Cambridge: Polity Press, 2001); Chandran Kukathas, *The Liberal Archipelago: A Theory of Diversity and Freedom* (Oxford: Oxford University Press, 2003).

[104] See, for example, Anghie, 'Human Rights and Cultural Identity'. I discuss this position in detail in the following chapter.

at minority rights more visible and the need for a reconciliatory approach to these competing traditions more compelling.

The UN Declaration on the Rights of Persons Belonging to National or Ethnic, Religious and Linguistic Minorities (UNDM, 1992) is the iconic document in this context, accommodating the post–Cold War consciousness about the ethnic dimensions of minority protection.[105] Although designed to address the rights of individuals, the declaration formulates state responsibilities towards minority groups. Unlike Article 27, this declaration makes it clear that these rights often require action, including protective measures and the encouragement of conditions for the promotion of minority groups' identity,[106] and it specifies active measures by the state.[107] In his oft-cited commentary on Article 4 of the declaration, Asbjørn Eide held that these measures may require economic resources from the state; thus, in the same way as the state provides funding for the development of the culture and language of the majority, it shall provide resources for similar activities of the minority.[108] Such a positive attitude towards minorities certainly underscores the conservative group dimension of minority protection.

However, the process was not as straightforward as it might appear. Breaking with the dominant liberal-individualist approach to minority protection was not an easy task; a consistent balance had to be found. Thus, at first, the declaration advocated rights for individuals in line with Article 27 and not for any group. Eide confirms this in his commentary: 'The rights of persons belonging to minorities are individual rights, even if they in most cases can only be enjoyed in community with others'.[109] Therefore, the right to self-determination, which is a collective right of peoples, is outside the purview of the declaration; the issue of autonomy shares the same status. Moreover, as Henrard claims, the declaration has little or no concrete content in relation to the right to enjoy one's own culture, the right to profess and practise one's own religion, or the right to participate in the religious life of the state.[110] Thus, in the final evaluation, Henrard depicts the provisions of the declaration as some mere open 'guidelines' for states who are positive about minority protection.[111]

[105] UN General Assembly, UN Doc. A/RES/47/135 (1992).
[106] Article 1 of the declaration. [107] Article 4 of the declaration.
[108] Asbjørn Eide, *Final Text of the Commentary to the Declaration on the Rights of National or Ethnic, Religious and Linguistic Minorities* (2001), UN Doc. E/CN4/Sub.2/AC5/2001/2, para 56.
[109] *Ibid.*, para 15. [110] Henrard, *Devising an Adequate System*, 192. [111] *Ibid.*, 193.

Three years after adoption of the UNDM, in 1995, the United Nations Working Group on Minorities (WGM) was established under the then Sub-Commission on Prevention of Discrimination and Protection of Minorities; the declaration was its normative basis.[112] The WGM was the first mechanism to promote implementation of the declaration and to facilitate peaceful accommodation of minorities within states by reviewing the promotion and practical realisation of the declaration, examining possible solutions to problems involving minorities, and recommending further appropriate measures for the promotion and protection of the rights of persons belonging to minorities.[113] It was unique in allowing participation by representatives of minorities, NGOs concerned with minority issues, and all governments as observers with full speaking rights and the right to submit proposals. An even more special feature of the WGM was its openness to participation by scholars and researchers in the field of minority rights.[114] However, as its openness indicates, the WGM was not a monitoring body, and it had no mechanism for dealing with complaints; also, states are under no obligation to report on their implementation of the declaration. As Eide characterises it: 'The WGM itself can best be described as a forum. It serves as an ongoing *workshop* exploring ways to promote constructive group accommodation based on the UNDM, and plays an important role in creating awareness of problematic situations'.[115] However, the Human Rights Council replaced the WGM with the UN Forum on Minority Issues on 28 September 2007.[116]

This forum, very much in line with its predecessor, WGM, merely provides a platform for dialogue and cooperation on minority issues. It attracted more than four hundred participants in each session, including representatives of minority groups as well as states, regional intergovernmental bodies, UN bodies, mechanisms and specialised agencies,

[112] United Nations, UN Commission on Human Rights Resolution 1995/31, UN Doc. E/CN4/1995/31 (1995).

[113] United Nations, UN Commission on Human Rights Resolution 1995/24 on the rights of persons belonging to national or ethnic, religious and linguistic minorities, ESCOR Supp. (No.4) at p. 92, UN Doc. E/CN4/1995/24 (1995).

[114] Asbjørn Eide, 'The Role of the United Nations Working Group on Minorities' in *Mechanisms for the Implementation of Minority Rights*, ed. M. Weller and A. H. E. Morawa (Strasbourg: Council of Europe Publishing, 2004), 57.

[115] Eide, 'The Role of the United Nations Working Group on Minorities', 58. Emphasis added.

[116] United Nations, Human Rights Council Resolution 6/15. UN Doc. A/HRC/6/15.

and NGOs working on minority issues.[117] As its mandate from the council spells out, its main task is to identify and analyse best practices, challenges, opportunities, and initiatives for further implementation of the UNDM.[118] The forum, which meets annually in Geneva for two working days, provides thematic contributions and expertise to the work of the United Nations Independent Expert on minority issues, produces thematic recommendations for use by all those concerned with minority issues, and contributes to efforts to improve cooperation within the UN mechanism for minority issues.[119] In its sixth session in November 2013, the forum recommended, *inter alia*, that states should translate the provisions of the UNDM into domestic legislation.[120]

Thus, this account of the liberal notion of minority protection in the international context demonstrates a rigorous effort to manage the conservative passion about ethnicity in relation to minority protection. Instead of being static, the response to ethnicity entailed, from time to time, make-shift arrangements to reconcile norms with pragmatic needs. While the efforts to eliminate ethnicity from the idea of minority protection marked the dawn of a new universal regime of human rights drawn upon the liberal individualist philosophy in the aftermath of World War II, the *de facto* existence of ethnic minority groups and ensuing pragmatic needs gradually showed the necessity for accommodating minorities along the line of the conservative tradition. The latter gained momentum in the face of ethnic violence that followed the end of the Cold War. Therefore, as Gaetano Pentassuglia notes, 'most recent responses to minority issues rest on the recognition of a linkage between rights protection and preservation of peace and the resulting need for more flexible (non-judicial) models which envisage minority issues and minority rights compliance from a predominantly pragmatic context-specific perspective'.[121]

However, the overall individualist tone of the existing regime of rights, the celebrated universal norm, and also a policy prescribing ethnic peace

[117] United Nations, *United Nations Forum on Minority Issues: Compilations of Recommendations of the First Four Sessions 2008–2011* (Geneva: The Office of the High Commissioner for Human Rights, 2012), vii.

[118] *Ibid.* [119] *Ibid.*

[120] United Nations, UN Forum on Minority Rights, 6th session on Guaranteeing the Rights of Religious Minorities, 26–27 November 2013. UN Doc. A/HRC/25/66.

[121] Gaetano Pentassuglia, 'Minority Rights, Human Rights: A Review of Basic Concepts, Entitlements and Implementation Procedures under International Law' in *Mechanisms for the Implementation of Minority Rights*, ed. M. Weller and A. H. E. Morawa (Strasbourg: Council of Europe Publishing, 2004), 23.

continued to be obstacles to the effective accommodation of minorities. What appears as a result is the rhetoric of protection of minority groups without any actual legal norm to this effect that would undercut liberalism itself. Ethnicity, thus, remains in the UN mechanism of minority protection as a symbol of constant tension between the liberal and conservative traditions: it is there at the core of the liberal understanding of the 'minority' as a conservative connotation but simultaneously avoided in the case of minority protection.

The post–Cold War European context: minorities as a problem of the East

The peculiarity of the post–Cold War moment of international law in relation to ethnicity lies in the fact that, on the one hand, the collapse of the Soviet Union is celebrated as the landslide of liberalism, the End of History, and a time of liberal-democratic progress and peace, and, on the other hand, the eruption of violent ethnic conflicts even in Europe brought the issue of ethnicity – a primitive notion in liberal understanding – to the forefront. During this troubled time of ethno-nationalist upheaval, Europe inclined towards more accommodative policies vis-à-vis national minorities.

Starting in 1989, the Conference on Security and Co-operation in Europe (CSCE) included statements of national minority rights in all of its texts setting the human rights standards, which, among other official documents, formed the basis of the activities of the organisation – Organisation for Security and Co-operation in Europe (OSCE) – that it became in 1995. These included the Copenhagen Document (1990), the Charter of Paris for a New Europe (1990), the Geneva Report on National Minorities (1991), the Moscow Document (1991), the Helsinki Document (1992), and the Budapest Document (1994).[122] Among them, the Copenhagen Document, although formulated in a very cautious way and including several escape clauses and loopholes giving states a large margin of discretion, makes explicit recognition of positive state obligations to protect and promote the minority identity.[123] It contains the first commitment at the level of the OSCE to take special measures concerning members of national minorities to make them substantially equal in position to the rest of the population.[124]

[122] See Preece, 'National Minorities and the International System', 21.
[123] Paragraph 33 of the document.
[124] Paragraph 31 of the document. See Henrard, *Devising an Adequate System*, 206–207.

Another instrument of this time – Recommendation 1201 of the Council of Europe Parliamentary Assembly (1993) – stipulates that 'in regions where there are a majority, persons belonging to national minorities shall have the right to have at their disposal appropriate local or autonomous authorities or to have a special status, matching this specific historical and territorial situation and in accordance with the domestic legislation of the State'.[125] This provision on autonomy is quite significant in relation to minority protection, for autonomy offers the guarantee that, as Will Kymlicka claims, the minority 'will not be outvoted or outbid on matters that are fundamental to the survival and flourishing of its culture and community. [...] it involves some explicit form of power-sharing, to reduce the vulnerability of the minority to the economic and political power of the majority'.[126] Despite the non-binding legal status of the recommendation, at that time there was a trend towards endorsing power-sharing mechanisms, including granting territorial autonomy.[127]

Yet, the European system of minority protection shared with the UN system the liberal hesitancy at the idea of creating uniformly applicable legal norms. Some Western countries not only opposed the idea of granting self-government rights to national minorities but also showed reluctance to bring their own minority protection system under a supranational monitoring mechanism.[128] The idea of entrenching national minorities' right to territorial autonomy was strongly resisted in the West. What appeared even more disturbing to these states was the proposition that there would be international monitoring of how Western states treated their minorities. As a result, those Western countries that accorded autonomy to their national minorities did not necessarily want their laws and policies regarding minorities subject to international monitoring mechanism.[129]

Kymlicka argues that under the new system, the West relied on two different and contradictory tracks – a universal justice–based track and a security-based track. In the universal justice–based minority rights

[125] Article 11 of the recommendation.

[126] Will Kymlicka, 'Reply and Conclusion' in *Can Liberal Pluralism be Exported? Western Political Theory and Ethnic Relations in Eastern Europe*, ed. Will Kymlicka and Magda Opalski (Oxford: Oxford University Press, 2001), 371.

[127] *Ibid.*, 371.

[128] *Ibid.*, 374. Cf. Will Kymlicka, 'Multiculturalism and Minority Rights: West and East', *Journal on Ethnopolitics and Minority Issues in Europe* 4 (2002), 1–25.

[129] Will Kymlicka, *Multicultural Odysseys: Navigating the New International Politics of Diversity* (Oxford: Oxford University Press, 2006), 210.

track, applicable to the whole of Europe, he argues, the liberal West systematically endeavoured to lower the standard of minority protection, while in the security-based track only ECE states were put under special minority protection obligations on the grounds that minorities in these countries pose a security threat to Europe.[130] Indeed, a critical examination of the FCNM, which was meant to translate the political commitments of the OSCE into legal obligations, reveals that it consists of vague programme declarations, including several escape clauses, and grants member states a wide range of discretion. Instead of providing an inter-state or individual complaints procedure, the convention basically aims at encouraging state parties to implement the convention properly, rather than sanctioning those states which breach it. Therefore, the Committee of Ministers, which is entrusted with the task of monitoring implementation of the convention, has no authority to adopt a binding decision against any state party.[131] The non-judicial character of the procedure also substantiates how little stringent the treaty as a whole is.[132] The Explanatory Report to the convention too confirms this fact:

> In view of the range of different situations and problems to be resolved, a choice was made for a Framework Convention which contains mostly programme-type provisions setting out objectives which the Parties undertake to pursue. These provisions, which will not be directly applicable, leave the States concerned with a measure of discretion in the implementation of the objectives which they have undertaken to achieve, thus enabling them to take particular circumstances into account.[133]

Compared to the earlier OSCE Declarations or COE Recommendation 1201, the convention is also weaker, in that it makes no reference to the right to autonomy or any other form of power-sharing for minorities, nor does it mention anything about official language status or mother-tongue universities or consociational measures.[134]

Regarding the framework convention's approach to group rights, the Explanatory Report categorically states that the convention does not imply the recognition of collective rights; instead, the emphasis is placed on the 'protection of persons belonging to national minorities' in conformity with the approach adopted by other international instruments in this regard.[135] Reinforcing this individualist approach, the parties

[130] For the details of this analytical framework, see Kymlicka, 'Reply and Conclusion', 369–387.

[131] Under Article 24, para. 1.

[132] Pentassuglia, 'Minority Rights, Human rights', 22.

[133] *Explanatory Report*, para. 11.

[134] Kymlicka, 'Reply and Conclusion', 373.

[135] *Explanatory Report*, para. 13.

recognised that protection of national minorities may be achieved through the protection of the rights of individuals belonging to such minorities.[136] On other matters, such as prohibiting forced assimilation but at the same time approving of integration[137] and the omission of specific financial obligations for state parties,[138] the convention adopts the tone of the UN Minority Rights Declaration (1992). As Hurst Hannum notes, both documents are circumscribed by terms such as 'encourage [. . .] effectively [. . .] where appropriate [. . .] favourable' or 'where necessary [. . .] adequate measures [. . .] take due account of the specific conditions [. . .] where [a] request responds to a real need [. . .] as far as possible'.[139]

As a side note, the same can also be said about the European Convention on Human Rights (ECHR, 1950) itself. In line with its contemporaries – UN Charter and UDHR – the ECHR contains no minority rights provision similar to Article 27 of the ICCPR.[140] The ECHR does not even make any mention of minorities as such, except for Article 14, which stipulates that 'the enjoyment of the rights and freedoms set forth in this Convention shall be secured without discrimination on any ground such as [. . .] association with a national minority'. Early proposals to include minority rights in the ECHR are largely associated with H. Lannung, the Danish representative to the Consultative Assembly who observed in the general debate on the draft convention that while fundamental human rights are important, 'it is necessary to extend, supplement and elaborate [them] in order that national minorities may secure the right to a free national life and protection against persecution and encroachment on account of their national convictions, aspirations and activities'.[141] However, his proposal that 'national minorities should be assured a free life with a free enjoyment of their own cultural development' did not find support and

136 *Ibid.*, on Article 1, para. 31. 137 *Ibid.*, on Article 5, paras. 45, 46.

138 *Ibid.*, on Articles 13.2 and 14.1, paras. 73, 74.

139 Hannum, 'The Concept and Definition of Minorities', 69.

140 Asbjørn Eide, 'Mechanism for Supervision and Remedial Action' in *Universal Minority Rights*, ed. Marc Weller (Oxford: Oxford University Press, 2007), 23. See also Fernand de Varennes, 'Using the European Court of Human Rights to Protect the Rights of Minorities' in *Mechanisms for the Implementation of Minority Rights*, ed. M. Weller and A. H. E. Morawa (Strasbourg: Council of Europe Publishing, 2004), 83.

141 *Collected Edition of the Travaux Preparatoires [Travaux]*, vol. I (The Hague: Martinus Nijhoff, 1975–85), 54. See also Christian Hillgruber and Matthias Jestaedt, *The European Convention on Human Rights and the Protection of National Minorities* (Cologne: Verlag Wissenschaft und Politik, 1994), 13–21.

was finally withdrawn.[142] Although the ECtHR subsequently made good use of Article 14 to offer protection to individuals belonging to minority groups,[143] minority groups as such do not have rights under the convention; rather, individual members can act jointly if each of them can establish a claim as a victim.[144]

Thus, when it came to the question of creating specific legal obligations to be uniformly applied to all European states vis-à-vis the protection of minorities in the conservative sense, the framework convention, in line with others, took an evasive stance. As a matter of fact, the sorts of universal *norms* which have been developed by the Western organisations since 1995 are quite weak, substantively as well as procedurally, so as to appease those Western states that opposed substantive and/or enforceable minority rights. In the bid for appeasement, the obligations of all states were lessened.[145] This stands in sharp contrast to the state practice in a number of Western democracies, such as the UK, Spain, Belgium and Canada, where national minorities have been offered a significant degree of territorial autonomy for pragmatic reasons. In this sense, this contrast between the norm and the practice is analogous to the universal mechanism of minority protection under the UN, in that in the post–Cold War period, both systems frequently underscored the importance of minority protection in the face of pragmatic needs such as preventing ethnic conflicts but hardly engendered any binding norm to this effect. In contrast, time and again, the liberal-individualist approach is reinforced in the functioning of these systems.

European organisations in the post–Cold War context essentially faced this challenging task of formulating norms of minority protection that would, on the one hand, reflect distinctively liberal democratic values and, on the other hand, provide effective means for dealing with ethnic violence. Although the framework convention in Article 1 refers to the protection of national minorities as well as their members, and thereby gives an indication that it addresses the issue of the protection of these

[142] *Collected Edition of the Travaux Preparatoires [Travaux]*, vol. I, 180–182.

[143] The ECtHR has been consistent in ruling against restrictions which affect a minority's identity and may be connected to the exercise of freedom of expression, freedom of religion, or freedom of association, unless there is a clear incitement to violence or a clear necessity to restrict private activities for reasons of public safety. See Fernand de Varennes, 'Using the European Court of Human Rights to Protect the Rights of Minorities', 88.

[144] Patrick Thornberry and Maria Amor Martin Estebanez, *Minority Rights in Europe* (Strasbourg: Council of Europe Publishing, 2004), 40–41.

[145] Kymlicka, 'Reply and Conclusion', 373.

minorities as groups, the Explanatory Report to the convention, as we have already seen, expressly states that the convention is not intended to grant group rights or collective rights to national minorities. In other words, as the framework convention illustrates, the generally applicable European minority rights system – the justice-based universal minority rights track, to use Kymlicka's phrase – does not go beyond the non-binding provisions of the UN guidelines that emerged at nearly the same time. Thus, in the post–Cold War European context of minority protection, efforts are evident to keep the conservative phenomenon of ethnicity at a distance from the liberal understanding of minority protection.

However, this is only one aspect of the relationship between ethnicity and minority protection in this context. Another aspect of this relationship is seen in the way at the same time the politics of minority protection in Europe referred to the salience of ethnicity in the political organisation of nation-states in Eastern and Central Europe as a reflection of the conservative tradition of this region. It is to be noted here that in a number of Western democracies, too, minorities are seen as a 'problem', and they threaten the political stability as well as national and international security with secessionist claims and violence, though the degree of violence is much lower than what the East has experienced in the recent past. Nevertheless, the liberal West found it necessary to devise a more accommodative and effective minority protection regime for only the Eastern countries to respond efficiently to the potential violent ethnic conflicts in these countries. Thus, a justification had to be made for differential treatments of minorities in two parts of Europe within a single European system of minority protection. It was made by drawing a demarcating line between the conservative 'ethnic' East and the liberal 'post-ethnic' West very much in line with the minority protection regime under the League.

The OSCE High Commissioner on National Minorities (HCNM) was put in place to pressure the Eastern European countries to protect their minorities by 'securitising' the minority issue. The mandate of the HCNM crafted in the 1992 OSCE meeting held in Helsinki made it clear that the position of the HCNM was not created to implement international norms concerning minorities; instead, the foremost responsibility of this position was conflict prevention.[146] Although the HCNM quite successfully used 'minority protection' as a norm to prevent

[146] Steven Ratner, 'Does International Law Matter in Preventing Ethnic Conflict?' *International Law and Politics* 32 (2000), 620.

ethnic conflict in Eastern Europe, the mechanism itself is premised on the perception that only these countries' minorities are security threats to European stability, whereas the minority issues in the West can be effectively addressed through existing national legislation, democratic institutions, and international as well as European instruments with an individualist approach to rights. Therefore, the HCNM has not so far initiated an investigation into, or offered recommendations regarding, any Western country's minority rights record.[147]

Kymlicka argues that by securitising the 'minority', the West justified a differential treatment of national minorities in the two parts of Europe.[148] This approach of securitising minority issues appeared against the backdrop of Western Europe's dominant public rhetoric that minorities not only lack loyalty to the state they live in but also collaborate with co-ethnics beyond its borders who are often seen as the enemies of the host state; therefore, a strong and stable state requires weak and disempowered minorities. In this sense, the treatment of minorities is above all a question of national security.[149] Now, if the popular view in the ECE states is to oppress minorities for greater stability of these states, the European mechanism perceived this very notion itself as a potential cause of further ethnic violence and a security threat for European instability. This is why the HCNM's security mandate allows him to recommend forms of minority rights beyond the limited ones required by the framework convention, if in his opinion they would help to ensure stability. Whereas the framework convention does not mention anything about territorial autonomy, which is considered an important safeguard for the maintenance of a minority's culture and political voice, the HCNM can recommend that Eastern states provide territorial autonomy or official language status or consociational veto rights or mother-tongue universities.[150] It is to be noted that although these recommendations are not legally binding, the EU has repeatedly emphasised that countries 'seeking accession to the EU are expected to follow the HCNM's advice. The EU and NATO have in effect delegated to the HCNM the task of judging whether [the Eastern and Central European (ECE)] countries have "done enough" in terms of minority rights'.[151] In each of the Western interventions in the major post–Cold War cases of ethnic

[147] Kymlicka, 'Reply and Conclusion', 374. [148] *Ibid.*, 374.
[149] Kymlicka, *Multicultural Odysseys*, 187. [150] Kymlicka, 'Reply and Conclusion', 374.
[151] Kymlicka, *Multicultural Odysseys*, 196–197.

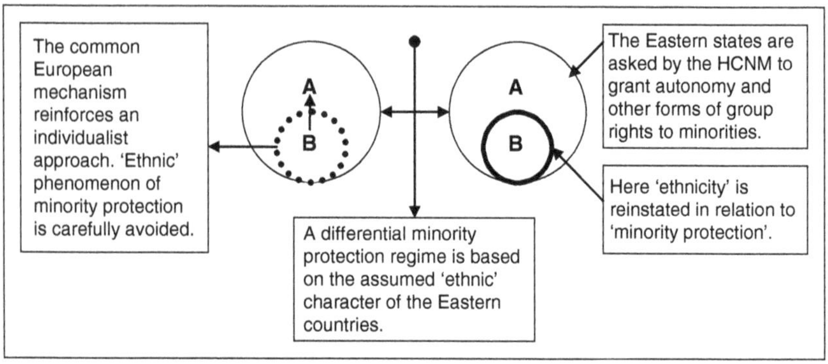

Figure 4.3 The post-Cold War European context of minority protection

violence, Western organisations have pushed the ECE states to go beyond the requirements of the FCNM and accept either some form of territorial autonomy, for example, in Moldova, Georgia, Azerbaijan, and Kosovo, and/or some form of constitutional power-sharing and official language status, as in Macedonia and Bosnia.[152]

However, Kymlicka's argument – that the pragmatic need for protection of minorities in the ECE states beyond what the West granted their minorities engendered a differential treatment justified by 'securitising' the concept of 'minority' – ignores a very significant aspect of the dichotomy. His acknowledgement in one work that even the very understanding of the term 'security' is informed by the East–West dichotomy – in the West 'security' is narrowly interpreted to mean absence of war between states, whereas in the East it expanded in various directions to justify intervention in countries where there is little or no prospect of interstate war[153] – in fact contradicts the proposition that a differential treatment is dictated by value-free pragmatic needs, a mere state of affairs. Instead, it is quite evident from the structure of the specific minority protection mechanism for the East that the West attributes a notion to the minorities in these countries which it carefully avoids in the discourse on the protection of its own minorities. And it is this conservative notion of ethnicity and its significance in the political organisation of the nation-state that informs the liberal West's concept of 'minority protection' in relation to Eastern European countries (Figure 4.3).

This role of ethnicity in this context is a historical phenomenon that can be traced to the minority protection mechanism under the League.

[152] *Ibid.*, 233–234. [153] See Kymlicka, 'Reply and Conclusion', 378.

As discussed in the preceding chapter, despite the existence of significant minority problems in Great Britain, Italy, France, Denmark, and the defeated Germany at that time and the efforts to bind all member-states of the League with minority protection obligations, the interwar international law of minority rights brought only the ECE countries under the minority protection mechanism with a series of bilateral minority rights treaties. Not only the concept of minority but also the very character of Eastern Europe was thereby constructed in ethnic terms.[154] This attribution of ethnicity to the conservative Eastern culture justified the exemption of the Western countries from international scrutiny of their treatment of minorities.

This interwar perception of non–Western Europe reappeared in the post–Cold War context. The outbreak of ethnic violence with the collapse of Yugoslavia was closely linked to the salience of ethnicity in the conservative tradition of perceiving the self-image of the people in this region. In the liberal understanding, if ethnic primitiveness leads to irrationality and ensuing violence, the ethnic characteristics of the people in this region necessarily offer a fertile field for violent confrontations. Maria Todorova demonstrates, in line with Said's deconstructivist approach to the West's imagination of the Orient, how 'as in the case of Orient, the Balkans have served as a *repository of negative characteristics* against which a positive and self-congratulatory image of the "European" and the "West" has been constructed'.[155] Bakic-Hayden argues that this 'Balkanism', to use Todorova's term, has been internalised by the Balkans themselves, who then attempt to get rid of the 'Balkan' label by claiming themselves to be 'European' and simultaneously designating their neighbouring nations as 'Balkans'.[156] This pattern not only reinforces the interwar ethnic dichotomy within Europe of the liberal, civilised West and the conservative, primitive East but also the process of 'othering' on the grounds of ethnic violence. Sumantra Bose notes that the stereotyping of the Balkans as primitive and, hence, a source of conflict, has drawn so many 'adventure-seekers,

[154] As discussed earlier, in *the Greco-Bulgarian Communities* case, the Permanent Court held the view that the 'sentiment of solidarity' and the importance of collective identity – in other words, the ethnic phenomenon – were attributes of the 'Eastern Countries'.

[155] Maria Todorova, *Imagining the Balkans* (New York: Oxford University Press, 1997), 188. Emphasis added. See also Edward W. Said, *Orientalism* (London: Penguin Books, 1995 [1978]).

[156] Malica Bakic-Hayden, 'Nesting Orientalisms: The Case of Former Yugoslavia', *Slavic Review* 54, no. 4 (1995), 917–931.

missionary zealots on civilising field expeditions, and careerists from contemporary dull and boring post-industrial Western societies' to 'exotic and tortured' post-conflict Bosnia.[157]

It is, therefore, no surprise that the European Community (EC) made recognition of the new states (those that came into being as independent states due to the dissolution of Yugoslavia) subject to the guarantee of minority rights in these states. The Declaration on the Guidelines on the Recognition of New States in Eastern Europe and in the Soviet Union declares that the EC and its member states have adopted a common position on the process of recognition of these new states, which requires 'guarantees for the rights of ethnic and national groups and minorities in accordance with the commitments subscribed to in the framework of the CSCE'.[158] Similarly, the Declaration on Yugoslavia categorically mentions that the EC and its member states agree to recognise the independence of all the Yugoslav Republics provided that they accept, *inter alia*, 'the provisions laid down in the draft Convention – especially those in Chapter 2 on human rights and rights of national or ethnic groups – under consideration by the Conference on Yugoslavia'.[159]

With reference to these declarations, the Arbitration Commission of the Conference on Yugoslavia (hereinafter, the Badinter Commission) decided that in the cases of Slovenia[160] and Macedonia[161] all criteria were fulfilled and that in the cases of Croatia[162] and Bosnia and

[157] Sumantra Bose, *Bosnia after Dayton: Nationalist Partition and International Intervention* (London: Hurst and Company, 2002), 12.

[158] The Declaration on the Guidelines on the Recognition of New States in Eastern Europe and in the Soviet Union (16 December 1991), *European Journal of International Law* 3 (1993), 72.

[159] Declaration on Yugoslavia (Extraordinary EPC Ministerial Meeting), Brussels, 16 December 1991, *European Journal of International Law* 3 (1993), 73. Rich argues that EC guidelines have 'moved away from the process of recognition as the formal acceptance of a fact to a process based on value judgments and through which the international community tries to create a fact'. Although these guidelines are stated to be subject to the normal standards of international practice, he notes, their application has 'thrown doubt on the relevance of the traditional criteria for statehood'. See Ronald Rich, 'Recognition of States: The Collapse of Yugoslavia and the Soviet Union', *European Journal of International Law* 4 (1993), 56. Cf. Danilo Turk, 'Recognition of States: A Comment', *European Journal of International Law* 4 (1993), 66–71.

[160] Conference on Yugoslavia, Arbitration Commission Opinion No. 7 (1992), *European Journal of International Law* 4 (1993), 80–84.

[161] Arbitration Commission Opinion No. 6 (1992), *European Journal of International Law* 4 (1993), 77–80.

[162] Arbitration Commission Opinion No. 5 (1992), *European Journal of International Law* 4 (1993), 76–77.

Herzegovina[163] additional activities were necessary (provision for an appropriate status of minorities and a referendum, respectively). Regarding Serbia and Montenegro, the commission held that they constituted a new state – the Federal Republic of Yugoslavia – and therefore, 'its recognition by the Member States of the European Community would be subject to its compliance with the conditions laid down by general international law for such an act and the joint statement and Guidelines [of 16 December 1991]', which stipulated the protection of minorities in the conservative sense.[164]

Reinforcing this dichotomy of liberal and conservative traditions regarding ethnicity, the OSCE/HCNM advances for the minorities in Eastern and Central Europe a number of group rights of varying strengths, ranging from mild forms of non-territorial cultural rights, to confederation, to associated statehood. Now the concept of 'minority' is an ethnic phenomenon that necessarily has a conservative group dimension. At the same time, this ethnic character of minorities is attributed to the Eastern culture alone, given their conservative tradition of perceiving nationalism along the ethnic line, in contrast with liberal Western values. While the West is more inclined to the liberal democratic norms that sanctify individual freedom, the East arguably keeps emphasising ethnic solidarity. And once the East is conceived of as an 'ethnic' entity, minorities within it would automatically require effective protection from exclusionist state-sponsored measures. In other words, the liberal construction of the East in conservative ethnic terms once again justifies the imposition of special minority protection obligations on ECE states to suppress the threat to minorities – with both the states and the minorities defined as conservative phenomena.

Therefore, it is this very nature of the Eastern states that defines the pragmatic needs now expressed as a 'security issue'. The emphasis on this ethnic character helps the liberal West to distance itself from the East and also to avoid additional minority protection obligations. This ethnic dimension explains Kymlicka's observation that the concept of security is understood by the HCNM in two different ways in relation to the West and the non-West. Here the ethnic notion of 'otherness' silently informs

163 Arbitration Commission Opinion No. 4 (1992), *European Journal of International Law* 4 (1993), 74–76.

164 Arbitration Commission Opinion No. 10 (1992), *European Journal of International Law* 4 (1993), 90–91.

an understanding of 'security' in the same way it explained 'civilisation' and 'backwardness' in various epochs of international law.

Thus, the security mandate of the HCNM, in a two-step process, justifies a differential system of minority protection for the East and the West within Europe. First, ethnicity is reinstated in the discourse of 'minority protection', understood as the protection of minorities as groups with distinct characteristics. Secondly, the conservative tradition of the Eastern countries as to ethnicity, which in itself is arguably a historical phenomenon and distinct from the West's culturally advanced liberal world view, then defines the pragmatic needs for ensuring 'security'.

Conclusion

This narrative of the international protection of minorities in these three contexts – in defining minorities internally in a state, in the liberal individualist response to minority protection, and in post-Cold War Europe – demonstrates how the contemporary liberal understanding of minority protection engages with the conservative notion of ethnicity against the historical backdrop of their uneasy relationship. While efforts to eliminate ethnicity from the minority marked the dawn of a new universal regime of human rights in the aftermath of World War II, the existence of minorities as an ethnic phenomenon and the ensuing pragmatic needs in the face of the post-Cold War ethnic violence gradually brought ethnicity to the surface of the current discourse on minority protection. Although ethnicity has consistently played a crucial role in the international law of minority protection, the post-Cold War period of international law is a significant era, in which the conservative appeal of ethnicity re-emerges in the most complex manner to coexist with the liberal-individualist notion of human rights. Thus, instead of being the era of mere enforcement of the norms of international human rights law, this post-Cold War era appears as the moment of reconciliation between 'progressive' human rights and ethnic 'primitiveness'.

The liberal approach of translating minority groups into 'individuals belonging to minorities' by eliminating the ethnic phenomenon from the notion of minority protection has serious implications for ethnic conflicts, among other concerns. If in the liberal understanding the primitive notion of ethnicity is the problem to be addressed in ethnic conflicts, it would be interesting to see to what extent the international legal denial of, or at least hesitancy at, ethnicity in relation to the conservative notion of minority protection can uphold its normative force in the discourse on ethnic conflicts. In this connection, the final chapter of this book explores with reference to ethnic conflicts the implications of dismantling ethnicity in the liberal international legal architecture.

5

Liberal individualism meets conservative passion

International law responses to ethnicity in ethnic conflicts

Introduction

The liberal ambivalence vis-à-vis the conservative notion of ethnicity, and the related international protection of minorities, is clearly seen in the context of ethnic conflicts. On the one hand, liberal individualism denies the need to 'protect' the ethnic elements of a minority group, and, within this liberal framework, international human rights mechanisms attempt to remove the conservative notion of ethnicity from the notion of 'minority'. On the other hand, the eruption of violent ethnic conflicts, undermining the liberal hope of a post-ethnic world, provides a fresh impetus for the protection of at least some of the conservative ethnic aspects of the minority identity. This is because in the post–Cold War context minority issues were seen as causing ethnic conflicts. OSCE, for example, perceived minority rights as a pre-condition for peace and security in Europe when it declared

> Stability and security are best served by ensuring that persons belonging to national minorities can effectively enjoy their rights. [. . .] Lasting peace and stability on this continent are possible only if the United Nations Declaration on the Rights of Minorities and the Framework Convention on National Minorities are fully implemented.[1]

Similarly, at the global level the UN recognised a relationship between ethnic conflicts, economic development, and minority rights, among others:

> Conflicts are most frequent in poor countries, especially in those that are ill governed and where there are sharp inequalities between ethnic or religious groups. The best way to prevent them is to promote healthy and balanced economic development, combined with human rights, minority

[1] OSCE, *Lund Recommendations on Effective Participation of National Minorities* (1999). Available at: www.osce.org.

> rights and political arrangements in which all groups are fairly represented.[2]

As we saw in the preceding chapter, this interaction between liberal individualism and the need for ethnic accommodation necessitates reconciliatory moves in current international law.

This dual depiction of ethnicity – for some, passively in the background; for others, at the forefront and *the* issue to be addressed – also informs an understanding of ethnic conflicts. In other words, the manner in which one understands the process of ethnic construction along the lines of the liberal and conservative traditions has significant implications for the way one then perceives the role of ethnicity in ethnic conflicts. In this sense, the pattern of dealing with ethnicity in ethnic conflicts has its root in the liberal and conservative traditions of the nineteenth century regarding the role of ethnicity in the political organisation of nation-states.

Against this backdrop, in this chapter I argue that international lawyers' treatment of ethnicity in the liberal and conservative senses informs their response to ethnic conflicts. I also demonstrate how, as in the case of minority protection, here too international lawyers have to rely on a reconciliatory approach to these philosophical traditions in order to work out pragmatic solutions to ethnic conflicts. My argument then is that the success of any international legal engagement with ethnic minorities and ethnic conflicts largely depends on the means and extent of such reconciliation between these two traditions. This in return exposes that even in the era of the normative primacy of liberalism, individualism as an ideology in international law is not sufficient in itself to deal with minority protection and ethnic conflicts.

To substantiate this proposition, I begin with a general discussion of the international legal response to ethnicity in ethnic conflicts along the lines of the liberal and conservative traditions, the reconciliation of these two traditions for pragmatic purposes, and the normative repercussions of this reconciliation for international law. To this end, I focus on the post–Cold War moment that, on the one hand, pronounced the landslide of liberalism as the end of human progress and the obvious philosophy of global peace but, on the other hand, recorded the worst form of ethnic violence, which paradoxically brought the conservative notion of ethnicity into the core of the international legal discourse. I follow this by discussing a specific case of such a reconciliation of these philosophical

[2] UNDP, *Overcoming Human Poverty* (New York: UNDP, 2000).

traditions in practice. Taking the example of conflicts in Bosnia and Herzegovina, I demonstrate how the international legal response to ethnicity in Bosnian conflicts initially phrased in liberal terms (exemplified by the Bandinter Commission Opinions in 1992) was later compelled to lean towards a conservative approach (exemplified by the Dayton Peace Agreement in 1995) in the face of escalating ethnocentrism. Although my focus in this chapter is the post–Cold War moment, given that no major change in the liberal architecture of international law has taken place since then, my account of this particular moment remains relevant for current international law as well. As one observer candidly says, '[t]he time for a real push on minority rights may have passed. The early 1990s offered an unprecedented window of opportunity for dramatic and creative innovations in the field of minority rights, but the window has gradually closed, with the job only half-done'.[3]

Ethnicity, ethnic conflicts, and international law

A 'conflict' may be defined as 'a relationship between two or more parties [. . .] who have, or think they have, incompatible goals',[4] and it arises from imbalances in social, economic, or power relations, for such imbalances lead to problems such as discrimination, unemployment, poverty, oppression, and many more. 'Each level connects to the others, forming a potentially powerful chain of forces either for constructive change or for destructive violence'.[5] Conflicts are generally categorised depending on the sphere of imbalances. Ethnic conflicts are those in which ethnic groups hold the protagonist positions, though the centrality of 'ethnicity' in such conflicts is often debated. As we discussed in Chapter 1, the discourse on ethnicity, in terms of the process of the construction of its constitutive elements, is informed by three mainstream schools of thought, namely, primordialism, instrumentalism, and elite-constructivism. These approaches to the construction of ethnicity shape the way ethnic conflicts are understood.

Primordialists argue that primordial attachments that define one's entity in a broader society have enormous emotional value. What make an ethnic group distinct from other social groups are its formative

[3] Will Kymlicka, *Multicultural Odysseys: Navigating the New International Politics of Diversity* (Oxford: Oxford University Press, 2007), 315.

[4] Simon Fisher, 'Understanding Conflict: Towards a Conceptual Framework' in *Working with Conflict: Skills and Strategies for Action* (London: Zed Books, 2000), 4.

[5] *Ibid.*

criteria – the 'given' or 'assumed given' or socio-historically constructed features. The belief that these features exist, which might not always be the case in reality, claims individuals' loyalty to and sacrifice for the ethnic group. Therefore, unless these 'given' or 'assumed given' or 'constructed' features that engender attachment among group members sustain, the very existence of an ethnic group will be jeopardised. Hence, any real, perceived, or constructed threat to language, religion, culture, and similar features, the argument follows, plays a significant role in mobilising ethnic groups for collective action.

In contrast, instrumentalists typically assume that human beings are rational individuals, who act primarily for the purposes of optimising their profit in a given situation. Ethnic groups are, thus, conceived as a collection of profit-maximising individuals, and consequently, ethnic conflicts are seen as a form of competition over scarce economic resources between or among coalitions identified along ethnic lines. For example, Caselli and Coleman II's instrumentalist position perceives ethnic conflicts as competitions over economic resources and ethnicity as a mere tool for a rational choice, at the individual level, which will make for peace or conflict. Their theory is premised on the assumption that in each society there is an incentive for agents to form coalitions to wrest control of the wealth-creating assets of that society from the rest of the population. Now, once such a coalition takes control of the assets, its primary task is to enforce the exclusion of non-members. In large communities of millions of citizens, it can be quite costly to keep track of the genuine members so as to successfully discriminate against the non-members. Under such circumstances, the authors assert,

> if the population is ethnically heterogeneous, coalitions can be formed along ethnic lines, and ethnic identity can therefore be used as a marker to recognise potential infiltrators. By lowering the cost of enforcing membership in the winning coalition, ethnic diversity makes it less susceptible to *ex-post* infiltration by members of the losing one.[6]

In other words, the role of ethnicity, according to these authors, is to enforce coalition membership by keeping imposters out.

On the other hand, the assertion that ethnic conflicts are mere elite constructs assumes that various political, religious, or military elites mobilise individuals by accentuating and inventing individuals' ethnic attachments as well as claims to economic resources. Berch Berberoglu's

[6] Francesco Caselli and Wilbur J. Coleman II, 'On the Theory of Ethnic Conflict', *Journal of the European Economic Association* 11, no. 1 (2013), 162.

socialist theory of ethnic conflict, for instance, perceives ethnicity as a mobilisational tool in the hands of the bourgeoisie. For him, nationalism and ethnic conflict are a manifestation of class interests and class forces that invoke national and ethnic symbolism to advance their own narrow class project and do so in the name of the nation or ethnic group they claim to represent.[7] Berberoglu accepts the real (not imagined) existence of nations as collective units with definite cultural, linguistic, territorial, and social characteristics but asserts that, in the absence of ruling class manipulation, the existence of nations does not *ipso facto* give rise to ethnic tension. Thus, ethnic conflicts and ethno-national strife are, in fact, the outcome of dominant class forces in society attempting to advance their class interests, both domestically and on a world scale.[8]

These approaches to ethnicity touch upon only limited aspects of the complexities involved in ethnic conflicts. Elite-constructive positions do not sufficiently explain why the followers follow the political elites who mobilise the mass for their own ambitions,[9] while instrumentalism hardly explains why rational human beings, who are otherwise unlikely to sacrifice their lives for better jobs or economic resources, do die for nationalist or religious causes. In this sense, Donald Horowitz's theory of group entitlement offers a more comprehensive explanation of ethnic conflicts. He addresses some of these aspects by showing how relative group worth and relative group legitimacy merge into a politics of ethnic entitlement.[10] He claims that in interactions between groups, favouritism towards 'ingroup' and discrimination against 'outgroup' are demonstrated.[11] This tendency to differentiate is presumably higher in real life, where ethnic groups have to experience group comparison and when such comparisons are historically rooted. Colonial juxtaposition, Horowitz argues, paved the way for ethnic group comparison, which naturally produced a sense of relative group worth and relative group legitimacy. For example, colonial practices of differential distribution of resources and benefits to different ethnic groups, as well as

[7] Berch Berberoglu, *Nationalism and Ethnic Conflict: Class, State, and Nation in the Age of Globalization* (Lanham, Maryland: Rowman and Littlefield, 2004), 107.

[8] *Ibid.*

[9] Donald L. Horowitz, *Ethnic Groups in Conflict*, 2nd edn (Berkeley, California: University of California Press, 2000), 140.

[10] *Ibid.*, 186. See also Donald L. Horowitz, *The Deadly Ethnic Riot* (Berkeley, California: University of California Press, 2001); Donald L. Horowitz, 'Structures and Strategy in Ethnic Conflict', paper presented in Annual World Bank Conference on Development Economies (Washington, DC, April, 1998).

[11] *Ibid.*, 144.

authentication of superiority of one ethnic group over others, and ethnic groups' response to differential colonial practices helped create relative group worth and legitimacy issues in a number of colonies.[12] Sometimes such differentiation was pursued as a policy goal. Colonisation is over, but the images of groups thus constructed still persist. As a direct result of such colonial policies, Horowitz argues, the concepts of relative group worth and relative group entitlement were cemented among many ethnic groups in the postcolonial world, providing fertile premises for fatal ethnic conflicts.[13]

In Horowitz's theoretical framework, relative group worth is related to relative group legitimacy, in that the fundamental need to feel worthy is satisfied in considerable measure by belonging to groups that are regarded as worthy. Since collective social recognition as worthy is conferred by political affirmation, Horowitz concludes that struggles over relative group worth are readily transferred to the political system: 'Groups that do suffer from [...] comparisons tend, therefore, to make stronger claims to priority by virtue of legitimacy, so as to make up on one front what they have lost on the other'.[14] Groups may claim legitimacy on the basis of a number of issues. Horowitz identifies four such foundations: prior occupation (relating to territory), special mission (often religious in character), traditional rule (earlier domination), and the right to succeed the colonial power (due to a close relationship with the colonisers).[15] In many cases, the colonial powers have endorsed these claims of legitimacy. He argues that the inter-relationship between the competing groups is reshaped on the basis of such differential claims of legitimacy. The parallels are as follows:

> The intensity of any conflict is, in large part, a function of the relative strength of group claims. The more invidious the intergroup *comparison* and the larger the area of unacknowledged claims to *group legitimacy*, the more intense the conflict, all else being equal.[16]

With this framework, Horowitz interlinks three of his key concepts – group comparison, relative group worth, and relative group legitimacy – which collectively constitute his theory of ethnic conflict.

Similarly, Ted Gurr's framework for analysing ethno-political mobilisation highlights the centrality of ethnicity, understood in terms of socio-historically constructed primordial attachments, to a comprehensive understanding of ethnic conflicts. After examining 275 cases of ethnic

[12] See, generally, *ibid.*, 151–166. [13] *Ibid.*, 164. [14] *Ibid.*, 186.
[15] See, generally, *ibid.*, 202–207. [16] *Ibid.*, 215. Emphasis added.

conflicts globally under the 'Minorities at Risk' (MAR) project,[17] Gurr concluded that the 'strong global trends' towards greater recognition of minority rights have contained the incidence of new ethno-political conflicts and, in this connection, recommended that the international community should continue to provide 'international support for non-discriminatory policies, recognition of group rights and provision of sub-state autonomy'.[18]

Thus, while the primordial theories of ethnic conflicts understand ethnicity essentially in conservative terms, the instrumental and elite-constructive theories of ethnic conflicts follow the liberal tradition in refuting the idea that ethnicity has a central role in ethnic conflicts. On the other hand, in order to offer a comprehensive understanding of ethnic conflicts, Horowitz and Gurr take a reconciliatory approach and recognise the relevance of both traditions.

So far as international lawyers' engagement with ethnic conflicts is concerned, three major streams can be identified, according to the approach they take to the centrality of ethnicity in ethnic conflicts. The first stream argues that individuals constitute the primary unit of international law, and therefore, the empowerment of individuals is the key to securing peace. This Kantian proposition gave birth to the idea of democratic peace at the global level and also to the liberal view that the democratic peace thesis is equally relevant for addressing ethnic conflicts. The second stream holds that although liberal individualism is the foundational norm of international law and therefore the idea of group 'rights' has no normative relevance, it is permissible for the sake of pragmatism to formulate policies favouring ethnic groups where ethnic tension erupts. In this process, some kind of 'liberal exceptionalism' is endorsed. And finally, the third stream recognises the relevance of ethnicity in ethnic conflicts and therefore proposes conflict prevention mechanisms that incorporate ethnicity-defined group measures such as ethnic federalism and consociationalism. I will demonstrate that the foundational notions of these three streams fall within the framework of liberal and conservative traditions of dealing with ethnicity and thereby reveal a general pattern of reconciling these traditions in contemporary international law in relation to ethnic conflicts.

[17] Ted R. Gurr, *Minorities at Risk: A Global View of Ethnopolitical Conflict* (Washington, DC: Institute of Peace Press, 1993). See also Barbara Harff and Ted R. Gurr, *Ethnic Conflict in World Politics* (Boulder, Colorado: Westview Press, 2004).

[18] Ted R. Gurr, *Peoples versus States: Minorities at Risk in the New Century* (Washington, DC: Institute of Peace Press, 2000), 211.

Democratic peace and ethnic conflicts

In an article published in 1983, Michael Doyle provokingly asserts that although wars between liberal and non-liberal states are a historical fact, constitutionally secure liberal states have yet to engage in war with one another; there exists a significant predisposition, if not guarantee, against warfare between liberal states. Thus, despite numerous particular conflicts of economic and strategic interests, Doyle argues, a 'liberal zone of peace' has been maintained and has expanded over years.[19] Such a regime of international peace is premised on liberal democratic norms. Given that the right to liberty belongs to morally autonomous citizens alone, only the state that democratically represents its citizens can exercise the right to political independence. At the international level, states with a democratic character respect each other's right to independence, while individuals enjoy a liberal environment in which they can freely establish private international ties of various kinds without state interference to create a web of mutual advantages and commitments. With this analogy of mutual respect, Doyle rationalises the formation of 'a cooperative foundation for relations' among liberal democracies, leading to peace among them.[20]

As the title of his article suggests, Doyle's proposition is largely drawn upon what Kant claimed in 1795. In *Perpetual Peace*, Kant offered a vision of permanent world peace that has its root in the freedom of each citizen in a polity. Thus, the first definitive article of his perpetual peace thesis claims that republicanism, which in itself is the original basis of every kind of civil constitution, would lead to perpetual peace, in that under such a republican constitution the consent of the citizens is required to decide whether or not war is to be declared. The citizens will hesitate to decide in favour of a war and will do so only under compelling circumstances.[21] This impact a republican constitution has for peace is markedly different from the impact of a non-republican

[19] Michael W. Doyle, 'Kant, Liberal Legacies, and Foreign Affairs', *Philosophy and Public Affairs* 12, no. 3 (1983), 213–215. For a detailed discussion on this topic, see Michael E. Brown, Sean M. Lynn-Jones, and Steven E. Miller (eds.), *Debating the Democratic Peace* (Cambridge, Massachusetts: MIT Press, 1996); Tarak Barkawi and Mark Laffey (eds.), *Democracy, Liberalism, and War* (London: Lynne Reinner, 2001); Steven W. Hook (ed.), *Democratic Peace in Theory and Practice* (Kent, Ohio: Kent State University Press, 2010).

[20] Doyle, 213.

[21] Kant, 'Perpetual Peace: A Philosophical Sketch (1795)' in *Kant: Political Writings*, ed. H. S. Reiss, trans. H. B. Nisbet (New York: Cambridge University Press, 1970), 100. See also Kant, 'The Metaphysics of Morals (1797)' in *Kant: Political Writings*, 164–173.

constitution, which permits war 'as the simplest thing in the world' because the individuals are not citizens and so have no voice in the decision-making process.[22] Having linked the exercise of state power to the primacy of individual freedom, in the second definitive article Kant then envisages a constitution at the global level, to be drawn up in the light of a republican constitution within which each nation would guarantee each other's rights. This would mean establishing a federation of peoples, but not an international state of hegemonic character, with the aim of preventing war and expanding the zone of peace.[23] Fernando Tesón claims that by 'republican', Kant refers to 'what we would call today a liberal democracy, a form of political organisation that provides full respect for human rights'.[24]

The Kantian vision of global peace, which linked the idea of democracy and individual human rights to peace,[25] has been extremely popular among liberal international lawyers, especially after the collapse of the Soviet Union. In 1992, Thomas Franck, in his pioneering article, *The Emerging Right to Democratic Governance*, claimed that in international law, a new norm was emerging that required democracy to legitimise the governance of the state. While governance has always fallen within the internal affairs of a state and been protected under its sovereign veil, Franck argues, this emerging law is becoming 'a requirement of international law, applicable to all and implemented through global standards, with the help of regional and international organisations'.[26] He locates the norm of democratic entitlement in the normative hierarchy by relating it to the peremptory norm of non-aggression in international law. 'If that principle of non-aggression', Franck argues,

> indeed stands at the apex of the global normative system, the democratic governance of states must be recognised as a necessary, although certainly not a sufficient, means to that end. Peace is the consequence of many circumstances: economic well-being, security, and the unimpeded movement of persons, ideas and goods. States' nonaggressiveness, however, depends fundamentally on domestic democracy'.[27]

Franck referred to Kant and his *Perpetual Peace Thesis* on this score.[28]

[22] Kant, 'Perpetual Peace', 100. [23] *Ibid.*, 102.
[24] Fernando Tesón, 'The Kantian Theory of International Law', *Columbia Law Review* 92 (1992), 61.
[25] See Tesón, 'Kantian Theory of International Law'. See also Thomas Franck, 'The Emerging Right to Democratic Governance', *American Journal of International Law* 86 (1992), 88.
[26] Franck, 47. [27] *Ibid.*, 88. [28] *Ibid.*

On the other hand, having traced the pedigree of the individual's right to democratic entitlement to the early twentieth-century idea of self-determination, which was initially meant for communities, Franck defuses the 'collective' entitlement of self-determination and reconceptualises it as a collection of the individuals' rights to political participation, which flourished in post–World War II international law.[29] Yet, elsewhere, he locates peoples' (collective) right to self-determination in the concept of fairness: instead of being a general principle, he argues, self-determination of peoples is a principle that should be applied on a case-by-case basis using the fairness paradigm. Thus, the right to self-determination can prevail over territorial integrity in limited cases, such as the disintegration of existing states or where there would be economically maldistributive side-effects.[30] In this liberal fairness discourse, ethnicity, in relation to the conservative claims for self-determination and to ensuing conflicts, is thus essentially perceived as 'post-modern neo-tribalism'. It is post-modern because ethnic tribalism is a direct challenge to modernism, in that it tends to reverse the modernist process of globalising commerce, homogenising culture, and creating a global village, among other reasons.[31] It is neo-tribalism because ethnicity is no longer the monopoly of backward peoples, in that minority elites in modern societies also present their claims along ethnic lines.[32]

However, the proposition that democracy guarantees peace draws criticism. Francis Fukuyama, in his *Second Thoughts* on the End of History thesis asserts, within the Hegelian tradition, that it is liberalism as an ideology, more than democracy, that is the true institutional basis for democratic peace. Setting the liberal ideology as his major premise, he offers a three-part syllogism, in which 'liberalisation of economic policy would lead to the rapid economic growth, which in turn would lead to the

[29] *Ibid.*, 52–56.

[30] See, generally, Thomas Franck, *Fairness in International Law and Institutions* (Oxford: Oxford University Press, 1995), 140–169.

[31] *Ibid.*, 140–141. See also T. Franck, 'Postmodern Tribalism and the Right to Secession' in *Peoples and Minorities in International Law*, ed. Catherine Brölmann, René Lefeber, and Marjoleine Zieck (Dordrecht: Martinus Nijhoff, 1993), 3–27; Rosalyn Higgins, 'Postmodern Tribalism and the Right to Secession: Comments' in *Peoples and Minorities in International Law*, 29–35. Koskenniemi notes that the Romantic ethnic challenge to statehood in the form of self-determination is 'post- (not pre-) modern precisely because of the urgent sense that these emerging identifications are not capable of being carried out by the creation of new States to represent them, with the unified, formal political structure of the modern state'. See Koskenniemi, 'National Self-determination Today', 259.

[32] Franck, *Fairness*, 143–144.

development of democratic political institutions, which would then enlarge the democratic zone of peace and promote the security of those nations inside it'.[33] While Fukuyama emphasises liberal ideology, not democracy per se, for promoting peace and finds only a 'correlation and not an iron-clad relationship' between the degree of liberal democratic consolidation and peace,[34] Susan Marks portrays democracy itself as an 'ideology' and comprehensively explains how the propagation of 'low intensity democracy' – democracy that focuses merely on electoral rituals – is used in international legal processes to legitimise, obscure, deny, reify, naturalise, or otherwise support asymmetrical power relations.[35]

In the context of ethnic conflicts, political theorist Frederick Whelan notes that when ethnic groups rely on radically different notions of 'the appropriate boundaries, or the extent and composition of the political community', the legitimacy of the sovereign unit itself becomes the core of the conflict, which is 'insoluble within the framework of democratic theory'.[36] This is partly because the legitimacy of the boundaries of the political community is a precondition to the operation of democratic institutions and decision-making processes.[37] Similarly, Robert Dahl asserts that given that any democratic process presupposes the 'rightfulness of the unit', which in itself is *the* issue of contention in many ethnic conflicts, the problem of the proper scope and domain of the unit of citizenship and governance cannot be solved from within the democratic theory.[38]

While talking about ethnic conflicts, Ann-Marie Slaughter also registers her scepticism about liberal democracy's ability to engender sufficient pacific effect. Although 'the deep inculcation of democratic norms of peaceful change and positive-sum bargaining that flow from long experience of alternating parties in power' provide only some hints about the possible effectiveness of liberal democracy in mitigating ethnic

33 Francis Fukuyama, 'Second Thoughts: The Last Man in a Bottle', *The National Interest* 65 (Summer, 1999), 16–44. See also F. Fukuyama, 'The End of History?' *The National Interest* 16 (Summer, 1989), 3–18.

34 Fukuyama, 'Second Thoughts'.

35 Susan Marks, *The Riddle of All Constitutions* (Oxford: Oxford University Press, 2000).

36 Frederick Whelan, 'Democratic Theory and the Boundaries Problem' in *Liberal Democracy: NOMOS* XXV, ed. J. R. Pencock and J. Chapman (New York: New York University Press, 1983), 13–47.

37 *Ibid.*

38 Robert Dahl, *Democracy and Its Critics* (New Haven, Connecticut: Yale University Press, 1989), 207.

conflicts, Slaughter nonetheless acknowledges that 'to the extent that ethnic conflicts result from the desire of persistent minorities to secure the rights and privileges accompanying majority political power, they are by definition unlikely ever to have had the experience of such alternation'.[39] Nevertheless, she keeps the liberal faith by concluding that '[l]iberal democracy may not be a cure for ethnic conflict. But it may be the best that the international legal order has to offer'.[40]

As a matter of fact, this is what has been offered as a policy prescription to post–Cold War ethnic conflicts. Liberal democracy has provided the framework for practically all peace-building operations in post-conflict societies since the end of the Cold War.[41] In the context of post-conflict Bosnia, David Chandler offers a critical perspective on how this liberal political agenda of 'democratisation' has adversely affected democracy itself. Chandler not only challenges the fundamental tenets of the international fantasy of the democratisation of Bosnia by tracing its root to the nineteenth-century colonial notion of the 'White Man's Burden'[42] but also explains how democratisation policies in practice help perpetuate, if not prolong, the regulatory and disempowering contents behind the language of human rights, multi-ethnic governance, freedom of expression, and civil society-building.[43]

On the other hand, Ronald Paris holds that the liberal democratic project is premised on the understanding that in order to secure a sustainable peace, it is imperative 'to transform war-shattered states into stable societies that resemble the industrialised market democracies of the West as closely as possible'.[44] One fundamental drawback of this liberal internationalist venture, Paris notes, is that it expects the

[39] Anne-Marie Slaughter, 'Pushing the Limits of the Liberal Peace: Ethnic Conflict and the "Ideal Polity"' in *International Law and Ethnic Conflict*, ed. David Wippman (Ithaca, New York: Cornell University Press, 1998), 143. For an account of Slaughter's liberal approach to international law in general, see A. Slaughter, 'Law Among Liberal States: Liberal Internationalism and the Act of State Doctrine', *Columbia Law Review* 92 (1992), 1907–1996; A. Slaughter, 'Toward an Age of Liberal Nations', *Harvard Journal of International Law* 33 (1992), 393–405; A. Slaughter, *A New World Order* (Princeton, New Jersey: Princeton University Press, 2004); A. Slaughter, *The Idea That Is America: Keeping Faith with Our Values in a Dangerous World* (New York: Basic Books, 2007).

[40] Slaughter, 'Pushing the Limits of the Liberal Peace', 143.

[41] Roland Paris, 'Peace-Building and the Limitations of Liberal Internationalism', *International Security* 22, no.2 (1997), 63.

[42] David Chandler, *Bosnia: Faking Democracy after Dayton* (London: Pluto Press, 1999), 7–33. Cf. Wilde, *International Territorial Administration*, 289–431.

[43] See, generally, Chandler, 66–153.

[44] Paris, 'Peace-Building and the Limitations of Liberal Internationalism', 63.

'beneficiaries' of this venture 'to become democracies and market economies in the space of a few years – effectively completing a transformation that took several centuries in the oldest European states' and, most importantly, within fragile political structures.[45] This leads to an interesting causal relationship – not between the existence of liberal democracy and ethnic peace but, ironically, between liberal democracy and ethnic conflict, at least under some circumstances. As Paris argues, given the inherently mutual conflictual character of democracy and capitalism, their implantation by international design can further destabilise the weak, unstable, and damaged social and political framework of post-conflict societies.[46]

Very much in this line, Amy Chua provides a persuasive argument about how the globalisation of democracy has created ethnic hatred in many parts of the non-Western world. She argues that in many countries outside the West, the economic impact of globalisation has created market-dominant ethnic minority groups but the simultaneous exporting of democracy to these countries has politically empowered the economically impoverished majority. Ethnic hatred and backlash have been the obvious results of this process.[47] Although these ethnic minorities were dominant long before the market economy phase, Chua argues that globalisation gave them an enormous opportunity to accumulate prodigious amounts of resources, making their dominance more visible. Simultaneously, the political impact of globalisation in the form of a global campaign for democracy has empowered impoverished majorities in these countries. The competition for votes fosters the emergence of demagogues who scapegoat the resented minorities and foment active ethno-nationalist movements demanding that the country's wealth and identity be reclaimed by the 'true owners of the nation'. Under such circumstances, backlash against the market-dominant ethnic minority in the form of expulsion or even genocide is quite predictable.[48] In this sense, Chua's thesis not only refutes the universal claim that liberal democracy prevents ethnic conflicts but also highlights the poverty of

[45] *Ibid.*, 78. [46] *Ibid.*

[47] Amy Chua, *World on Fire: How Exporting Free Market Democracy Breeds Ethnic Hatred and Global Instability* (New York: Doubleday, 2003), 9–12. See also Zlatko Isakovic, 'Democracy, Human Rights and Ethnic Conflicts in the Globalised World', *East European Human Rights Review* 8, no. 2 (2002), 199–236.

[48] To substantiate this argument, she selects the examples, among others, of genocides in post–Cold War Rwanda and the former Yugoslavia. She also discusses backlashes against market-dominant ethnic minorities in other countries including Indonesia and Uganda in her work. However, those incidents were of limited scale.

such a liberal notion by identifying it as a *cause* of ethnic conflicts when coupled with the imposition of a market economy, at least in the non-Western world.

Liberal exceptionalism vis-à-vis ethnicity

While liberal international lawyers' engagement with the democratic peace theory tends to rely on the individualist version of democracy as the way to peace and so to keep ethnicity (perceived as a conservative primitive notion and therefore a source of conflict) at a distance from the discourse on ethnic conflicts, pragmatic needs compel them to acknowledge the instrumental relevance of ethnicity in ethnic conflicts. This is often done by introducing a certain degree of exceptionalism into liberal international legal philosophy. To explain this phenomenon, we now turn to Tesón's version of the international legal engagement with ethnic conflicts.

Like the democratic peace theorists, Tesón borrows directly from the Kantian framework to claim that the legitimacy of the rights of states under international law is merely derivative of the rights and interests of individuals who reside within them.[49] In his *The Kantian Theory of International Law*, criticising traditional international legal scholarship for not acknowledging this normative structure and thus perceiving international law as a matter between and among states, Tesón contends that 'the sovereignty of the state is dependent upon the state's domestic legitimacy; and therefore, the principles of international justice must be congruent with the principles of internal justice'.[50] This idea of 'internal justice' and its significance for the international legitimacy of states as well as its being a condition of peace, as Kant suggests, led Tesón to reinterpret Kant's most basic proposition – that any kind of intervention against another state is invalid. He argues that the validity of non-intervention depends on the internal legitimacy of a state. Tesón claims that 'citizens in a liberal democracy should be free to argue that, in some admittedly rare cases, the only morally acceptable alternative is to intervene to help the victims of serious human rights deprivations'.[51]

Against this backdrop of the Kantian conception of the individual as the building block of international law, Tesón argues that liberal theory

[49] Tesón, 'The Kantian Theory of International Law', 53. [50] *Ibid.*, 54.
[51] *Ibid.*, 92, 93. One may wish to explain the Western intervention against the Gaddafi regime in Libya within this framework.

commits itself to 'normative individualism' – the idea that individuals constitute the primary units of a state.[52] Thus, for him, as a matter of general principle, groups defined by ethnic characteristics should not enjoy any special privilege '*merely by virtue of the fact that they possess some common ethnic trait*'.[53] His key criticism of the conservative position on the right of 'groups' to self-determination therefore follows: that such a position perceives the encompassing group as entitled to the right to self-determination on the basis of non-voluntary ethnic traits. This, according to Tesón, violates the very fundamental liberal notion of consent and individual preference as the basis of political institutions.[54] In the liberal theory, an ethnic group has no right to cultural protection if a majority of its members do not want it to survive.[55] He, therefore, concludes: '[I]f a majority discriminates against a culture [. . .], then that majority violates the rights to equal treatment of the members of the culture'.[56]

On the other hand, if the culture decays spontaneously, as a result of 'market failure' – where individual members rationally prefer another culture over their own or fail to contribute to the survival of their culture due to ignorance or a free-riding tendency – Tesón argues, 'it is hard to see how that fact would justify special group rights or secession from a liberal state'.[57] Similarly, regarding the territorial claims thesis of the right to self-determination, Tesón endorses Lea Brilmayer's position that ethnicity has only the limited role of identifying the people making the territorial claim and that claims to territory do not follow *ipso facto* from ethnic distinctiveness.[58] Thus a claim to a separate territory on the grounds of the oppression of a people within a territory can be addressed by simply eliminating such oppression.[59]

Having outlined the general normative liberal framework, Tesón then moves towards exceptionalism by offering specific conditions under which special group rights can be granted to ethnic groups. In the first place, if any despotic government flagrantly violates human rights, then members of a group have the right to take necessary steps, even secession in relevant cases, to free themselves from oppression, provided that no other means of redress is available.[60] Secondly, in the case of injustice to groups in the form of discriminatory redistribution, groups with

[52] *Ibid.*, 54.
[53] Fernando Tesón, 'Ethnicity, Human Rights, and Self-Determination' in *International Law and Ethnic Conflict*, 86. Italics in original.
[54] *Ibid.*, 88–89. [55] *Ibid.*, 94. [56] *Ibid.* [57] *Ibid.* [58] *Ibid.*, 95. [59] *Ibid.*
[60] *Ibid.*, 99.

a territorial claim attain a moral right to greater autonomy or even to break up the existing state. However, if the group with territorial title does not intend to observe the human rights of its individual members, then its title to territory alone does not suffice to engender any right to self-determination.[61] On the other hand, in the absence of any territorial claim and of any other specific right that by conservative tradition would engender a special right to self-determination for such a group, no such group right can be granted, for such discriminatory redistribution brings similar sufferings to all other social classes that form part of an 'economic programme adopted in a democratic political system that respects individual rights and abides by the strictures of democratic fairness'.[62] And finally and most significantly, Tesón addresses the conservative notion of ethnic 'group rights' by deconstructing the concept itself and claiming that group rights or collective rights are not distinct categories in the liberal theory. Philosophically, rights are individualised, non-aggregative, and distributive, in contrast to social policies, which are non-individualised, aggregative, and non-distributive.[63] In the classical liberal understanding of 'right', Tesón continues, collective rights in the conservative sense are not rights but aggregative social policies lacking 'deontological bite', and the word 'right' in 'collective right' is used only for rhetorical purposes.[64] He thus concludes that various conservative claims framed in the rhetorical language of collective or group rights cannot be called rights in the same sense that liberal theory defines rights.[65]

Nevertheless, in the final step of his argument, Tesón opens up avenues for pragmatism to cope with his normative denial of the conservative notion of group entitlement. While he re-emphasises that the recognition of collective rights has the potential to restrict individual freedoms, he categorically mentions that 'nothing in [his argument] precludes the establishment of legal group rights or other forms of group autonomy for weighty pragmatic or prudential reasons, such as the need to avert ethnic conflict'.[66] This reconciliation is achieved by limiting the scope of his normative position to the claim that 'while legal collective rights may sometimes be an appropriate remedy, they are never required by justice. They are not supported by principled, deontological reasons nor by popular public goods argument. There are no moral collective rights – at least

[61] *Ibid.*, 107. [62] *Ibid.*, 100. [63] *Ibid.*, 103.
[64] *Ibid.*, 105. Cf. Jones, 'Human Rights, Group Rights and Peoples' Rights', 82–83.
[65] *Ibid.*, 106. [66] *Ibid.*, 111.

none that is consistent with rights-based liberalism'.[67] Thus, by redefining the conservative notion of collective 'rights' as 'policies', Tesón's thesis endeavours to mitigate the tension between the pragmatic need to recognise ethnicity in the conservative sense and the normative values of liberal individualism. Conservative collective rights may exist as 'rights' in rhetorical uses for pragmatic ends but not in the liberal theory of rights. In other words, the liberal denial of the conservative tradition of putting ethnicity at the forefront dwells within the pragmatic recognition of the same phenomenon.

Tesón's thesis that ethnicity itself does not suffice to create special group rights but that only to the extent that ethnicity is linked to political or territorial injustice may ethnic groups legitimately claim special rights implies that acts of oppression and political subordination have constructive effects on rights if only in the rhetorical sense. We, therefore, trace a reverse flow here: it is not liberal international law that prohibits the oppression of ethnic 'groups' and thereby prevents ethnic tension from erupting; rather, it is the act of oppression that generates a reconciliatory approach in international law towards the conservative notion of group entitlement. This argument has the potential of offering the elites incentives to mobilise ethnic groups in a particular way so as to develop a normative argument for collective rights (policies). As a corollary, the pragmatic reconciliation of the liberal norm with the conservative notion of ethnicity in Tesón's thesis also implies that special ethnic group entitlements only prevail in a condition of 'abnormality', while liberal individualism must dominate the 'normal' state of affairs.[68]

The Advisory Opinion of the International Court Justice on the legality of the unilateral declaration of independence of post-conflict Kosovo can be explained within this framework of liberal exceptionalism.[69] First of all, the court explicitly exhibits the classical liberal hesitancy at the conservative notion of self-determination in dealing with the case. On the one hand, the court indicates that although in the aftermath of World War II the international law of self-determination developed so as to grant especially peoples of non-self-governing territories and peoples subject to alien rule

[67] *Ibid.*

[68] Cf. *Aaland Islands Case*, Report of the International Commission of Jurists, *League of Nations Official Journal*, Sp. Supp. No. 3 (1920).

[69] See *Accordance with International Law of Unilateral Declaration of Independence in Respect of Kosovo*, Advisory Opinion, ICJ Report (2010); the Dissenting Opinion of Mohamed Bennouna, paras. 1–16; the Dissenting Opinion of Judge Leonid Skotnikov, paras. 1–18; the Dissenting Opinion of Jude Abdul G. Koroma.

the right to independence,[70] there were also instances of declarations of independence outside this colonial/alien rule context. The court then asserts that '[t]he practice of States in these latter cases does not point to the emergence in international law of a new rule prohibiting the making of a declaration of independence in such cases'.[71] On the other hand, the court carefully refrains from telling us whether such state practice has led to the creation of any positive norm in this regard and simply notes that the issue was highly contentious among the participants in the proceedings of the case.[72] The court, thus, bypassed the question of the legality of the conservative ethnic right to self-determination altogether by claiming that since the General Assembly had requested the court's opinion 'only on whether or not the declaration of independence was in accordance with international law', the issue 'regarding the extent of the right of self-determination and the existence of any right of "remedial secession"', which according to the court 'concerned the right to separate from a State', fell beyond the scope of the question posed by the General Assembly; hence, it was unnecessary to resolve these questions in the present case.[73]

Conversely, in his dissenting opinion, Judge Abdul Koroma held the view that the question put before the court was a legal question (as opposed to a political issue) that required a legal response that the court failed to deliver.[74] Instead of avoiding the key question of the

[70] The court referred to these oft-cited cases: *Legal Consequences for States of the Continued Presence of South Africa in Namibia (South West Africa)*, Advisory Opinion, ICJ Reports (1971), paras. 52–53; *East Timor (Portugal* v. *Australia)*, Judgment, ICJ Reports (1995), para. 29; *Legal Consequences of the Construction of a Wall in the Occupied Palestinian Territory*, Advisory Opinion, ICJ Reports (2004), para. 88. Cf. *Western Sahara* Case, Advisory Opinion, ICJ Reports (1975).

[71] Advisory Opinion in the *Kosovo* case, para. 79. [72] *Ibid.*, para. 82.

[73] *Ibid.*, para. 83. While the court in its opinion avoided the problematic question of self-determination, in his dissenting opinion, Judge Mohamed Bennouna held the view that the court should have exercised its discretion to refrain from giving any opinion on a political process that the Security Council initiated but could not finalise. See the Dissenting Opinion of Mohamed Bennouna in the *Kosovo* case, paras. 1–16; especially, paras. 2, 3, 5. According to him, by doing so, the court 'could have put a stop to any "frivolous" requests which political organs might be tempted to submit to it in future, and indeed thereby protected the integrity of its judicial function'. See *ibid.*, para. 3. The same view is taken by Judge Leonid Skotnikov on the grounds that the court, for the first time in its history, dealt with a question (posed by the General Assembly), the answer to which entirely depended on the interpretation of a decision taken by the Security Council – another United Nations organ. See the Dissenting Opinion of Judge Leonid Skotnikov in the *Kosovo* case, paras. 1–18.

[74] The Dissenting Opinion of Judge Abdul G. Koroma in the *Kosovo* case, para. 20.

legality of self-determination and secession in international law with reference to a mere general statement that international law does not authorise or prohibit declarations of independence, Koroma asserts, the court should have concluded that the unilateral declaration of independence by the Provisional Institutions of Self-Government of Kosovo amounted to secession and was not in accordance with international law. Given that respect for the sovereignty and territorial integrity of states is the cardinal principle of contemporary international law, '[n]ot even the principles of equal rights and self-determination of peoples as precepts of international law allow for the dismemberment of an existing state without its consent'.[75]

Koroma also referred to Resolution 1244[76] (which is *lex specialis* in relation to the political as well as legal matters concerning Kosovo) and the Rambouillet Accords[77] (the Interim Agreement for Peace and Self-Government in Kosovo of 1999, drafted by NATO), which reaffirm the sovereignty and territorial integrity of the Federal Republic of Yugoslavia and do not provide for the unilateral secession of Kosovo. He thus concluded that the actual intention of the resolution was for Kosovo to enjoy substantial autonomy and self-government but as an integral part of the Federal Republic of Yugoslavia.[78] In other words, the resolution provides for 'substantial autonomy [for the ethnic Albanian people of Kosovo] *within* the Federal Republic of Yugoslavia'.[79] Koroma's account of the special rights of the Albanians in Kosovo, within the general principle of territorial integrity, thus appears to be a fallback position for the ethnic right to self-determination leading to secession, an 'exception' to the general liberal principle that substantiates Tesón's formula of liberal exceptionalism. This is a special regime of rights for the oppressed Albanians in Kosovo (in that neither the framework convention nor any other international convention grants the right to autonomy to any minority group), which is legitimised by the very act of oppression and, hence, remains in the sphere of abnormality.

On the other hand, Tesón's proposition that the granting of the right to self-determination to any oppressed minority group is subject to that

[75] *Ibid.*, para. 22.

[76] United Nations, *Official Records of the Security Council*, 4011th meeting, S/RES/1244 (1999), annexes 1 and 2. These annexes provide that the political process must take 'full account' of the 'principles of sovereignty and territorial integrity of the Federal Republic of Yugoslavia and the other countries of the region'.

[77] United Nations, *Official Records of the Security Council*, Doc. S/1999/648.

[78] Dissenting Opinion of Judge Abdul G. Koroma, para. 13.

[79] *Ibid.* Emphasis added.

minority's intention to maintain liberal human rights in the new regime, as we have seen before, is reflected in the Unilateral Declaration of Independence of Kosovo. For example, paragraph 2 of the declaration declares Kosovo to be 'a democratic, secular and multi-ethnic republic, guided by the principles of non-discrimination and equal protection under the law', in which the rights of all communities in Kosovo shall be protected and promoted, and the necessary conditions for their 'effective participation in political and decision-making processes' will be created.[80] Similarly, the authors of the declaration assert in paragraph 5 that they welcome the international community's continued support of democratic development in Kosovo 'through international presences established in Kosovo on the basis of UN Security Council resolution 1244 (1999)'. Within Tesón's framework of liberal exceptionalism, such a liberal projection of the future state of Kosovo not only offers justification for Kosovo's right to self-determination but also reinforces the primacy of liberal individualism as the applicable norm in the normal state of affairs.

Ethnic accommodation and the liberal challenge

While Tesón's thesis implies that the suppression of ethnic groups and the ensuing conflicts may give rise to ethnic group entitlements in liberal international law, international lawyers in the third stream argue to the contrary that the failure to recognise ethnic group rights in international law leads to ethnic conflicts. They therefore propose an inclusive international legal framework that accommodates the conservative tradition of perceiving ethnicity as a significant element of identity formation. Anghie, for example, argues that ethnic violence is the dramatic expression of the struggle for cultural survival, and therefore, to prevent ethnic conflicts, cultural identity should be recognised in international law.[81] His thesis is premised on the normative recognition of ethnicity in the conservative sense, in that he argues that far from being some ornamental aspects of an individual's existence, culture acts as a framework within which individuals comprehend themselves and their relation to the world; hence, cultural identity is central to the very being of the individuals who belong to that group.[82] Ironically, he continues, the current

[80] See Advisory Opinion in the *Kosovo* case, para. 75.

[81] Anthony Anghie, 'Human Rights and Cultural Identity: New Hope for Ethnic Peace?' *Harvard International Law Journal* 33, no. 2 (1992), 341.

[82] *Ibid.*, 349, 352.

individualist regime of international law, by endorsing assimilation, not only conceives of culture as a 'peripheral element of human existence' but also conceals the systematic subordination of ethnic minorities using the rhetoric of liberal neutrality and the principle of non-discrimination.[83] In the absence of any effective forum to voice their grievances, ethnic groups then have recourse to violence to redress the wrong inflicted upon them.[84] Having perceived the salience of ethnicity in the conservative sense and thereby linked the lack of group rights in international law with the eruption of ethnic tension and violence, Anghie concludes with optimism that *by expanding the ambit of individual human rights* to incorporate cultural rights, a framework could be developed in which the competing demands of states and minorities may be assessed and settled, and consequently, the need to resort to violence may be reduced.[85]

While Anghie presents a causal relationship between liberal individualist international law and ethnic conflicts and proposes the introduction of ethnic group rights to prevent ethnic conflicts, other jurists within this stream rely on various interpretative techniques to justify their normative recognition and pragmatic accommodation of the conservative notion of ethnicity vis-à-vis ethnic conflicts. For David Wippman, too, ethnicity constitutes the basis for the most viable pragmatic responses to ethnic conflicts, namely, ethnic federalism and consociationalism.[86] In ethnically divided societies, he argues, the recognition of ethnicity through the adoption of such measures is of great significance, for a system premised exclusively on the respect for individual rights, even if it succeeds, will not address all of the concerns of subnational ethnolinguistic groups. To quote him:

> Even if the members of such groups are not, as individuals, subject to discrimination or mistreatment, their aspirations for fulfilling community

[83] *Ibid.*, 348, 352. [84] *Ibid.* [85] *Ibid.*, 351.

[86] For a detailed theoretical account of consociationalism, see Arend Lijphart, 'Consociation and Federalism: Conceptual and Empirical Links', *Canadian Journal of Political Science* 12, no. 3 (1979), 499–515; A. Lijphart, *Democracy in Plural Societies: A Comparative Exploration* (New Haven, Connecticut: Yale University Press, 1977); A. Lijphart, 'Consociational Theory: Problems and Prospects. A Reply', *Comparative Politics* 13, no. 3 (1981), 355–360. See also Charles E. Ehrlich, 'Democratic Alternatives to Ethnic Conflict: Consociationalism and Neoseparatism', *Brooklyn Journal of International Law* 26 (2000), 447–483. For a critical evaluation of ethnic federalism, see Alemante G. Selassie, 'Ethnic Federalism: Its Promise and Pitfalls for Africa', *Yale Journal of International Law* 28 (2003), 51–107; Nicole B. Herther-Spiro, '"Can Ethnic Federalism Prevent Recourse to Rebellion?" – A Comparative Analysis of Ethiopian and Iraqi Constitutional Structures', *Emory International Law Review* 21 (2007), 321–371.

> life may be frustrated absent some measure of self-governance. In a one-person, one-vote system, members of such groups may simply be out-voted and thus permanently frozen out of national political life.[87]

That is why separatist movements – primarily based on concerns over group identity – are active in countries (such as Canada and Spain) where individual rights are well protected.[88]

Although Wippman highlights the success of ethnicity-based power-sharing mechanisms in dealing with ethnic conflicts, he is nonetheless aware that such measures encounter the problem of compatibility with the existing liberal architecture of international law. In general, power-sharing mechanisms tend to favour collective rights (the conservative tradition) over individual rights (the liberal tradition), as a result of which many such practices appear discriminatory when viewed from a liberal-individualist perspective.[89] From an individual-rights standpoint, Wippman identifies at least three specific human rights norms that are infringed by power-sharing practices: first, these practices are drawn upon characteristics such as race, religion, and language rather than on neutral merit-based criteria and thereby violate the fundamental liberal principle of non-discrimination on these grounds. Secondly, ethnic power-sharing practices may violate the participatory rights of individuals who are not members of a protected ethnic group. And, finally, some of the autonomy schemes place restrictions on individuals' efforts to settle in areas controlled by members of another ethnic group and, therefore, violate the right to freedom of movement and residence.[90]

Indeed, using power-sharing devices to confer power on particular groups in excess of what is reasonably necessary to protect their interests and in ways that are designed to deny other groups meaningful participation in the governance of the state may be taken as a violation of international human rights obligations. For example, the power-sharing aspects of consociationalism are challenged by established norms of equal rights to political participation for all, including the right to take part in the conduct of public affairs, the right to vote and to be elected at genuine periodic elections, and the right to have access, on general terms of equality, to public services in the

[87] David Wippman, 'International Law and Ethnic Conflict in Cyprus', *Texas International Law Journal* 31 (1996), 168.

[88] *Ibid.*, 169.

[89] David Wippman, 'Practical and Legal Constraints on Internal Power Sharing' in *International Law and Ethnic Conflict*, 240.

[90] *Ibid.*, 231.

country.[91] Consociational arrangements violate these rights of the members of the majority community by providing minority ethnic groups with political power disproportionate to their number through reserved seats and offices, minority veto rights, or similar devices.[92] And finally, territorial autonomy for a particular ethnic group prevents the rest of the citizens from full enjoyment of the freedom of movement and residence stipulated in Article 12(1) of the ICCPR, which reads: 'Everyone lawfully within the territory of a State shall, within that territory, have the right to liberty of movement and freedom to choose his residence'. Similar provisions can also be found in Article 13 of the UDHR and Protocol No. 4, Article 2(1) of the European Convention for the Protection of Human Rights and Fundamental Freedoms.

In order to accommodate his normative and pragmatic recognition of the conservative notion of ethnicity within the liberal international legal regime, Wippman therefore seeks refuge in interpretative techniques to expand the relevant human rights provisions in a way that would open up space, albeit limited, to incorporate ethnicity-defined power-sharing measures. He thus argues that despite being violations of the international human rights instruments from an individualist perspective, power-sharing arrangements are not *ipso facto* violations of established human rights norms from a group perspective, and hence, they are compatible with international human rights law. Consociational practices, he continues, should be viewed not as creating separate or discriminatory rights for ethnic minorities but as enabling ethnic minorities to exercise their rights on a level as close as possible to parity with the dominant groups and thereby ensuring equality among groups.[93]

Therefore, in relation to the International Convention on the Elimination of All Forms of Racial Discrimination (CERD, 1965), which permits special measures for the advancement of particular racial or ethnic groups but stipulates that such measures 'should not lead to the maintenance of separate rights for different racial groups',[94] Wippman holds that

[91] Such rights are incorporated in Article 21 of the UDHR and Article 25 of the ICCPR.

[92] Wippman, 'Practical and Legal Constraints', 234. [93] *Ibid.*, 233.

[94] Articles 1(4) of the CERD. Moreover, the convention also requires that special measures be discontinued after the objectives for which they were taken have been achieved. See United Nations, *General Assembly Resolution 2106A* (1965), UN GAOR, 20th Session, Supp. No. 14. UN Doc. A/6014, 48.

> [a]s an instrument designed primarily to protect individual human rights, it may be that the CERD, strictly interpreted, should be understood to place significant constraints on ethnic federalism. But it seems unduly formalistic to interpret the CERD as a blanket prohibition of political systems designed to enable different racial and ethnic groups to co-exist harmoniously. Moreover, if the CERD is so interpreted, a conflict would be created with the emerging principle that minorities are entitled to effective political participation, going beyond the principle of one person, one vote.[95]

This view was endorsed later by the Committee on Elimination of Racial Discrimination in its General Recommendation No. 32 on the provision of special measures under Articles 1(4) and 2(2) of the convention. On this point the committee asserted that this provision is narrowly drawn to refer to 'racial groups' in relation to the practices of apartheid and racial segregation. Therefore, such 'separate rights' that the convention finds inadmissible 'must be distinguished from rights accepted and recognised by the international community to secure the existence and identity of groups such as minorities', for these rights are also accepted and recognised within the framework of universal human rights.[96] With reference to the specific context in which this restriction on special measures was placed in the convention, the committee reiterated that the convention is a 'living instrument that must be interpreted and applied taking into account the circumstances of contemporary society'.[97]

However, while extending this analogy to the ICCPR, Wippman takes note of the limitations of his argument in favour of ethnic group-based equality within the liberal individualistic framework of the ICCPR. In his words:

> It might be possible to interpret general 'terms of equality' broadly enough to encompass political systems that focus on the equality of groups rather than of individuals, in keeping with present trends toward recognition of collective rights, but such an interpretation seems inconsistent with the predominantly individual rights focus of the Covenant itself.[98]

Thus, in order to reconcile the liberal and conservative approaches in international law vis-à-vis the salience of ethnicity and thereby develop

[95] Wippman, 'International Law and Ethnic Conflict in Cyprus', 179.

[96] CERD, General Recommendation No. 32, *The Meaning and Scope of Special Measures in the International Convention on the Elimination of Racial Discrimination*, UN Doc. CERF/C/GC/32, 24 September 2009, para. 26.

[97] *Ibid.*, para. 5.

[98] Wippman, 'Practical and Legal Constraints', 237.

a legal justification for power-sharing, Wippman ultimately takes a 'purely pragmatic standpoint' and concludes: '[Power-sharing practices] may compromise some human rights ideals, but they may also help avoid the even greater injustices associated with other possible solutions'.[99] One can rephrase this assertion in this way: power-sharing devices are the most viable ways of addressing injustices towards ethnic minorities and thereby minimising the potential for ethnic conflicts, but being premised on the conservative tradition of emphasising ethnicity in identity formation, these ethnicity-defined mechanisms are to a large extent in tension with liberal-individualistic norms of international law.

In short, international lawyers within this stream rely on different techniques to put forward their normative recognition and pragmatic accommodation of ethnicity in ethnic conflicts and thereby exhibit a constant effort to reconcile the liberal and conservative traditions. While Anghie argues for the incorporation of ethnic group rights within the existing individualist human rights regime, Wippman reinterprets human rights norms to help them appear compatible with pragmatic, ethnicity-defined power-sharing mechanisms. Despite the diversity in their approaches and techniques, they essentially recognise the conservative tradition of perceiving ethnicity as an important element of identity formation and, hence, a relevant factor in dealing with ethnic conflicts. Accordingly, they propose guidelines that keep the conservative notion of ethnicity at the core of their proposed conflict prevention mechanisms.

International legal responses to ethnic conflicts, thus, represent three main streams: the first stream relies on the democratic peace thesis as a viable response to ethnic conflicts, while the second stream, despite highlighting liberal primacy, accepts ethnic accommodation in the conservative sense for the sake of pragmatism. And, finally, the third stream recognises the relevance of ethnicity in ethnic conflicts and, therefore, proposes conflict prevention mechanisms that incorporate ethnicity-defined group measures such as ethnic federalism and consociationalism.

As we have seen, the foundational notions of these three streams fall within the framework of liberal and conservative traditions of dealing with ethnicity. The democratic peace thesis follows the classical liberal tradition in bypassing the conservative notion of ethnicity in dealing with ethnic conflicts. The second stream denies the normative relevance of the conservative tradition of perceiving ethnicity as an important element of

[99] *Ibid.*, 241.

identity formation but in practice relies on this understanding of ethnicity on instrumental grounds, as an exception to the general primacy of individualism. In contrast, the third stream recognises the salience of ethnicity along conservative lines and attempts to accommodate ethnicity within the dominant liberal international legal architecture. Taken together, these three approaches to ethnicity in ethnic conflicts reveal a general pattern in contemporary international law of reconciling liberal and conservative traditions for pragmatic purposes in relation to ethnic conflicts. Against this theoretical backdrop, in the following section I turn to a specific case of such a reconciliation of these philosophical traditions in practice. Taking the example of conflicts in Bosnia and Herzegovina, I demonstrate how the initial international legal response to ethnicity in Bosnian conflicts in liberal terms (exemplified by the Badinter Commission Opinions in 1992) was later supplanted with a more conservative approach (exemplified by the Dayton Peace Agreement in 1995) in the face of escalated ethnocentrism.

Ethnicity: from the Badinter Commission to the Dayton Agreement

Following the breakup of the Socialist Federal Republic of Yugoslavia (SFRY), Bosnia and Herzegovina experienced one of the deadliest conflicts since World War II. The degree of violence exerted in these conflicts from 1992 to 1995 – by both state and non-state actors, including NATO – is less debated than are the factors that turned the Serbs, Croats, and Muslims (Bosniacs), who co-existed peacefully for centuries,[100] into protagonists of this bloody affair. For those who conceived of these protagonists in terms of the conservative passion that defines the self-image along ethnic lines, the conflict was obvious. They argue that the demise of the powerful central authority of the SFRY, which kept the contending ethnic groups together within Bosnia and Herzegovina by suppressing their ethnic allegiance, provoked the resurgence of old bitterness among the groups, a new zeal for redefining their frontiers along the lines of ethnicity, and ethnic hatred towards the 'other'.[101]

[100] See, generally, Robert J. Donia and John V. A. Fine, Jr., *Bosnia and Hercegovina: A Tradition Betrayed* (London: Hurst and Co., 1994).

[101] See, generally, Gale Stokes, John Lampe, Dennison Rusinow and Julie Mostov, 'Instant History: Understanding the Wars of Yugoslav Succession', *Slavic Review* 55, no. 1 (1996), 136–160.

This pattern of explaining the conflict can be traced even to a much earlier image of Bosnia. In his description of Bosnia, recorded in 1943, Fitzroy Maclean sensed an inherent tension among the three constituent communities: 'The population was made up of violently Catholic Croats and no less violently Orthodox Serbs, with a strong admixture of equally fanatical local Moslems. It is hard to imagine the savage intensity of the passions that were aroused or the extremes of bitterness which they engendered'.[102] More recently, Thomas Friedman reiterates this view in the context of post-war Bosnian state crafted by the Dayton Agreement when he projects the future of the state in two dichotomous visions: forcing Bosnian Serbs, Croats, and Muslims to live together in an artificial Bosnian state by using NATO military power or letting the Serbs merge with Serbia and the Croats with Croatia and leaving the remaining Muslim sector as an independent mini-state.[103] His scepticism about the prospect of a self-sustaining democracy and peaceful co-existence of different communities within the state of Bosnia and Herzegovina is premised on a strong sense of ethnic identity and hatred with deep roots in the Balkans.[104] Being aware of the salience of ethnicity in the political organisation in Bosnia, commentators within this stream have had recourse to ethnic partition as a viable solution to Bosnian conflicts.[105]

On the other hand, the liberal approach to the conflict is directed towards keeping 'ethnicity' to the minimum. British journalist Allan Little, questioning the notion of 'artificiality' that scholars often relate to the Bosnian state, claimed that

> there is nothing artificial about Bosnia as an integrated entity. [...] In 1992, when you asked a Sarajevan how many students in his final-year high school class were Serb, how many Muslim and so on, they could not answer the question. It seems to me that it is these distinctions that are artificial.[106]

Such a view leads to the understanding of conflicts essentially in non-ethnic, liberal statist terms – that is, the conflict resulted from the

[102] Fitzroy Maclean, *Eastern Approaches* (London: Penguin, 1991 [1949]), 337–338.

[103] Thomas Friedman, 'Democracy Isn't Happening in Bosnia', *New York Times*, 24 January 2001.

[104] *Ibid.*

[105] For example, see *ibid.* For an account of such a proposition, see Sumantra Bose, *Bosnia after Dayton: Nationalist Partition and International Intervention* (London: Hurst and Company, 2002), 48–50.

[106] Allan Little, Transcript of BBC Radio 4 broadcast, 20 November 2000, quoted in Bose, *Bosnia after Dayton*, 41–42. See also Gale Stokes et al., 'Instant History', 136–160.

aggression of Serbia and Montenegro against Bosnia and Herzegovina. Proponents of this approach are, therefore, also advocates of preserving and developing Bosnia and Herzegovina as a single and united sovereign state and demand concerted action by the international community to this effect.[107] David Campbell, for example, argues that ethnic nationalism is by its very nature exclusionist and, therefore, demands a violent relationship with the 'other'.[108] Although no community is completely free from violent tendencies, given that all forms of communities are bounded to some extent, he concludes that non-ethnic and non-national forms of communities involve less violent relationships with each other, for these communities have the capacity to accommodate more difference.[109] In this sense, the various responses to the Bosnian conflicts are informed by different understandings of the salience of ethnicity in the political organisation of nation-states along the line of the liberal and conservative traditions.

Since the very beginning, international lawyers have attempted to engage with the breakup of the SFRY as well as the ensuing conflicts in liberal terms and, therefore, endeavoured to suppress the increasing conservative desire to create new ethnic states in the Balkans. Their attitude was expressed, first of all, in the process of internationalising the conflict, which would have otherwise amounted to an ethnic secession of Bosnia and Herzegovina from the SFRY – an internal affair of the latter. When Lord Carrington, president of the Conference on Yugoslavia, referred to the Badinter Commission the question of whether the act of declaring independence by the republics amounted to secession from the SFRY, the commission held:

> [I]n the case of a federal-type state, which embraces communities that possess a degree of autonomy and, moreover, participate in the exercise of political power within the framework of institutions common to the Federation, the existence of the state implies that the federal organs represent the components of the Federation and wield effective power.[110]

Given that the republics had declared their independence and the composition and workings of the essential organs of the federation ceased to meet the criteria of participation and representatives inherent in a federal

107 See Bose, *Bosnia after Dayton*, 18.
108 David Campbell, *National Deconstruction: Violence, Identity, and Justice for Bosnia* (Minneapolis, Minnesota: University of Minnesota Press, 1998), 13.
109 *Ibid.*
110 Conference on Yugoslavia, Arbitration Commission Opinion No. 1 (1991), *European Journal of International Law* 3 (1992), 182.

state, the commission decided in Opinion No. 1 that the SFRY was in the process of dissolution.[111]

This opinion was accompanied by recognition of the republics as independent states by the European Community and the United States, subject to the provisions stipulated in the twin declarations on the guidelines for recognition of these states.[112] The opinion of the commission and the recognition policy of the West cemented the statehood of these new states and thereby turned the ostensibly ethnic conflict into an interstate non-ethnic conflict – an issue of Serbian aggression.

As a corollary, the commission declared in Opinion No. 3 (concerning the question of whether the internal boundaries between Croatia and Serbia and between Bosnia and Herzegovina and Serbia should be regarded as frontiers in terms of public international law) that in the circumstances of the emergence of new states following dissolution of the SFRY, both the external and internal frontiers of the SFRY had to be respected.[113] The commission categorically mentioned that this conclusion followed from the principle of respect for the territorial *status quo* and, in particular, from the principle of *uti possidetis*, which, though initially applied in settling decolonisation issues, was recognised as a general principle, as stated by the International Court of Justice in the *Burkina Faso–Mali* case.[114] In other words, the internal boundaries of the SFRY were converted to protected international frontiers, which could only be altered by agreement. The commission, thus, moved away from the conservative, ethnicity-oriented political organisation of these new states and offered a liberal international legal vision of post-conflict regional order in the Balkans.[115]

[111] *Ibid.*, 183. In its Opinion No. 8 on 8 July 1992, the commission declared that the process of dissolution of the SFRY was completed. See Arbitration Commission Opinion No. 8 (1992), *European Journal of International Law* 4 (1993), 87–88.

[112] See the Declaration on the Guidelines on the Recognition of New States in Eastern Europe and in the Soviet Union (16 December 1991), *European Journal of International Law* 3 (1993), 72; The Declaration on Yugoslavia (Extraordinary EPC Ministerial Meeting, Brussels, 16 December 1991), *European Journal of International Law* 3 (1993), 73.

[113] Arbitration Commission Opinion No. 3 (1991), *European Journal of International Law* 3 (1992), 185. The commission, in its support, specifically referred to the principles stated in the United Nations Charter, in the Declaration on Principles of International Law concerning Friendly Relations and Cooperation among States in accordance with the Charter of the United Nations (General Assembly Resolution 2625 [XXV]) and in the Helsinki Final Act.

[114] *Ibid.* See also *Frontier Dispute* (Burkina Faso and Mali) Case, ICJ Reports (1986).

[115] In an approving note, Pallet writes that the application of this principle was indispensable for maintaining peace. He further asserts that 'the principle is not as rigid as some

Taken together, these two commission opinions reinforced the political organisation of Bosnia and Herzegovina under the SFRY, in which the conservative notion of ethnicity had little relevance. By considering the dissolution of the SFRY to be a breaking up of the federal units and then endorsing the existing boundaries of the republics, the commission envisaged Bosnia and Herzegovina as a non-ethnic unit in which Bosniac, Croat, and Serb ethnic groups would continue to live together.

The commission's liberal vision was essentially in conflict with the conservative notion of the right to self-determination as claimed by Bosnian Serbs and Croats, who were keen to join their co-ethnics in Yugoslavia and Croatia, respectively. The commission had to address this issue formally when Lord Carrington requested the commission's opinion on whether the Serbian population in Croatia, Bosnia and Herzegovina, as one of the constituent peoples of Yugoslavia, had the right to self-determination. In conformity with its earlier opinions, the commission held in Opinion no. 2 that 'whatever the circumstances, the right to self-determination must not involve changes to existing frontiers at the time of independence *(uti possidetis juris)* except where the states concerned agree otherwise'.[116]

In this regard, the commission did not deviate from the general international legal attitude towards this issue. The International Commission of Jurists in the *Aaland Island* case declared the right to self-determination, in the conservative sense, legally inapplicable as long as it challenges state sovereignty and international peace and stability.[117] However, the commission held that the right to self-determination can be applied when statehood itself was in question.[118] Similarly, although the Helsinki Final Act (1975) of the OSCE recognised that the right to self-determination goes beyond the colonial context, it nonetheless

might feel it ought to be. Stability does not mean intangibility. Although States are prohibited from acquiring a territory by force, they might freely decide, as the Committee made clear, to a modification of their frontiers "by agreement"'. See Alain Pellet, 'The Opinions of the Badinter Arbitration Committee: A Second Breath for the Self-Determination of Peoples', *European Journal of International Law* 3 (1992), 180. For a critical perspective on the 'Badinter frontiers principle', see Peter Radan, 'Post-secession International Borders: A Critical Analysis of the Opinions of the Badinter Arbitration Commission', *Melbourne University Law Review* 24 (2000), 50–76.

116 Arbitration Commission Opinion No. 2 (1991), *European Journal of International Law* 3 (1992), 184.

117 See *Aaland Islands* Case, Report of the International Commission of Jurists, *League of Nations Official Journal*, Sp. Supp. No. 3 (1920); cf. *Aaland Islands* Case, Report of the Commission of Rapporteurs (1921), League of Nations Council Doc. B7 [C] 21/68/106.

118 *Ibid.*

reiterated the primacy of the norms of territorial integrity and preservation of existing boundaries in international law.[119] The same is equally true of the Declaration on Principles of International Law concerning Friendly Relations and Cooperation among states in accordance with the Charter of the United Nations (1970).[120]

However, while upholding the territorial integrity of Bosnia and Herzegovina (a symbol for the liberal design of a post-ethnic world) as the supreme value and thereby denying the conservative claim of the Serbs to the right to self-determination (seen as ethnic primitiveness contrary to liberal progress and peace), the Badinter Commission had recourse to the idea of minority protection as a fallback position very much in line with the interwar arrangement. Asserting that ethnic, religious, or language communities within a state have the right to recognition of their identity under international law and that the peremptory norms of international law require states to ensure respect for the rights of minorities, the commission held that this requirement applies to all the republics vis-à-vis the minorities on their territories. The commission concluded that

> the Serbian population in Bosnia-Herzegovina and Croatia must therefore be afforded every right accorded to minorities under international conventions as well as national and international guarantees consistent with the principles of international law and the provisions of Chapter 2 of the draft Convention of 4 November 1991, which has been accepted by these Republics.[121]

In addition to the special minority rights provisions, the commission also extended all individual human rights and fundamental freedoms recognised in international law to individual members of those ethnic minority groups and thereby created a hybrid regime of rights.[122] More importantly, in an effort to reconcile the conservative notion of self-determination with the liberal regime of individualist rights, the commission interpreted the right to self-determination (as enumerated in Article 1 of twin International Covenants of 1966) in liberal terms, linking it to the individual right to choose to belong to whatever ethnic, religious, or language community one wishes.[123] The commission envisaged that

[119] Cf. Principles IV and VI and Principle VIII of the Helsinki Final Act.
[120] General Assembly Resolution 2625 (XXV), 25th session, 24 October 1970.
[121] Arbitration Commission Opinion No. 2 (1991), *European Journal of International Law* 3 (1992), 184.
[122] See *ibid.* [123] *Ibid.*

a possible consequence of this principle might be that the individual members of the Serbian population in Bosnia and Herzegovina and Croatia would be recognised as having the nationality of their choice, 'with all the rights and obligations which that entails with respect to the states concerned'.[124]

However, the commission's liberal approach to Balkan conflicts soon proved inadequate in the face of the violent ethno-centrism in Bosnia and Herzegovina that marked the years between 1992 and 1995. The tripartite conflict among Muslims (Bosniacs), Croats, and Serbs during these years came to an end with the General Framework Agreement for Peace in Bosnia and Herzegovina (hereinafter the Dayton Agreement), reached at an Air Force base near Dayton, Ohio in November 1995 and formally signed in Paris on 14 December 1995. The Dayton Agreement is a product of, on the one hand, the liberal vision of its architects (the US and European Community) of a civic, as opposed to an ethnic, Bosnian state and, on the other, the pragmatic realisation that the liberal approach of suppressing ethnicity in relation to the Balkan conflicts, which the Badinter Commission adopted in its opinions, was mere wishful thinking. As we shall see in the following discussion, the Dayton Agreement thus reconciled the liberal and conservative traditions vis-à-vis the relevance of ethnicity in the political organisation of post-war Bosnia and Herzegovina.

This reconciliatory approach in the Dayton Agreement is perhaps best exemplified by the three-layered constitutional structure of Bosnia and Herzegovina that it crafted: the common Federal State of Bosnia and Herzegovina; the Entity of the Bosniac-Croat Federation (Federation of Bosnia and Herzegovina); and the Entity of the Republic of Srpska (RS).[125] The common state of Bosnia and Herzegovina reflects the liberal vision of the peacemakers: it goes beyond the narrow ethnicity-defined perception of the state, to serve as a non-ethnic outer shell of the Bosnian state keeping all three contending ethnic groups under its liberal protection. This vision of constructing a common multi-ethnic state, which was seen as a safeguard against ethnic nationalism and therefore vital for both regional and international stability, was expressed by then US Deputy Secretary of State Strobe Talbott during the Dayton negotiations:

[124] *Ibid.*

[125] For a detailed account of the constitutional structure of the administration in Bosnia and Herzegovina, see Chandler, *Bosnia: Faking Democracy after Dayton*, 66–89. See also Bose, *Bosnia after Dayton*, 60–89; Paola Gaeta, 'The Dayton Agreements and International Law', *European Journal of International Law* 7 (1996), 160–162.

> If there is to be a post–Cold War peace in Europe – and not a cold peace, but a real one – it must be based on the principle of multi-ethnic democracy [. . .]. The United States is one of the first and one of the greatest examples of that principle. What's more, the civic behavior and constitutional structures associated with pluralism are conducive to regional peace and international trade. Hence, it is in our interest that multi-ethnic democracy ultimately prevails.[126]

The constitution of Bosnia and Herzegovina, which is primarily the work of lawyers from the US Department of State, affirms in the preamble the status of Bosniacs, Serbs, and Croats as constituent peoples (along with others) of the state.[127] Article 2 (para. 4) of the constitution guarantees that the enjoyment of the rights and freedoms shall be secured to all individuals in Bosnia and Herzegovina without discrimination on any ground such as sex, race, colour, language, religion, political, or other opinion, national or social origin, association with a national minority, property, birth, or other status.[128] Article 2 (para. 5) grants all refugees and displaced persons the right to freely return to their home of origin, while Article 1 (para. 4) guarantees freedom of movement of persons, goods, services, and capital throughout Bosnia and Herzegovina.[129] These provisions significantly highlight the conventional 'human rights tone' of liberal constitutionalism.

Given its international orientation, the constitution also explicitly exhibits its liberal internationalist character.[130] For example, Article 2 (para. 2) of the constitution mentions that the 'rights and freedoms set forth in the European Convention for the Protection of Human Rights and Fundamental Freedoms and its Protocols shall apply *directly* in Bosnia and Herzegovina. These shall have priority over all other laws'.[131] The supremacy of these rights is guaranteed in Article 10

126 US Department of State, *US Leadership and the Balkan Challenge. Deputy Secretary of State Strobe Talbott, remarks at the National Press Club, Washington, DC, 9 November 1995, released by the Office of the Spokesman*. Available at: www.state.gov.

127 See *The Constitution of Bosnia and Herzegovina*; available at the official website of the Constitutional Court of Bosnia and Herzegovina. www.ccbh.ba.

128 See Article 2, para. 4 of the constitution.

129 See Article 2, para. 5 and Article 1, para. 4 of the constitution.

130 Gaeta notes that the constitution was drafted and agreed upon in an international forum (negotiated between Bosnia and Herzegovina with its three ethnic components, on the one hand, and a group of foreign states including Serbia and Croatia, on the other) and subsequently entered into force by virtue of international transactions. It is therefore 'no coincidence that the Constitution was drafted in English and not in the three languages of the peoples concerned'. See Gaeta, 'The Dayton Agreements and International Law', 160.

131 See Article 10, para. 2 of the constitution. Emphasis added.

(para. 2), which makes all constitutional provisions on human rights non-amendable by constitutional process.[132]

The liberal internationalist character of the State of Bosnia and Herzegovina is further demonstrated by the fact that in a number of key central institutions of the state, the ultimate decision-making authority has been devolved to international agencies. Wilde presents a detailed account of international appointments in Bosnia and Herzegovina made by international actors (sometimes without the obligation to consult local actors first) to international individuals.[133] For example, the Constitutional Court of Bosnia and Herzegovina, the supreme judicial organ of the country, is composed of nine judges, of whom three may not be citizens of Bosnia and Herzegovina or of any neighbouring countries and appointed by the European Court of Human Rights, while the other six judges are Bosniacs, Serbs, and Croats in equal numbers.[134] Similarly, the Governor of the Central Bank, who must also be a non-citizen of Bosnia and Herzegovina and of all neighbouring states, is appointed by the International Monetary Fund (IMF).[135] Chandler notes that although the Dayton Agreement provided for a one-year transitional international administration until the first state-level elections in September 1996, 'this one-year "transitional" administration has been indefinitely extended and the democratisation process in Bosnia has become a major international experiment in "political engineering"'.[136] Therefore, it is no surprise that the High Representative in Bosnia is allowed to exercise key executive and legislative powers, including the power to directly impose legislation, to veto political candidates, and to dismiss 'uncooperative' elected members of Bosnian governing bodies.[137] Bose thus rightly asserts that the liberal state of Bosnia is a 'state by international design and of international design'.[138]

132 This article reads: 'No amendment to this Constitution may eliminate or diminish any of the rights and freedoms referred to in Article 2 of this Constitution or alter the present paragraph'.

133 See Ralph Wilde, *International Territorial Administration – How Trusteeship and the Civilizing Mission Never Went Away* (Oxford: Oxford University Press, 2008), 70–75.

134 *Ibid.*, 71. See also Bose, *Bosnia after Dayton*, 65.

135 Wilde, *International Territorial Administration*, 67.

136 Chandler, *Bosnia: Faking Democracy after Dayton*, 2.

137 Wilde, *International Territorial Administration*, 68–69. Wilde notes that the High Representative considers the dismissals to be automatically effective and imposed legislations to be directly the law of the country without parliamentary ratification.

138 Bose, *Bosnia after Dayton*, 60.

At the same time, the Dayton Agreement outlined the constitutional procedures and powers in relation to the Presidency, Council of Ministers, and the Parliamentary Assembly in ethnic terms.[139] In order to safeguard the interests of the three ethnic groups and thereby maintain the existence of the state, the central state institutions were organised on the basis of ethnicity-defined consociational power-sharing mechanisms. Such an accommodation of the conservative notion of ethnicity within the liberal internationalist architecture of the Dayton Agreement guaranteed the representation of all three sides and the protection of their vital interests. For example, the three-member presidency was organised in such a way that each of the three ethnic groups can elect a representative from their group, and only from their group.[140]

The Dayton Agreement also perceived the constituent entities of Bosnia and Herzegovina in conservative terms, in that the salience of ethnicity in the organisation of these entities is explicitly demonstrated. Article 3 (para. 2) of the constitution of Bosnia and Herzegovina categorically mentions that 'the Entities shall have the right to establish special parallel relationships with neighbouring states, consistent with the sovereignty and territorial integrity of Bosnia [and] Herzegovina'.[141] The Bosniac–Croat Federation (Federation of Bosnia and Herzegovina) signed such a framework agreement with the Republic of Croatia in 1998 and the Republic of Srpska with the Federal Republic of Yugoslavia in 2001.[142] As a matter of fact, the Dayton peace process on Bosnia and Herzegovina itself engaged the Serbian and Croatian republics; it was none other than the President of Serbia, Slobodan Milosevic, who represented the Bosnian Serbs in the peace process.[143] The Dayton Agreement also includes declarations from these republics guaranteeing compliance with various annexes primarily concluded by Bosnia and Herzegovina, the Republic of Srpska, and the Federation of Bosnia and Herzegovina; in fact, Croatia and the Federal Republic of Yugoslavia have been given the formal status of 'third parties' in relation to the annexed agreements.[144]

Compared to the minority treaties under the League, which restricted the involvement of kin-states in the minority affairs of the host-states, the Dayton Agreement offered significantly more leverage to kin-states and thereby acknowledged the importance of cross-border ethnic affiliation

[139] See Annex 4 of the Dayton Agreement. [140] See Chandler, 68.

[141] See Article 3, para. 2 of the Constitution of Bosnia and Herzegovina. [142] Bose, 61.

[143] For an explanation of such a 'media portrayal' of Milosevic as the representative of the Serbs, see Gaeta, 'The Dayton Agreements and International Law', 150–153.

[144] See *ibid.*, 153.

for securing stability and peace in Bosnia and Herzegovina. However, it must be noted that Serbs and Croats within Bosnia and Herzegovina were not in fact perceived as minorities; as Bose notes, the Republic of Srpska qualifies as a 'State within a State' within Bosnia and Herzegovina.[145] It has its own radio and television broadcasting network as well as a national bank.[146] On the other hand, the Bosniac–Croat Federation (Federation of Bosnia and Herzegovina) – the other entity – is again another liberal venture to keep Bosniacs and Croats within one federal unit in order to 'end bitter Muslim–Croat hostilities and lay the foundation for a working military collaboration that could turn the tide of the war against Serbs'.[147] However, this is a mere *de jure* union; in reality, little integration has been achieved between these two communities.[148] For the sake of its existence as an entity, it had to be radically decentralised.[149] Although 'the Federation's armed forces are formally integrated, with a standard uniform for personnel and insignia reflecting the national symbols of both Croats and Bosniacs', in practice the units continue to exist separately.[150]

Bose offers a clear picture of the dichotomy in post-war Bosnia. On the one hand, the international community (especially OSCE and the United States) has been trying to safeguard the continuation of a viable joint state of Muslims, Serbs, and Croats very much as a microcosmic model of pre-war Bosnia under the former Yugoslavia. On the other hand, Bosniacs (Muslims) are advocating for an integrationist revision of the Dayton Agreement that devolves more power to the central state, while Serbs and Croats are asking for a partitionist revision of the agreement to facilitate an even closer association with their respective kin-states.[151]

In other words, the situation can be seen as an example of the persisting tension between two competing traditions: the liberal vision of a civic state with little or no focus on ethnicity in the political organisation of the state and the conservative tradition of defining the self-image of the constituent groups along ethnic lines. The latter tends to result in a quest to rejoin co-ethnics at the cost of the very existence of the state. Bose claims that Western politicians and diplomats in Bosnia are typically reluctant to entertain either integrationist or partitionist revisionism, for any revision of the Dayton arrangement will open a Pandora's box; hence, they tend to work within the parameters of the *status quo*.[152]

[145] Bose, 74. [146] *Ibid.* [147] *Ibid.*, 75. [148] *Ibid.* [149] *Ibid.*, 23. [150] *Ibid.*, 77–78.
[151] *Ibid.*, 22–28. [152] *Ibid.*, 30.

What the foregoing brief sketch of the international legal response to Bosnian conflicts demonstrates is the manner in which the dichotomous liberal and conservative traditions of perceiving the role of ethnicity in nation-states inform the response of international lawyers to Bosnian conflicts. While international policy-makers in the early days of the breakup of Yugoslavia and jurists in the Badinter Commission had high hopes for a post-ethnic regional order in the Balkans, the escalation of conflict to eventually the worst in recent European history made them realise that in the real world the liberal and conservative traditions of dealing with ethnicity must find some common ground for the sake of pragmatic paths to peace. Therefore, in the Dayton Agreement we see a combination of liberal democratic arrangements with a series of consociational power-sharing elements along ethnic lines.

This pattern is not peculiar to the Bosnian conflicts between 1992 and 1995; as the preceding section demonstrates, this compromise represents the general attitude of international law towards ethnicity in ethnic conflicts. Given that ethnic groups involved in conflicts over the control of political institutions are invariably capable of exercising self-government and of sustaining their own public institutions, norms developed within the framework of the FCNM or UNDM that accepted the primacy of individualism proved largely ineffective: some sort of ethnic power sharing was necessary.[153] 'None of these conflicts revolved around the right of individuals to join with others to enjoy their cultures. The violation of such rights was not the cause of violent conflicts, and respect for such rights would not resolve the conflicts'.[154] As a result, responses to most such conflicts involved some degree of ethnic accommodation for purely pragmatic reasons, on a case-specific basis. As one critic has noted, the EU's country-specific recommendations have 'demonstrated their preparedness to follow virtually any policy measure to create stability'.[155] In the process, ethnic federalism and various other formulations of ethnic group-specific rights bypassed existing legal regimes. However, the emphasis on the *ad hoc* nature of such interventions undermined the potential to generate norms in favour of minority group rights.

[153] Kymlicka, *Multicultural Odysseys*, 216, 234. [154] *Ibid.*, 215.

[155] Carter Johnson, 'The Use and Abuse of Minority Rights: Assessing Past and Future EU Policies towards Accession Countries of Central, Eastern, and South-Eastern Europe', *International Journal of Minority and Group Rights* 13 (2006), 51.

Conclusion

The foregoing narrative of international legal responses to ethnic conflicts demonstrates that the liberal world view falls short in the face of violent conflicts defined along ethnic lines by the protagonists themselves or outsiders or both. International law attempts to address this shortfall by accommodating the conservative notion of ethnicity within the predominant liberal architecture of international law. As we have already seen, the Bosnian case exposes a shift in the international legal attitude towards ethnicity: from the liberal understanding of ethnicity in the Badinter Commission to the conservative accommodation of ethnicity within the liberal framework in the Dayton Agreement. Dealing with ethnicity in ethnic conflicts more generally, jurists follow exactly the same trend. It thus transpires that however strong the normative pull of the liberal peace thesis is claimed to be, pragmatism demands ethnic accommodation in the conservative sense – a tension that results in the effort to reconcile these two broadly drawn traditions.

Yet, such a reconciliatory approach, against the backdrop of the dominant liberal ideology, brings forth normative inconsistency. Although Anghie speaks for a much broader accommodation of ethnic minority rights in international law, he does so without actually considering the issue of the normative compatibility of the conservative cultural rights with the liberal-individualist human rights regime. Similarly, while Wippman endeavours to reconcile the conservative ethnic measures with normative liberal individualism, in the end he submits to pragmatism. In this sense, this narrative of the international legal engagement with ethnicity in ethnic conflicts brings forth the issue of the normative compatibility of current liberal legal norms with an effective response to ethnic conflicts that entails ethnic accommodation along the line of the conservative tradition, in one form or another.[156]

[156] To explain the limitation of the liberal-individualist approach to ethnic conflicts, Koshy describes the proceedings involving the Sri Lankan ethnic conflict before the Human Rights Commission and the Sub-Commission in which almost exclusive attention was given to the violations of core individual rights rather than to the ethnic and political structures giving rise to the conflict as such or to the related claims of some Tamil groups for an autonomy scheme. See Ninan Koshy, 'Ethnic Conflicts in Sri Lanka and the UN Human Rights System' in *Ethnic Conflicts and the UN Human Rights System*, ed. Henry J. Steiner, cited in Henry J. Steiner, 'Ideals and Counter-Ideals in the Struggle over Autonomy Regimes for Minorities', *Notre Dame Law Review* 66 (1991), footnote 33. Similarly, in the context of Nigeria, Osaghae registers his distrust of individualist human rights as the sole system for addressing ethnic conflicts and argues that although individual rights are necessary, group rights which 'regard ethnic groups as deserving

This gap between the normative stance and pragmatic needs implies that international law, with its normative reliance on liberal individualism, deals with ethnic conflicts in a 'quasi-legal' realm.

However, this ostensible failure of liberalism paradoxically opens up avenues for the flexible accommodation of ethnicity for securing peace on pragmatic grounds, as various institutional responses – both domestic and international – to ethnic conflicts demonstrate. We have already seen such an ethnic accommodation within the liberal framework of the Dayton Agreement; other contemporary peace agreements are no different.[157] This dichotomous way of perceiving ethnicity in ethnic conflicts reflects back on the nineteenth-century traditions of perceiving the role of ethnicity in the political organisation of nation-states. The same is true of the international legal response to ethnicity in minority protection. In this sense, it would be arbitrary to think of any pragmatic regime dealing with ethnic conflicts outside the normative realm addressing the issue of ethnicity itself. I address some of these normative issues, their challenges, and the way forward in the conclusion of this book.

of protection of justice in competition with others are also needed' for ethnic conflict management. See Eghosa E. Osaghae, 'Human Rights and Ethnic Conflict Management: The Case of Nigeria', *Journal of Peace Research* 33, no. 2 (1996), 171. Absent these rights, he asserts, the continued existence of ethnic groups cannot be guaranteed, nor can their subjugation by other groups be prevented, in that the entrenchment of individual rights alone cannot serve the purposes which group rights are meant to serve (178). Using the example of ethnic tension in Nigeria, Osaghae thus concludes that there are important ethnic group interests which cannot be served by individual rights; at least some fundamental group rights, such as the rights of the ethnic group to exist, to preserve and protect its language and culture, and to participate equally with others in the affairs of the state, including the sharing of power and resources, have to be recognised, which would then become 'a meaningful basis for trying to redress the imbalances and inequalities among the various groups' (186). This claim is equally true for other conflict situations as well.

[157] See, for example, the Chittagong Hill Tracts Peace Accord (Agreement between the National Committee on Chittagong Hill Tracts Constituted by the Government of Bangladesh and the Parbattya Chattagram Jana Samhati Samiti – PCJSS, Dhaka, 3 December 1997); the Belfast Agreement (Agreement Reached in the Multiparty Negotiations, Belfast, 10 April 1998). See also Christine Bell, *Peace Agreements and Human Rights* (Oxford: Oxford University Press, 2000); C. Bell, 'Peace Agreements: Their Nature and Legal Status', *American Journal of International Law* 100, no. 2 (2006), 373–412; C. Bell, *On the Law of Peace: Peace Agreements and the Lex Pacificatoria* (Oxford: Oxford University Press, 2008).

Conclusion

Immanuel Kant, in the conclusion of *The Metaphysics of Morals*, writes:

> If a person cannot prove that a thing exists, he may attempt to prove that it does not exist. If neither approach succeeds (as often happens), he may still ask whether it is *in his interest to assume* one or other possibility as a hypothesis, either from theoretical or from practical considerations. In other words, he may wish on the one hand simply to explain a certain phenomenon (as the astronomer, for example, may wish to explain the sporadic movements of the planets), or on the other, to achieve a certain end which may itself be either *pragmatic* (purely technical) or *moral* (i.e. an end which it is our duty to take as a maxim).[1]

While no one is duty bound to make an assumption that this moral end can be realised, Kant continues, it is nonetheless the duty of each individual to act as if it is possible to realise this end, especially when it is possible to guarantee neither its realisation nor non-realisation. Here Kant's hope and the urge for the pursuit of this hope came in the context of his formula of perpetual peace among nations.

However, the legacy of this eighteenth-century proposition has currency for the manner in which liberal international lawyers deal with the idea of ethnicity even today. Bypassing any serious normative discourse on ethnicity, they pursue instead the moral end of a post-ethnic world order that suitably fits the liberal-individualist premise of international law. This is a form of 'liberal expectancy', to take Nancy Rosenblum's phrase, by which she indicates the hope and expectation that liberal democratic values will grow over time and take firm root across ethnic, racial, and religious lines, within both majority and minority groups.[2]

But, at the same time, the conservative tradition of perceiving ethnicity as being at the forefront of the political organisation of at least some of

[1] Kant, 'The Metaphysics of Morals (1797)' in *Kant: Political Writings*, 173. Italics in original.

[2] Nancy Rosenblum, *Membership and Morals: The Personal Uses of Pluralism in America* (Princeton, New Jersey: Princeton University Press, 1998), 55–61.

the nation-states has kept the relevance of ethnicity alive in relation to minorities and ethnic conflicts, among other matters. In the face of pragmatic needs, liberal international lawyers then tend to recognise the 'practical use' of ethnicity and its relevance in identity formation at least among non-Western communities and thereby engender reconciliation between the liberal and conservative traditions – between moral end and crude reality. As a result, at the normative level, ethnicity remains a peripheral issue in the international legal discourse and appears relevant only as a descriptive criterion, as in ethnic minorities and ethnic conflicts. In this book I have attempted to reverse this understanding of the relationship between ethnicity and international law by tracing the central role that ethnicity plays in the historical development of international law. However, two aspects of this story of ethnicity in international law need to be honed before we conclude: what does this engagement between ethnicity and international law tell us, and where do we go from here?

Ethnicity and international law: an engagement with consequences

In the preceding chapters, I have demonstrated that ethnicity, expressed in the dichotomy of the 'self' and the 'other' along the lines of the liberal and conservative traditions, has shaped not only the way in which international law engaged with the major events of each of its developmental phases but also the consequences such interactions between international law and ethnicity have engendered over centuries. Taken together, a number of major themes flow from my narrative of the ethnic underpinning of international law. First, the political meaning of ethnicity as 'otherness' plays a crucial role in shaping international law. This role is historical and took different forms in different phases of the development of international law. However, in the nineteenth-century Romantic literature, ethnicity appeared as the core of a nation, while in the liberal tradition, ethnicity remained as a symbol of primitiveness and, hence, irrelevant in the political organisation of nation-states. This is a trend that persists even in current international law, exemplified by the perception of minorities as the ethnic 'other'. As we have demonstrated earlier, in almost all the definitions of the 'minority' incorporated in various post–World War II international and regional human rights instruments, this phenomenon of identifying a 'minority' as an ethnic 'other' is evident. In ethnic conflicts too, the very notion of ethnicity as a defining category constructs ethnic conflicts as a problem specifically relevant for the non-Western 'other'. Therefore, since the interwar period, whenever addressing the conservative notion of ethnicity was deemed necessary for an understanding of minority protection, the international mechanism invariably targeted the non-Western countries even within Europe.

In this sense, as this book argues, the ethnic dichotomy of 'self' and 'other' is not a monolithic phenomenon; instead, it essentially finds expression within the dominant political philosophies of each epoch. Throughout the history of modern international law, ethnicity acquired different meanings as the contrasting liberal and conservative traditions went through the process of constructing the 'self' and the 'other'. Thus, the treatment of ethnicity in these two traditions had different implications: while the liberal nation perceived ethnicity as primitiveness and therefore set an agenda of assimilating the ethnic 'other' into the liberal high culture, the Romantic-conservative notion of national 'self' aimed to exclude the 'other' to ensure ethno-cultural homogeneity. The logic of liberal assimilation and conservative exclusion sought their 'scientific' explanation and justification in another dominant nineteenth-century doctrine, social Darwinism, with its two streams, each matching a political philosophy. While for the liberals the monogenic stream of social Darwinism explained ethnicity as backwardness in the march towards 'progress' and justified the assimilation of the ethnic 'other', the polygenic stream advanced the idea of racial segregation to the satisfaction of the conservatives.

Within this liberal–conservative dichotomy, nineteenth-century international law, far from being monolithic, demonstrated different perceptions of the nation-state and sovereignty. On one side, the liberal self-image of a nation within the Enlightenment tradition was reflected on the understanding of international law, which, going beyond the notion of specific ethnic culture, envisioned a common supra-national, universal cultural domain. On the other side, German international jurisprudence under the influence of the German Historical School glorified the notion of the state as an omnipotent entity, much more than a mere collection of individuals as the liberals suggest. Seen through this dichotomy of liberal and conservative traditions, the story of colonialism explains why the assimilationist thrust of liberal international lawyers, as expressed in the notion of 'civilising mission', remained very different from the conservative-exclusionist project of German colonialism as endorsed by international lawyers in the conservative Romantic camp. Similarly, the minority protection mechanisms under the League and the UN revealed the inherent tension between the liberal progressiveness of the Western cultures and the conservative ethnic 'primitiveness' in the concept of minorities and their protection. The same phenomenon is also traced in the international legal responses to ethnicity in ethnic conflicts.

These philosophical traditions coexisted, one emerged dominant over the other, or they mutually confronted each other for political salience; the relevance of ethnicity and, hence, the meaning of the 'self' and the 'other' changed accordingly. While the ascendancy of the conservative tradition was witnessed in the nineteenth century and again during Nazi rule, liberalism has gained dominance since the end of World War II and declared ultimate victory in the post–Cold War world order. The shifting primacy of these traditions has always been reflected in international law and also in the consequences of international legal engagement with ethnicity. In this dynamic process, liberal individualism now dominates the current international legal plane and the conservative notion of ethnicity is naturally conceived as primitiveness, backwardness, and 'post-modern tribalism'. Yet, ethnicity remains relevant for the pragmatic need of dealing with ethnicity-defined phenomena such as ethnic minorities and ethnic conflicts. In this contrasting way, the conservative understanding of ethnicity also remains relevant in reinforcing the 'progressive' image of the liberal tradition and its emancipatory potential. In other words, the liberal and conservative traditions are mutually constitutive; they rely on each other for their existence.

In this connection, the final theme that flows from my narrative is that international law demonstrates a liberal anxiety apropos of the conservative notion of ethnicity. As a matter of fact, liberal international lawyers do engage with ethnic minorities and ethnic conflicts in a variety of ways, and, for sure, they will continue to do so in future as well. The tension emanating from this juxtaposition of their normative stance of denying the relevance of ethnicity in the political organisation of nation-states, and the pragmatic need to recognise the same, consistently highlights that individualism is not a self-sufficient ideology in international law. Even in the era of the normative primacy of liberalism, it is not sufficient to deal with minority protection and ethnic conflicts. Hence, reconciliatory efforts are quite often put in place to find some sort of workable solutions to these problems. In other words, the liberal anxiety regarding ethnicity reveals the limitations of normative individualism as the sole foundation of international law. What is the way forward, then?

Ethnicity and international law: a future direction?

This normative drawback in international law is not merely an issue for international legal scholars reluctant to accommodate ethnicity within their intellectual framework. Rather, this drawback is inherent in nature, for normative individualism (the foundation of the liberal international legal architecture) is often seen as incompatible with the conservative notion of the centrality of ethnicity in identity formation. Therefore, in the absence of any concrete headway towards the remodelling of liberalism in relation to ethnicity, international law will continue to deal with ethnic minorities and ethnic conflicts in an environment of ambivalence. And as I demonstrated in preceding chapters, the success of any future international legal engagement with ethnic minorities and ethnic conflicts will largely depend on the efforts to reconcile both the liberal and conservative traditions. This also indicates that to effectively counteract this drawback of international law vis-à-vis ethnic conflicts and ethnic minorities, international lawyers must look beyond international law to find the root of the problem as well as the seed of a hope.

One prudent way of doing so is to rethink liberalism itself. The shortcoming of liberal international law in accommodating the conservative ethnic group phenomenon within its individualist framework is inherent and therefore demands a drastic remodelling of the normative relationship between ethnicity and international law. Since international law is shaped by the dominant political philosophy of each epoch, the normative accommodation of ethnicity within liberalism is naturally expected to reorganise the normative foundation of international law vis-à-vis ethnicity. As a matter of fact, the post–Cold War ethnic violence has already facilitated a fresh discourse on the necessity of ethnic accommodation within liberal political philosophy itself. Indeed, there is a hope for a more accommodative international law in the 'liberal' proposition that individual and group rights are not mutually exclusive and that it is possible to accommodate group rights within the liberal framework. The proponents of this argument – Yael Tamir, Joseph Raz, and Will Kymlicka, among others – acknowledge that there are compelling interests related to culture and identity, which are fully consistent with the liberal principles of individual freedom and equality and justify granting special rights to minorities.[3]

[3] Yael Tamir, *Liberal Nationalism* (Princeton, New Jersey: Princeton University Press, 1995); Joseph Raz, 'Multiculturalism: A Liberal Perspective', *Dissent* (Winter, 1994),

Kymlicka famously advanced his theory of liberal culturalism, which is based on the fact that modern states invariably develop and consolidate a 'societal culture' which requires the standardisation and diffusion of a common language and the creation and diffusion of common educational, political, and legal institutions. [4] These societal cultures are profoundly important to liberalism as liberal values of freedom and equality must be defined and understood in relation to such societal cultures. Therefore, in his theory, while freedom and equality for immigrants entail freedom and equality within mainstream institutions – by promoting linguistic and institutional integration as well as by reforming those institutions so that immigrants can achieve linguistic and institutional integration without denying their ethno-cultural identities – freedom and equality for the 'national minorities' require something more.[5] Given that these groups already possess a societal culture and that they have fought to maintain these institutions, Kymlicka argues that their demands for special language rights and regional autonomy have increasingly been accepted by liberal democracies. He then contends that group-differentiated treatment of this sort is not a violation of liberal principles, for to expect the members of national minorities to integrate into the institutions of the dominant culture is neither necessary nor fair. Freedom for them involves the ability to live and work in their own societal culture. In short, the aim of the liberal theory of minority rights is to define fair terms of integration

67–79; J. Raz, 'Multiculturalism', *Ratio Juris* 11, no. 3 (1998), 193–205. For a detailed discussion on group rights within liberalism, see David Miller and Michael Walzer (eds.), *Pluralism, Justice, and Equality* (Oxford: Oxford University Press, 1995); Jeremy Waldron (ed.), *Liberal Rights: Collected Papers (1981–1991)* (Cambridge: Cambridge University Press, 1993); Joel E. Oestreich, 'Liberal Theory and Minority Group Rights', *Human Rights Quarterly* 21, no. 1 (1999), 108–132; Steven Wheatley, 'Deliberative Democracy and Minorities', *European Journal of International Law* 14, no. 3 (2003), 507–527; Max Plog, 'Democratic Theory and Minority Rights: Internal and External Group Rights in a Global Democracy', *International Journal on Minority and Group Rights* 10 (2003), 52–82; Claus Offe, 'Political Liberalism, Group Rights, and the Politics of Fear and Trust', *Studies in East European Thought* 53 (2001), 167–182; Eric J. Mitnick, 'Three Models of Group-Differentiated Rights', *Columbia Human Rights Law Review* 35 (2004), 102–144; Geoff Gilbert, 'Autonomy and Minority Groups: A Right in International Law?' *Cornell International Law Journal* 35 (2002), 307–353.

4 Societal culture is defined as a set of institutions, covering both public and private life, with a common language, which has historically developed over time on a given territory, which provides people with a wide range of choices about how to lead their lives.

5 Kymlicka defines national minorities as groups who formed functioning societies on their historical homelands prior to being incorporated into a larger state.

for immigrants and to enable national minorities to maintain themselves as distinct societies.[6]

While, like the communitarians, Kymlicka recognises the paradoxical gap between the theory and the practice of group rights in the liberal societies – on the one hand, group-differentiated practices exist in the liberal societies in various forms for the sake of pragmatism; on the other hand, liberalism does not recognise group rights at the normative level – and urges the normative incorporation of group rights, he does so essentially within the liberal framework.[7] What makes Kymlicka different from a communitarian is his liberal justification for group-differentiated practices with the central argument that depriving minorities of their rights violates the liberal principles of autonomy and equality. According to him, multiculturalism is premised on the assumption that recognition and accommodation of ethnic diversity can in fact further 'develop liberal values of human freedom and human rights, diminish ethnic and racial hierarchies, and deepen democracy'.[8] However, he simultaneously notes his concerns that interpreting multiculturalism in conservative terms – as a right to preserve 'authentic' cultural traditions – would not only inhibit constructive relations between cultures 'by privileging cultural purity over cultural hybridity' but also deny the existence of universal human rights and thereby erode the freedom of individuals within groups.[9] But, to his satisfaction, he finds the emerging international discourses and norms of multiculturalism fundamentally liberal in character and broadly consistent with the foundational liberal commitment to principles of individual freedom and equality.[10]

So far as cultural rights of 'illiberal' groups are concerned, conforming to the core value of liberalism, Kymlicka categorically claims that minority rights are consistent with liberal multiculturalism if, first of all, 'they

[6] Will Kymlicka, *Multicultural Citizenship: A Liberal Theory of Minority Rights* (Oxford: Oxford University Press, 1995). See also Will Kymlicka, *Politics in the Vernacular: Nationalism, Multiculturalism, and Citizenship* (Oxford: Oxford University Press, 2001), 51–66; Leighton McDonald, 'Regrouping in Defence of Minority Rights: Kymlicka's Multicultural Citizenship', *Osgoode Hall Law Journal* 34, no. 2 (1996), 292–319.

[7] For a communitarian perspective on group rights, see, for example, Vernon van Dyke, 'The Individuals, the State, and Ethnic Communities in Political Theory', *World Politics* 29, no. 3 (1977), 343–369; also, V. van Dyke, 'Collective Entities and Moral Rights: Problems in Liberal-Democratic Thought (1982)' in *Group Rights – Perspective Since 1900*, ed. Julia Stapleton (Bristol: Theommes Press, 1995), 180–200.

[8] Will Kymlicka, *Multicultural Odysseys: Navigating the New International Politics of Diversity* (Oxford: Oxford University Press, 2007), 18.

[9] *Ibid.*, 102–103. [10] *Ibid.*, 7.

protect the freedom of individuals within the group' and, secondly, 'they promote relations of equality (non-dominance) between groups'.[11] In other words, his construction of liberal multiculturalism is a product of a dual function of human rights: on the one hand, it creates a political environment and space wherein different groups 'contest inherent hierarchies'; on the other hand, it 'requires groups to advance their claims in a very specific language – namely, the language of human rights, civil rights liberalism, and democratic constitutionalism'.[12]

This 'liberal' requirement that groups need to act in a particular manner to enjoy rights in a liberal regime essentially symbolises a kind of 'governmentality' by which Michel Foucault means a collective process involving institutions, procedures, analyses, reflections, calculations, and tactics 'that allow the exercise of the very specific albeit complex form of power, which has as its target population, as its principal form of knowledge political economy, and as its essential technical means apparatus of security'.[13] Seen through the lens of 'governmentality', the government then has as its purpose the welfare of the 'population', on which the government will 'act either directly, through large-scale campaigns, or indirectly, through techniques that will make possible, without the full awareness of the people, achieving certain goals'.[14] Conceptualised in this way, not only as the subject of the needs and aspirations of the government but also as the object in the hands of the government, in Foucauldian terms, the 'population', while aware of what the government wants from it, is ignorant of what is being done to it.[15]

However, this liberal shift, despite its promise for a better coherence with pragmatic needs, and also practice, is often depicted as counterproductive for liberalism itself. Liberal theorist Chandran Kukathas, for example, dismantles the notion of cultural rights altogether.[16] Despite his concerns for minority communities, he finds it unnecessary to abandon, modify, or reinterpret liberalism. According to him, the very emphasis of liberalism on individual rights and liberty reflects not hostility to the interests of communities but wariness of the power of the majority over

[11] Kymlicka, *Politics in the Vernacular*, 22–23.

[12] Kymlicka, *Multicultural Odysseys*, 92–93.

[13] Michel Foucault, 'Governmentality' in *Essential Works of Foucault 1954–1984*, vol. III (Power), ed. James D. Faubion (London: Penguin Books, 2002), 220.

[14] *Ibid.*, 217. [15] *Ibid.*

[16] See, generally, Chandran Kukathas, 'Are There Any Cultural Rights?' in *Group Rights – Perspective Since 1900*, ed. Julia Stapleton, 258–298. See also Chandran Kukathas, *The Liberal Archipelago: A Theory of Diversity and Freedom* (Oxford: Oxford University Press, 2003).

minorities. Thus, there is no need to look for alternatives to liberalism or to throw away the individualism that lies at its heart. Therefore, unlike Kymlicka, he finds it unnecessary to accommodate any idea of group rights to address the issues of minorities. To quote him: 'We need, rather, to reassert the fundamental importance of individual liberty and individual rights and question the idea that cultural minorities have collective rights'.[17] This proposition depends heavily on his assumption that the basis of collective rights is the rights of individuals. For Kukathas, while the interests given expression in groups do matter, they matter ultimately only to the extent that they affect actual individuals. Therefore, groups and communities have no special moral primacy in virtue of some natural priority.

Solely relying on the primacy of the individual's choice, Kukathas contends that as long as individuals choose to remain with a group, liberal or illiberal, the outside society is not entitled to intervene in the internal affairs of that group: '[T]he primacy of freedom of association is all-important; it has to take priority over other liberties – such as those of speech or worship – which lie at the core of the liberal tradition'.[18] Now, if membership in a cultural community is voluntary, and if the outside society has no right to intervene in the internal affairs of that community, it follows that to remain a member of that community, individuals must stick to the rules of that community. Kukathas believes that in this way individualism offers the cultural communities some protection without actually deviating from basic liberal principles.

Another prominent liberal philosopher, Brian Barry, vehemently opposes the idea of the state promoting communal identities, although he recognises the role of communities and associations in human well-being.[19] Like Kukathas, Barry believes that it is no part of liberalism to insist that every group must conform to liberal principles in its internal structure. For him, the fundamental liberal position on group rights is that individuals should be free to associate together in any way they like, provided that their taking part in the activities of the group comes about as a result of their voluntary decision and they are free to cease to take part whenever they want to.[20] However, what makes Barry distinct from Kukathas is Barry's deeper understanding of the term 'voluntariness'. When a member of a group quits or remains with the group 'voluntarily',

[17] *Ibid.*, 261. [18] *Ibid.*, 289.
[19] Brian Barry, *Culture and Equality* (Cambridge: Polity Press, 2001), 112–154.
[20] *Ibid.*, 148.

various factors actually work behind that apparently 'voluntary' decision. If an individual remains a member of an illiberal group 'voluntarily', Barry argues, such voluntary group membership might result from that individual's unwillingness to shoulder the costs that will follow his or her decision to leave that group. Therefore, membership in illiberal groups cannot always be seen as a voluntary decision, and Barry asks for state intervention in such cases. Yet, 'voluntariness' can also be examined from the other end of the spectrum: against the backdrop of a series of state-sponsored incentives for cultural assimilation, if a mother belonging to an ethnic minority group wants her daughter to be educated in the dominant language and get assimilated into mainstream culture to secure material gains, can such a decision be called 'voluntary' in the sense Barry understands the term?

Being a liberal, not surprisingly, Barry is not interested in this aspect of 'voluntary' assimilation. Instead, he argues that there should not be any liberal protection of 'group' rights, for '[t]he only ways of life that need to appeal to the value of cultural diversity are those that necessarily involve unjust inequalities or require powers of indoctrination and control incompatible with liberalism in order to maintain themselves'.[21] Given that such cultures are unfair and oppressive to at least some of their members, he finds it hard to see why they should be kept alive artificially, especially when he assumes that in embracing liberalism, groups will give up their demand for separate cultural rights.[22]

That the state does not lend any special weight to the norms of illiberal – or liberal – groups is, according to Barry, the essence of what it means to say that a society is a liberal society.[23] It is, therefore, unsurprising that Kymlicka's emphasis on 'diversity' and 'autonomy' for minorities came under his criticism; these notions refer to policies, he argues, that paradoxically would systematically undercut those rights of individuals to protection against groups that the liberal states should guarantee. His crucial question thus follows: 'How can a theory that would gut liberal principles be a form of liberalism?'[24] A more candid expression comes from him when he claims: 'If a liberal is not somebody who believes that liberalism is true (with or without inverted commas), what is a liberal?'[25] And, consequently, he refuses to recognise Kymlicka as a liberal:

> A theory that has the implication that nationalities (whether they control a state or a sub-state polity) have a fundamental right to violate liberal

[21] *Ibid.*, 135. [22] *Ibid.* [23] *Ibid.*, 125. [24] *Ibid.* [25] *Ibid.*, 132.

> principles is not a liberal theory of group rights. It is an *illiberal theory* with a bit of liberal hand-writing thrown in as an optional extra.[26]

This controversy *within* liberalism regarding the accommodation of the conservative notion of group rights indicates that it may take a bit longer for this age-old controversy between liberal individualism and conservative collectivism to reach a subtle compromise keeping their core values intact. For now, let ethnicity remain a symbol of the unaccomplished liberal dream of 'progress' and universal 'civilisation' and liberalism itself a part of the problem as much as a part of the solution of the exclusionist projects that the conservative way of defining the 'self' engenders.

*****

While a detailed agenda of action to mitigate the tension between these two traditions is not the aim of the present work, my narrative of the international legal response to ethnicity in minority protection and ethnic conflicts indicates that an effective response to the drawback of international law vis-à-vis minority protection and ethnic conflicts relies on the subtle normative reconciliation of the nineteenth-century traditions of liberalism and conservatism apropos of the role of ethnicity in the political organisation of nation-states. To this end, this book offers the necessary theoretical framework, as well as the historical background, by demonstrating how the treatment of ethnicity in the liberal and conservative philosophical traditions shaped the way international law engaged with the key events of each of its developmental phases. Although I discussed only a few specific events of international legal history in relation to colonialism, minority protection, and ethnic conflicts, the pattern of the engagement between ethnicity and international law that this book reveals has much wider implications.

As a whole, this book offers an opportunity to understand international law beyond the conventional (orthodox) narratives. At the same time, it also remains distinct from other critical approaches to international law, in that the paradigm of the ethnic dichotomy of 'self' and 'other', expressed in the liberal and conservative traditions, explains major events of international legal history in a new light. Explained through this framework, nineteenth-century colonialism, the interwar minority protection, the current minority protection regime, and the international legal response to ethnic conflicts – each of these events opens up

[26] *Ibid.*, 140. Emphasis added.

new avenues for a fresh critical analysis of other crucial issues involved in these events and international law's engagements with similar events in future.

The world witnessed such an event in 2014, one that involved, *inter alia*, the question of ethnicity in the political organisation of nation-states in a powerful way. Crimea, a southern part of Ukraine with ethnic Russians as the majority, held a referendum on 16 March 2014 on the question of whether to join their co-ethnics in Russia. Crimea was transferred from the Russian Soviet Federative Socialist Republic to the Ukrainian Soviet Socialist Republic in 1954 and remained part of Ukraine as an autonomous region following the dissolution of the Soviet Union. Crimea's political troubles of 2014 erupted when the Ukrainian 'revolution' in February that year overthrew the pro-Russia regime of President Victor Yanukovych, who had a popular support base in Crimea. The new Ukranian government, backed by the Western powers and rejected by Russia, soon faced resistance in Crimea, where ethnic Russians already feared they would be repressed. In response, while the Security Service of Ukraine (SBU) used military threat 'to prevent any action taken against diminishing the territorial integrity and sovereignty of Ukraine',[27] the Ukrainian parliament quickly passed a bill to repeal the 2012 law 'on the principles of the state language policy', making Ukrainian the sole state language at all levels. Although the acting president finally vetoed the bill, this move led ethnic Russians in Crimea to perceive the Ukrainian revolution in nationalist terms – as a process of their marginalisation under the new regime.[28] In the referendum, nearly 96 per cent decided in favour of independence, with a turnout of over 83 per cent.[29] The following day, the Crimean parliament declared independence from Ukraine and asked to join the Russian Federation.[30] Russia had no reason not to respond positively; President Vladimir Putin specifically mentioned the principle of self-determination when he claimed that Crimea is a part of Russia on both moral and material grounds.[31] However, the

[27] 'EuroMaidan Rallies in Ukraine', Kyiv Post, 21 February 2014. Available at: www.kyivpost.com.

[28] Sabra Ayres, 'Is It too Late for Kiev to Woo Russian-Speaking Ukraine?' *Christian Science Monitor*, 28 February 2014. Available at: www.csmonitor.com.

[29] 'Crimea referendum: Voters "Back" Russia Union', BBC News, 16 March 2014. Available at: www.bbc.co.uk.

[30] 'Crimean Parliament Formally Applies to Join Russia', BBC News, 17 March 2014. Available at: www.bbc.co.uk.

[31] Uriel Abulof, 'Self-Determination, Redux?' *Huffington Post*, 20 March 2014. Available at: www.huffingtonpost.com.

UN General Assembly passed a resolution declaring Crimea's referendum invalid and urged member states not to recognise a change in status of the Crimean region.[32]

This salience of ethnicity in the reconstruction of the national self-image of Russia, albeit as a part of its realist politics, symbolises the re-emergence of the nineteenth-century conservative tradition of understanding ethnicity as the central element in the political organisation of nation-states. For Crimea, ethnicity remains the basis for exercising the right to self-determination, as expressed in the referendum, to rejoin the co-ethnics. On the other hand, an ethnically based Russian nationalism as a ground for Russian expansion in the region in many ways resembles the treatment of ethnicity by interwar Germany, especially in relation to German minorities in Eastern and Central Europe, as we have seen in Chapter 3. This also indicates the implications for the region – from the perspectives of both minority rights and stability – if Russia continues to advance such a conservative ethno-nationalist campaign. Russia already had a war with neighbouring Georgia in 2008 on the ethnic grounds of protecting Russian minorities in South Ossetia and Abkhazia.

While the dichotomy of the liberal and conservative traditions of perceiving the salience of ethnicity in nationalism, as explained in this book, offers a useful framework to better understand some aspects of the complexities involved in the Crimean case in a historical continuum, this framework also demonstrates that liberal international law is insufficient to normatively engage with this ethnic phenomenon. Labelling the problem in Ukraine as a mere security issue to be addressed with *realpolitik* will not be helpful in the long run, for it will jeopardise minority interests and thereby cause further instability.

Another less helpful approach will be to glorify the non-ethnic notion of Scottish nationalism as the current phenomenon – demonstrated by the outcome of the independence referendum of 18 September 2014 in favour of remaining with the UK and also by the nationalists' campaigning for independence in non-ethnic terms[33] – and globally export this as

[32] United Nations, General Assembly Resolution No. 68/262, 27 March 2014. Yet, four UN members, *viz.*, Afghanistan, Nicaragua, Syria, and Venezuela, have explicitly recognised Crimea as a federal subject of Russia.

[33] Throughout the campaign, the Scottish National Party (SNP) highlighted issues of social welfare and economic justice to make a case for Scottish independence. See, for example, the SNP manifesto for independence: www.snp-bannockburn.org. Moreover, only the residents of Scotland were allowed to vote in the referendum, meaning resident non-Scots (e.g., the English and the Irish) were allowed to vote to decide on the vital question of

a model. Clearly, what looked like a refusal of ethno-nationalism in the referendum re-appeared as a national question in the general election of 7 May 2015. Then, the conservatives kindled a sense of English nationalism as opposed to Scottish nationalism, contributing to the Tories' victory over Labour. Also, the 'Scottish lesson' did not work in the case of Catalonia. The Spanish government, with the help of the Spanish Constitutional Court, blocked the referendum on independence that was approved by the Catalan parliament on 19 September 2014. Nevertheless, the Catalan government held, this time in violation of the Constitutional Court's embargo, a non-binding 'citizen participation process on the political future of Catalonia' on 9 November 2014 as an alternative to the original referendum. Although the turnout was low –41.6 per cent – more than 80 per cent of votes were in favour of 'an independent state of Catalonia'.[34] However, a more recent victory in favour of independence came in the regional election of 27 September 2015 when the pro-independence *Junts per Si* (Together for Yes) alliance along with far-left separatist CUP party secured an absolute majority (72 out of 135 seats) in the regional parliament.[35] The separatists considered this election as a *de facto* referendum on independence from Spain and therefore claimed the victory as a clear mandate to form an independent Catalan state. The Spanish government, however, pledged to challenge any unilateral move towards independence in the courts, as it did before. Despite conflicting claims regarding the true meaning of this election result in favour of the separatists, it is certain that any attempt to meaningfully engage with the Catalonian question in the near future will essentially involve further ethnic accommodation in terms of linguistic and cultural rights. The liberal nature of the Scottish nationalist campaign is going to be certainly less appealing to minorities outside Europe.

The analytical framework that I offer in this book is equally relevant in the context of postcolonial nationalism and statehood. It would also be a viable project to expose, with reference to the liberal underpinning of current international law, the connection between the self-image of the liberal West and postcolonial statehood. These postcolonial states can be considered the 'global other', while the process of constructing the

Scottish independence, while Scots resident outside of Scotland were not allowed to do the same. For details on voting eligibility, see www.scotreferendum.com.

34 Patrick Johnson, 'Catalonia Vote: No Smile for Spain', BBC News, 10 November 2014. Available at: www.bbc.co.uk.

35 'Catalonia vote: Pro-independence parties win elections', BBC News, 28 September 2015. Available at: www.bbc.co.uk.

national self in light of the liberal world view engenders a particular kind of identity for minorities – the 'local other' within a given polity – and thereby redefines the meaning of nationalism and allegiance. And also how, at the same time, the 'local other' then responds to this postcolonial nation-building process by redefining its identity as well as claims for self-determination along the conservative ethnic line. Such a project has the promise of revealing the central role of ethnicity in the international human rights regime in relation to minorities in the periphery and thereby opening up new avenues for a critical examination of the postcolonial order in general.

In this regard, the major contribution of this book remains in its potential for exploring ways to reveal the untold stories of other key events of international legal history or international law as a whole. In other words, the critical discourse on international law in the coming days can benefit from looking back to the nineteenth-century construction of ethnicity within liberal and conservative traditions for a fresh understanding of international law at present as well as in the future. *Ethnicity and International Law* is a humble contribution to this promising project.

BIBLIOGRAPHY

Acton, John Emerich Edward Dalberg. *The History of Freedom and Other Essays*, ed. John Neville Figgis and Reginald Vere Laurence (London: Macmillan, 1907), 270–300.

Adams, Herbert Baxter. *Bluntschli's Life-Work* (Baltimore, Maryland: Privately printed, 1884).

Alexandrowicz, C. H. *An Introduction to the History of the Law of Nations in the East Indies* (Oxford: Oxford University Press, 1967).

Allott, Philip. 'Self-Determination – Absolute Right or Social Poetry?' in *Modern Law of Self-Determination*, ed. Christian Tomuschat (Dordrecht: Martinus Nijhoff, 1993), 177–210.

Alston, Philip. 'Peoples' Rights: Their Rise and Fall' in *Peoples' Rights*, ed. Philip Alston (Oxford: Oxford University Press, 2001), 259–293.

Anand, Ram Prakash. *Studies in International Law and History: An Asian Perspective* (Leiden: Martinus Nijhoff, 2004).

Anaya, James. 'Self-Determination as a Collective Human Right under Contemporary International Law' in *Operationalizing the Right of Indigenous Peoples to Self-Determination*, ed. Pekka Aikio and Martin Scheinin (Turku: Åbo Akademi University, 2000), 3–18.

Anderson, Benedict. *Imagined Communities*, rev edn (London: Verso, 2006).

Anghie, Antony. 'Human Rights and Cultural Identity: New Hope for Ethnic Peace?'. *Harvard International Law Journal* 33, no. 2 (1992), 341–352.

'Francisco De Vitoria and the Colonial Origins of International Law'. *Social and Legal Studies* 5 (1996), 321–336.

'Finding the Peripheries: Sovereignty and Colonialism in Nineteenth-Century International Law'. *Harvard International Law Journal* 40, no. 1 (1999) 1–80.

'Colonialism and the Birth of International Institutions: Sovereignty, Economy, and the Mandate System of the League of Nations'. *New York University Journal of International Law and Politics* 34 (2001–2002), 513–633.

Imperialism, Sovereignty and the Making of International Law (Cambridge: Cambridge University Press, 2005).

The Armenian National Delegation to Peace Conference. *The Armenian Question Before the Peace Conference.* A Memorandum Officially Presented by the

Representatives of Armenia to the Peace Conference at Versailles on 26 February 1919. Appendix.

Ashmore, Richard D., Lee J. Jussim, and David Wilder (eds.). *Social Identity, Intergroup Conflict and Conflict Reduction* (Oxford: Oxford University Press, 2001).

Bakic-Hayden, Malica. 'Nesting Orientalisms: The Case of Former Yugoslavia'. *Slavic Review* 54, no. 4 (1995), 917–931.

Banton, Michael. *Racial and Ethnic Competition* (Cambridge: Cambridge University Press, 1983).

Barkawi, Tarak and Mark Laffey (eds.). *Democracy, Liberalism, and War* (London: Lynne Reinner, 2001).

Barry, Brian. *Culture and Equality* (Cambridge: Polity Press, 2001).

Barth, Fredrik (ed.). *Ethnic Groups and Boundaries: The Social Organisation of Culture Difference* (Prospect Heights, Illinois: Waveland Press, 1998).

Bell, Christine. *Peace Agreements and Human Rights* (Oxford: Oxford University Press, 2000).

'Peace Agreements: Their Nature and Legal Status'. *American Journal of International Law* 100, no. 2 (2006), 373–412.

On the Law of Peace: Peace Agreements and the Lex Pacificatoria (Oxford: Oxford University Press, 2008).

Berberoglu, Berch. *Nationalism and Ethnic Conflict: Class, State, and Nation in the Age of Globalisation* (Lanham, Maryland: Rowman and Littlefield, 2004).

Berman, Nathaniel. 'A Perilous Ambivalence: Nationalist Desire, Legal Autonomy, and the Limits of the Interwar Framework'. *Harvard International Law Journal* 33, no. 2 (1992), 353–380.

'"But the Alternative Is Despair": European Nationalism and the Modernist Renewal of International Law'. *Harvard Law Review* 106, no. 8 (1993), 1792–1904.

'International Law of Nationalism: Group Identity and Legal History' in *International Law and Ethnic Conflict*, ed. David Wippman (Ithaca, New York: Cornell University Press, 1998), 25–57.

Bernhardi, General Friedrich von. *Germany and the Next War*, trans. Allen H. Powels (New York: Chas A. Eron, 1914).

Betts, Raymond F. *Assimilation and Association in French Colonial Theory 1890–1914* (New York: Columbia University Press, 1961).

Biddis, Michael. 'Gobineau and the Origins of European Racism' in *Racism*, ed. Martin Bulmer and John Solomos (Oxford: Oxford University Press, 1999), 49–52.

Bluntschli, Johann Kaspar. *The Theory of the State* (Kitchener, Ontario: Batoche Books, 2000 [1885]).

Bose, Sumantra. *Bosnia after Dayton: Nationalist Partition and International Intervention* (London: Hurst and Company, 2002).

Bowden, Brett. 'The Colonial Origin of International Law: European Expansion and the Classical Standard of Civilisation'. *Journal of the History of International Law* 7, no. 1 (2005), 1–23.

Brass, Paul. 'Ethnic Groups and Ethnic Identity Formation' in *Ethnicity*, ed. John Hutchinson and Anthony D. Smith (Oxford: Oxford University Press, 1996), 301–305.

Brehl, Medardus. 'The Drama was Played Out on the Dark Stage of the Sandveldt: The Extermination of the Herero and Nama in German (Popular) Literature' in *Genocide in German South-West Africa*, ed. Jurgen Zimmerer and Joachim Zeller, trans. E. J. Neather (Monmouth: Merlin Press, 2008 [2003]), 100–112.

Breuilly, John. *Nationalism and the State*, 2nd edn (Chicago, Illinois: University of Chicago Press, 1994).

Brown, Michael E., Sean M. Lynn-Jones and Steven E. Miller (eds.). *Debating the Democratic Peace* (Cambridge, Massachusetts: MIT Press, 1996).

Brown, Michael E., Owen R. Coté, Sean M. Lynn-Jones and Steven E. Miller (eds.). *Nationalism and Ethnic Conflict* (Cambridge, Massachusetts: MIT Press, 1997).

Brubaker, Rogers. *Ethnicity without Groups* (Cambridge, Massachusetts: Harvard University Press, 2004).

Brunschwig, Henri. *French Colonialism 1871–1914: Myths and Realities*, trans. William G. Brown (London: Pall Mall Press, 1966 [1960]).

Buchanan, Allen. 'The Quebec Secession Issue: Democracy, Minority Rights, and the Rule of Law' in *Secession and Self-Determination*, ed. Stephen Macedo and Allen Buchanan (New York: New York University Press, 2003), 238–271.

Buchner, Friedrich Carl Christian Ludwig. *Man in the Past, Present and Future*, trans. William Sweetland Dallas (London: Asher and Co., 1872).

Burkey, Richard M. 'Discrimination and Racial Relations' in Report on the International Research Conference on Race Relations (Colorado, 7–9 June 1970).

Burleigh, Michael. *The Third Reich – A New Story* (London: Pan Books, 2001 [2000]).

Butkevych, Olga V. 'History of Ancient International Law: Challenges and Prospects'. *Journal of the History of International Law* 5 (2003), 189–236.

Campbell, David. *National Deconstruction: Violence, Identity, and Justice for Bosnia* (Minneapolis, Minnesota: University of Minnesota Press, 1998).

Capotorti, Francesco. 'Protection of Minorities under Multinational Agreements on Human Rights'. *Italian Yearbook of International Law* (1976), 3–32.

Study on the Rights of Persons Belonging to Ethnic, Religious or Linguistic Minorities (1977). UN Doc. E/CN4/Sub. 2/384/Rev.1.

Carty, Anthony. *The Decay of International Law? A Reappraisal of the Limits of Legal Imaginations in International Affairs* (Manchester: Manchester University Press, 1986).

'Carl Schmitt's Critique of Liberal International Legal Order Between 1933 and 1945'. *Leiden Journal of International Law* 14 (2001), 25–75.

'The Evolution of International Legal Scholarship in Germany during the Kaiserreich and the Weimarer Republic (1871–1933)'. *German Yearbook of International Law* 50 (2007), 29–90.

Caselli, Francesco and Wilbur J. Coleman II. 'On the Theory of Ethnic Conflict'. *Journal of the European Economic Association* 11, no. 1 (2013), 161–192.

Caspersen, N. 'Intragroup Divisions in Ethnic Conflicts: From Popular Grievances to Power Struggles'. *Nationalism and Ethnic Politics* 14, no. 2 (2008), 239–265.

Cassese, Anthony. *Self-determination of Peoples: A Legal Reappraisal* (Cambridge: Cambridge University Press, 1995).

Chambers 21st Century Dictionary, 2nd rev edn (London: Chambers, 1999).

Chandler, David. *Bosnia: Faking Democracy after Dayton* (London: Pluto Press, 1999).

Chowdhury, Subrata Roy. 'The Status and Norms of Self-Determination in Contemporary International Law'. *Netherlands International Law Review* 24 (1977), 72–84.

Chua, Amy. *World on Fire: How Exporting Free Market Democracy Breeds Ethnic Hatred and Global Instability* (New York: Doubleday, 2003).

Clark, Linda L. *Social Darwinism in France* (Alabama: University of Alabama Press, 1984).

Claude, Inis L. *National Minorities: An International Problem* (Cambridge, Massachusetts: Harvard University Press, 1955).

Collins Cobuild Advanced Learner's English Dictionary, 5th edn (Birmingham: Collins Cobuild, 2006).

Collinson, Susan. 'Robert Knox's Anatomy of Race'. *History Today* 40 (1990), 44–49.

Conference for Security and Co-operation in Europe. *CSCE Helsinki Document 1992: Challenges of Change* (9–10 July 1993). Available at: www.osce.org.

Conklin, Alice. *A Mission to Civilize: The Republican Idea of Empire in France and West Africa, 1895–1930* (Stanford, California: Stanford University Press, 1997).

Connor, Walker. 'A Nation Is a Nation, Is a State, Is an Ethnic Group, Is a . . .' in *Nationalism*, ed. John Hutchinson and Anthony D. Smith (Oxford: Oxford University Press, 1994), 36–46.

'Beyond Reason: The Nature of Ethnonational Bond' in *Ethnicity*, ed. John Hutchinson and Anthony D. Smith (Oxford: Oxford University Press, 1996), 69–75.

Craven, Matthew. *Decolonization of International Law – State Succession and the Law of Treaties* (Oxford: Oxford University Press, 2007).

'Introduction: International Law and Its Histories' in *Time, History and International Law*, ed. Matthew Craven, Malgosia Fitzmaurice, and Maria Vogiatzi (Leiden: Martinus Nijhoff, 2007), 1–26.

Crawford, James. *The Creation of States in International Law* (Oxford: Clarendon Press, 1979).

'The Right of Self-Determination in International Law: Its Development and Future' in *Peoples' Rights*, ed. Philip Alston (Oxford: Oxford University Press, 2001), 7–67.

Dahl, Robert. *Democracy and Its Critics* (New Haven, Connecticut: Yale University Press, 1989).

Dampierre, Jacques Marquis de. *German Imperialism and International Law – Based Upon German Authorities and the Archives of the French Government* (New York: Charles Scribner's Sons, 1917).

Daughton, James P. *An Empire Divided: Religion, Republicanism, and the Making of French Colonialism, 1880–1914* (Oxford: Oxford University Press, 2006).

Deschenes, Jules. *Proposals Concerning a Definition of the Term 'Minority'* (1985). UN Doc. E/CN.4/Sub.2/1985/31.

De Varennes, Fernand. 'Using the European Court of Human Rights to Protect the Rights of Minorities' in *Mechanisms for the Implementation of Minority Rights*, ed. Marc Weller and Alexander H. E. Morawa (Strasbourg: Council of Europe Publishing, 2004), 83–108.

Dickens, Peter. *Social Darwinism* (Buckingham: Open University Press, 2000).

Donaldson, Emma Brace (ed.). *The Life of Charles Loring Brace Chiefly Told in His Own Letters* (London: Sampson, Low, Marston and Co., 1894).

Donia, Robert J., and John V. A. Fine, Jr. *Bosnia and Hercegovina: A Tradition Betrayed* (London: Hurst and Co., 1994).

Doyle, Michael W. 'Kant, Liberal Legacies and Foreign Affairs'. *Philosophy and Public Affairs* 12, no. 3 (1983), 205–235.

Drew, Catriona. 'Self-Determination, Population Transfer and the Middle East Peace Accords' in *Human Rights, Self-determination and Political Change in the Occupied Palestinian Territories*, ed. Stephen Bowen (The Hague: Martinus Nijhoff, 1997), 119–168.

The East Timor Story: International Law on Trial'. *European Journal of International Law* 12, no. 4 (2001), 651–684.

Dumont, Louis. *German Ideology: From France to Germany and Back* (Chicago, Illinois: University of Chicago Press, 1994).

Dyke, Vernon van. 'The Individuals, the State, and Ethnic Communities in Political Theory'. *World Politics* 29, no. 3 (1977), 343–369.

'Collective Entities and Moral Rights: Problems in Liberal-Democratic Thought (1982)' in *Group Rights – Perspectives Since 1900*, ed. Julia Stapleton (Bristol: Theommes Press, 1995), 180–200.

Ehrlich, Charles E. 'Democratic Alternatives to Ethnic Conflict: Consociationalism and Neoseparatism'. *Brooklyn Journal of International Law* 26 (2000), 447–483.

Eide, Asbjørn. *Final Text of the Commentary to the Declaration on the Rights of National or Ethnic, Religious and Linguistic Minorities* (2001). UN Doc. E/CN4/Sub.2/AC5/2001/2.

'The Role of the United Nations Working Group on Minorities' in *Mechanisms for the Implementation of Minority Rights*, ed. Marc Weller and Alexander H. E. Morawa (Strasbourg: Council of Europe Publishing, 2004), 55–70.

Elias, Norbert. *The Civilizing Process: The Development of Manners. Changes in the Code of Conduct and Feeling in Early Modern Times* (New York: Urizen Books, 1978 [1939]).

Eller, Jack, and Michael R. Coughlan. 'The Poverty of Primordialism: The Demystification of Ethnic Attachment'. *Ethnic and Racial Studies* 16, no. 2 (1993), 83–102.

Erzberger, Matthias. *The League of Nations: The Way to World's Peace*, trans. Bernard Miall (New York: Henry Holt and Company, 1919).

Esman, Milton J. *An Introduction to Ethnic Conflict* (Cambridge: Polity Press, 2004).

European Community. 'Declaration on the Guidelines on the Recognition of New States in Eastern Europe and in the Soviet Union'. *European Journal of International Law* 3 (1993), 72.

'Declaration on Yugoslavia'. Extraordinary EPC Ministerial Meeting, Brussels, 16 December 1991. *European Journal of International Law* 3 (1993), 73.

Fenton, Steve. 'Beyond Ethnicity: The Global Comparative Analysis of Ethnic Conflict'. *International Journal of Comparative Sociology* 45, no. 3/4 (2004), 179–194.

Fichte, Johanne Gottlieb. 'Addresses to the German Nation – Thirteenth Address (1808)' in *The Political Thought of the German Romantics*, ed. H. S. Reiss and P. Brown (Oxford: Blackwell Publishers, 1955), 102–118.

'An Outline of International and Cosmopolitan Law (1796–97)' in *The Political Thought of the German Romantics*, ed. H. S. Reiss and P. Brown (Oxford: Basil Blackwell, 1955), 73–85.

Foreign Relations of the United States (FRUS). *Papers Relating to the Foreign Relations of the United States 1913–1921: Paris Peace Conference 1919*, vols. I–IV (Washington: Government Printing Press, 1942).

Foucault, Michel. 'Governmentality' in *Essential Works of Foucault 1954–1984*, vol. III (Power), ed. James D. Faubion (London: Penguin Books, 2002), 201–222.

Fowkes, Ben. *Ethnicity and Ethnic Conflict in the Post-Communist World* (Basingstoke: Palgrave, 2002).

Franck, Thomas. 'The Emerging Right to Democratic Governance'. *American Journal of International Law* 86 (1992), 46–91.

'Postmodern Tribalism and the Right to Secession' in *Peoples and Minorities in International Law*, ed. Catherine Brölmann, René Lefeber, and Marjoleine Zieck (Dordrecht: Martinus Nijhoff, 1993), 3–27.

Fairness in International Law and Institutions (Oxford: Oxford University Press, 1995).

Franklin, John Hope (ed.). *Colour and Race* (Boston, Massachusetts: Houghton Mifflin, 1968).

Frenz, Christian Raitz von. *A Lesson Forgotten – Minority Protection under the League of Nations. The Case of the German Minority in Poland, 1920–1934* (New York: St. Martin's Press, 1999).

Friedman, Thomas. 'Democracy Isn't Happening in Bosnia'. *New York Times* (24 January 2001).

Fukuyama, Francis. 'The End of History?'. *The National Interest* 16 (Summer, 1989), 3–18.

'Second Thoughts: The Last Man in a Bottle'. *The National Interest* 65 (Summer, 1999), 16–44.

Gaeta, Paola. 'The Dayton Agreements and International Law'. *European Journal of International Law* 7 (1996), 147–163.

Gagnon, Jr., V. P. *The Myth of Ethnic War: Serbia and Croatia in the 1990s* (Ithaca, New York: Cornell University Press, 2004).

Gathii, James Thuo. 'International Law and Eurocentricity'. *European Journal of International Law* 9 (1998), 184–211.

'Imperialism, Colonialism, and International Law'. *Buffalo Law Review* 54, no. 4 (2007), 1013–1066.

Gattinni, Andrea. 'Sense and Quasisense of Schmitt's Grossraum Theory in International Law – A Rejoinder to Carty's "Carl Schmitt's Critique of Liberal International Legal Order Between 1933 and 1945". *Leiden Journal of International Law* 15 (2002), 53–68.

Geertz, Clifford. *Old Societies and New States: The Quest for Modernity in Asia and Africa* (New York: Free Press, 1963).

The Interpretation of Cultures (New York: Basic Books, 1973).

Gellner, Ernest. *Nations and Nationalism* (Oxford: Basil Blackwell, 1983).

Culture, Identity, and Politics (Cambridge: Cambridge University Press, 1987).

Nationalism (London: Weidenfeld and Nicolson, 1997).

Gibson, Ralph. *A Social History of French Catholicism, 1789–1914* (New York: Routledge, 1989).

Gilbert, Geoff. 'Autonomy and Minority Groups: A Right in International Law?'. *Cornell International Law Journal* 35 (2002), 307–353.

Gilroy, Paul. *There Ain't No Black in the Union Jack* (London: Unwin Hyman, 1987).

Glazer, Nathan, and Daniel P. Moynihan (eds.). *Ethnicity* (Cambridge, Massachusetts: Harvard University Press, 1975).

Gobineau, Arthur de. 'Essay' in *Gobineau: Selected Political Writings*, ed. Michael Biddiss (London: Jonathan Cape, 1970).

Goldsmith, Jack L., and Eric A. Posner. *The Limits of International Law* (New York: Oxford University Press, 2005).

Gong, Gerritt W. *The Standard of 'Civilization' in International Society* (Oxford: Clarendon Press, 1984).

Greene, John C. *Science, Ideology and World View* (Berkeley, California: University of California Press, 1981).

Greenfeld, Liah. *Nationalism: Five Roads to Modernity* (Cambridge, Massachusetts: Harvard University Press, 1992).

Grosby, Steven. 'The Verdict of History: The Inexpungeable Tie of Primordiality – a Response to Eller and Coughlan'. *Ethnic and Racial Studies* 17, no. 1 (1994), 164–171.

Gumplowicz, Ludwig. *Outlines of Sociology*, trans. Frederick W. More (New York: Paine-Whitman, 1963).

Gurr, Ted R. *Minorities at Risk* (Washington, DC: US Institute of Peace Press, 1993).

Haeckel, Ernest Heinrich Philipp. *The History of Creation, or the Development of the Earth and Its Inhabitants by the Action of Natural Causes*, rev. trans. E. Ray Lankester (London: King, 1876).

Hall, William E. *A Treatise on International Law*, 2nd edn (Oxford: Clarendon Press, 1884 [1880]).

Hannum, Hurst. 'New Minority Rights for the Twenty-First Century' in *The Universal Declaration of Human Rights: Fifty Years and Beyond*, ed. Yael Danieli, Elsa Stamatopoulou, and Clarence J. Dias (Amityville, New York: Baywood Publishing, 1999), 163–173.

'The Concept and Definition of Minorities' in *Universal Minority Rights*, ed. Marc Weller (Oxford: Oxford University Press, 2007), 49–73.

Harff, Barbara, and Ted R. Gurr. *Ethnic Conflict in World Politics* (Oxford: Westview Press, 2004).

Harrison, Thomas. 'A Question of International Solidarity' in *Why Bosnia? Writings on the Balkan War*, ed. Rabia Ali and Lawrence Lifschultz (Stoney Creek, Connecticut: Pamphleteer's Press, 1993).

Hausrath, Adolf (com. and trans.). *Treitschke: His Doctrine of German Destiny and of International Relations Together with a Study of His Life and Work* (New York: G. P. Putnam and Sons, 1914).

Hawkins, Mike. *Social Darwinism in European and American Thought, 1860–1945* (Cambridge: Cambridge University Press, 1997).

Headlam-Morley, James W. *A Memoir of the Paris Peace Conference*, ed. Agnes Headlam-Moreley et al. (London: Methuen, 1972).

Healey, Joseph F. *Race, Ethnicity, Gender, and Class: The Sociology of Group Conflict and Change* (Thousand Oaks, California: Pine Forge Press, 2006).

Hechter, Michael. 'A Rational Choice Approach to Race and Ethnic Relations' in *Ethnicity*, ed. John Hutchinson and Anthony D. Smith (Oxford: Oxford University Press, 1996), 90–98.

Hegel, George Wilhelm Friedrich. *Lectures on the Philosophy of World History* (1837), ed. D. Forbes and H. B. Nisbet (New York: Cambridge University Press, 1975).

Henrard, Kristin. *Devising an Adequate System of Minority Protection* (The Hague: Martinus Nijhoff, 2000).

'The Protection of Minorities through the Equality Provisions of UN Human Rights Treaties: The UN Treaty Bodies'. *International Journal on Minority and Group Rights* 14, no. 1 (2007), 1–23.

Herder, Johann Gottfried von. 'Ideas towards a Philosophy of the History of Mankind (1785)' in *Modern Political Doctrines*, ed. Alfred Zimmern (Oxford: Oxford University Press, 1939), 164–167.

'Reflections on the Philosophy of the History of Mankind (1791)' in *The Nationalism Reader*, ed. Omar Dahbour and Micheline R. Ishay (Atlantic Highlands, New Jersey: Humanities Press, 1995), 48–57.

Herther-Spiro, Nicole B. '"Can Ethnic Federalism Prevent Recourse to Rebellion?" – A Comparative Analysis of Ethiopian and Iraqi Constitutional Structures'. *Emory International Law Review* 21 (2007), 321–371.

Herz, John H. 'The National Socialist Doctrine of International Law and the Problems of International Organisation'. *Political Science Quarterly* 54, no. 4 (1939), 536–554.

Heyden, Ulrich van der. 'The "Hottentot Elections" of 1907' in *Genocide in German South-West Africa*, ed. Jurgen Zimmerer and Joachim Zeller, trans. E. J. Neather (Monmouth: Merlin Press, 2008 [2003]), 113–122.

Higgins, Rosalyn. 'Postmodern Tribalism and the Right to Secession: Comments' in *Peoples and Minorities in International Law*, ed. Catherine Brölmann, René Lefeber, and Marjoleine Zieck (Dordrecht: Martinus Nijhoff, 1993), 29–35.

Problems and Process: International Law and How We Use It (Oxford: Oxford University Press, 1994).

Hillgruber, Christian, and Matthias Jestaedt. *The European Convention on Human Rights and the Protection of National Minorities* (Cologne: Verlag Wissenschaft und Politik, 1994).

Hobsbawm, Eric. *Nations and Nationalism since 1780*, 2nd edn (Cambridge: Cambridge University Press, 1992).

Hoddie, M. 'Ethnic Conflict's Dilemmas and Paradoxes'. *International Studies Review* 9, no. 3 (2007), 519–521.

Hook, Steven W. (ed.). *Democratic Peace in Theory and Practice* (Kent, Ohio: Kent State University Press, 2010).

Horowitz, Donald L. 'Structures and Strategy in Ethnic Conflict', paper presented in *Annual World Bank Conference on Development Economies* (Washington, DC, April 1998).

Ethnic Groups in Conflict, 2nd edn (Berkeley, California: University of California Press, 2000 [1985]).

The Deadly Ethnic Riot (Berkeley, California: University of California Press, 2001).

Hudson, Manley O. 'The Protection of Minorities and Natives in the Transferred Territories' in *What Really Happened at Paris? The Story of the Peace Conference, 1918–1919 by American Delegates*, ed. Edward Mandell House (New York: Charles Scribner's Sons, 1921), 204–230.

Hull, Isabel V. *Absolute Destruction* (Ithaca, New York: Cornell University Press, 2005).

Humphrey, John P. 'The United Nations Sub-Commission on the Prevention of Discrimination and the Protection of Minorities'. *American Journal of International Law* 62 (1968), 869–888.

Hurst, Michael (ed.). *Key Treaties for the Great Powers 1814–1914*, vol. I (Newton Abbot: David and Charles, 1971).

Isakovic, Zlatko. 'Democracy, Human Rights and Ethnic Conflicts in the Globalised World'. *East European Human Rights Review* 8, no. 2 (2002), 199–236.

Ishay, Micheline R. 'Introduction' in *The Nationalism Reader*, ed. Omar Dahbour and Micheline R. Ishay (Atlantic Highlands, New Jersey: Humanities Press, 1995), 1–19.

Johnson, Carter. 'The Use and Abuse of Minority Rights: Assessing Past and Future EU Policies towards Accession Countries of Central, Eastern, and South-Eastern Europe'. *International Journal of Minority and Group Rights* 13 (2006), 27–51.

Jones, Dorothy V. 'The League of Nations' Experiment in International Protection'. *Ethics and International Affairs* 8 (1994), 77–95.

Jones, Francis Clifford. *Extraterritoriality in Japan and the Diplomatic Relations in Its Abolition 1853–1899* (New York: AMS Press, 1970).

Jones, Peter. 'Human Rights, Group Rights and Peoples' Rights'. *Human Rights Quarterly* 21 (1999), 80–107.

Just, Roger. 'Some Problems for Mediterranean Anthropology'. *Journal of the Anthropology Society of Oxford* 6, no. 3 (1978), 81–97.

Kant, Immanuel. 'Perpetual Peace: A Philosophical Sketch (1795)' in *Kant: Political Writings*, ed. H. S. Reiss, trans. H. B. Nisbet (New York: Cambridge University Press, 1970), 93–130.

'The Metaphysics of Morals (1797)' in *Kant: Political Writings*, ed. H. S. Reiss, trans. H. B. Nisbet (New York: Cambridge University Press, 1970), 131–175.

Kaufmann, Arthur. 'National Socialism and German Jurisprudence from 1933 to 1945'. *Cardozo Law Review* 9 (1987–1988), 1629–1649.

Kennedy, David. 'International Human Rights Movement: Part of the Problem?'. *Harvard Human Rights Journal* 14 (2002), 101–126.

Dark Sides of Virtue: Reassessing International Humanitarianism (Princeton, New Jersey: Princeton University Press, 2004).

Of War and Law (Princeton, New Jersey: Princeton University Press, 2006).

'One, Two, Three, Many Legal Orders: Legal Pluralism and the Cosmopolitan Dream'. *New York University Review of Law and Social Change* 3 (2007), 441–459.

'The Mystery of Global Governance'. *Ohio Northern University Law Review* 34 (2008), 827–860.

Kingsbury, Benedict. 'Claims by Non-State Groups in International Law'. *Cornell International Law Journal* 25 (1992), 481–513.

'Self-Determination and "Indigenous Peoples"'. *Proceedings of the American Society of International Law* 86 (1992), 383–394.

'Reconstructing Self-Determination: A Relational Approach' in *Operationalizing the Right of Indigenous Peoples to Self-Determination*, ed. Pekka Aikio and Martin Scheinin (Turku: Åbo Akademi University, 2000), 19–37.

Knop, Karen. *Diversity and Self-Determination in International Law* (Cambridge: Cambridge University Press, 2002).

Komjathy, Anthony, and Rebecca Stockwell. *German Minorities and The Third Reich* (New York: Holmes and Meier Publishers, 1980).

Koskenniemi, Martti. 'National Self-determination Today: Problems of Legal Theory and Practice'. *International and Comparative Law Quarterly* 43, no. 1 (1994), 241–269.

'"Intolerant Democracies": A Reaction'. *Harvard International Law Journal* 37 (1996), 231–235.

Gentle Civilizer of Nations: The Rise and Fall of International Law 1870–1960 (Cambridge: Cambridge University Press, 2002).

Koszorus, Jr., Frank. 'The Forgotten Legacy of the League of Nations Minority Protection System' in *Essays on World War I: Total War and Peacemaking – A Case Study on Trianon*, ed. B. K. Kiraly (New York: Atlantic Research and Publications, 1982).

Kukathas, Chandran. 'Are There Any Cultural Rights?' in *Group Rights – Perspective Since 1900*, ed. Julia Stapleton (Bristol: Theommes Press, 1995), 258–298.

The Liberal Archipelago: A Theory of Diversity and Freedom (Oxford: Oxford University Press, 2003).

Kunz, Joseph. 'The Italo-Austria Agreement on the Austrian South Tyrol'. *American Journal of International Law* 41 (1947), 439–445.

'The Present Status of the International Law for the Protection of Minorities'. *American Journal of International Law* 48 (1954), 282–287.

Kuper, Adam. *Culture: The Anthropologists' Account* (Cambridge, Massachusetts: Harvard University Press, 1999).

Kymlicka, Will. *Multicultural Citizenship: A Liberal Theory of Minority Rights* (Oxford: Oxford University Press, 1995).

Politics in the Vernacular: Nationalism, Multiculturalism, and Citizenship (Oxford: Oxford University Press, 2001).

'Reply and Conclusion' in *Can Liberal Pluralism Be Exported? Western Political Theory and Ethnic Relations in Eastern Europe*, ed. Will Kymlicka and Magda Opalski (Oxford: Oxford University Press, 2001), 345–414.

'Multiculturalism and Minority Rights: West and East'. *Journal on Ethnopolitics and Minority Issues in Europe* 4 (2002), 1–25.

Multicultural Odysseys: Navigating the New International Politics of Diversity (Oxford: Oxford University Press 2006).

Lansing, Robert. *The Peace Negotiations: A Personal Narrative* (Boston, Massachusetts: Houghton Mifflin, 1921).

Lawrence, Thomas J. *The Principles of International Law* (London: Macmillan, 1895).

League of Nations Information Section. *The League of Nations and the Protection of Minorities of Race, Language, and Religion* (Geneva: League of Nations Secretariat, 1927).

League of Nations Secretariat. *Registry Files* (1919–1946). 41.681.681.

League of Nations Official Journal (1933). Special Supplement No. 120.

Lerner, Natan. *Group Rights and Discrimination in International Law*, 2nd edn (The Hague: Martinus Nijhoff, 2003).

Lijphart, Arend. *Democracy in Plural Societies: A Comparative Exploration* (New Haven, Connecticut: Yale University Press, 1977).

'Consociation and Federalism: Conceptual and Empirical Links'. *Canadian Journal of Political Science* 12, no. 3 (1979), 499–515.

'Consociational Theory: Problems and Prospects. A Reply'. *Comparative Politics* 13, no. 3 (1981), 355–360.

Lorimer, James. *The Institutes of the Law of Nations: A Treatise of the Jural Relations of Separate Political Communities* (Edinburgh: Blackwood, 1883).

Lusane, Clarence. *Hitler's Black Victims* (London: Routledge, 2002).

Luther, Timothy C. *Hegel's Critique of Modernity – Reconciling Individual Freedom and the Community* (New York: Lexington Books, 2009).

Maclean, Fitzroy. *Eastern Approaches* (London: Penguin, 1991 [1949]).

Mair, Lucy P. *The Protection of Minorities – The Workings and Scope of the Minorities Treaties under the League of Nations* (London: Christophers, 1928).

Malcolm, Noel. *Bosnia: A Short History* (London: Macmillan, 1994).

Marks, Susan. *The Riddle of All Constitutions* (Oxford: Oxford University Press, 2000).

Maunier, Rene. *The Sociology of Colonies*, vol. I, ed. and trans. E. O. Lorimer (London: Routledge and Kegan Paul, 1949).

Mazower, Mark. *Hitler's Empire – Nazi Rule in Occupied Europe* (London: Penguin Books, 2008).

McDonald, Leighton. 'Regrouping in Defence of Minority Rights: Kymlicka's Multicultural Citizenship'. *Osgoode Hall Law Journal* 34, no. 2 (1996), 292–319.

Meiertöns, Heiko. 'An International Lawyer in Democracy and Dictatorship – Re-Introducing Herbert Kraus'. *European Journal of International Law* 25, no. 1 (2014), 255–286.

Mello-Franco, Afranio de. 'Report of the Council Meeting of 9 December 1925'. *League of Nations Official Journal* 7, no. 2 (February, 1926), 138–144.

Mill, John Stuart. 'On Liberty (1859)' in *Utilitarianism, Liberty, Representative Government* (London: Everyman's Library, 1964 [1910]), 61–170.

'Representative Government (1861)' in *Utilitarianism, Liberty, Representative Government* (London: Everyman's Library, 1964 [1910]), 171–393.

Miller, David Hunter. *My Diary at the Conference at Paris*, vol. XIII (New York: Appeal Printing, 1924).

The Drafting of the Covenant, vols. I and II (New York: G. P. Putnam's Sons, 1928).

Miller, David, and Michael Walzer (eds.). *Pluralism, Justice, and Equality* (Oxford: Oxford University Press, 1995).

Mitnick, Eric J. 'Three Models of Group-Differentiated Rights'. *Columbia Human Rights Law Review* 35 (2004), 102–144.

Morawa, Alexander H. E. 'The United Nations Treaty Monitoring Bodies and Minority Rights, with particular Emphasis on the Human Rights Committee' in *Mechanisms for the Implementation of Minority Rights*, ed. Marc Weller and H. E. Morawa Alexander (Strasbourg: Council of Europe Publishing, 2004), 29–53.

Musgrave, Thomas D. *Self-Determination and National Minorities* (Oxford: Clarendon Press, 1997).

Neather, Edward J. 'Introduction to the English Edition' in *Genocide in German South-West Africa*, ed. Jurgen Zimmerer and Joachim Zeller, trans. E. J. Neather (Monmouth: Merlin Press, 2008 [2003]), xv–xxxii.

Neumann, Franz. *Behemoth: The Structure and Practice of National Socialism 1933–1944* (New York: Harper and Row, 1966 [1942]).

Nussbaum, Arthur. *A Concise History of the Law of Nations* (New York: Macmillan, 1947).

Oestreich, Joel E. 'Liberal Theory and Minority Group Rights'. *Human Rights Quarterly* 21, no. 1 (1999), 108–132.

Offe, Claus. 'Political Liberalism, Group Rights, and the Politics of Fear and Trust'. *Studies in East European Thought* 53 (2001), 167–182.

Olusoga, David, and Casper W. Erichsen. *Kaiser's Holocaust* (London: Faber & Faber, 2011).

Olzak, Susan. *The Global Dynamics of Racial and Ethnic Mobilisation* (Stanford, California: Stanford University Press, 2006).

Onuma, Yasuaki. 'When Was the Law of International Society Born? An Inquiry of the History of International Law from an Intercivilisational Perspective'. *Journal of the History of International Law* 2 (2000), 1–66.

Oppenheim, Lassa. *International Law* (London: Longmans, Green and Co., 1905).

Osaghae, Eghosa E. 'Human Rights and Ethnic Conflict Management: The Case of Nigeria'. *Journal of Peace Research* 33, no. 2 (1996), 171–188.

Oxford Advanced Learner's Dictionary (Oxford: Oxford University Press, 2000).

Packer, John. 'On the Definition of Minorities' in *The Protection of Ethnic and Linguistic Minorities in Europe*, ed. J. Packer and K. Myntti (Abo/Turku: Abo Akademi University Press, 1993), 23–65.

'Problems in Defining Minorities' in *Minority and Group Rights in the New Millennium*, ed. Deirdre Fottrell and Bill Bowring (Leiden: Brill Academic Publishers, 1999), 223–273.

'Making International Law Matter in Preventing Ethnic Conflict: A Practitioner's Perspective'. *International Law and Politics* 32 (2000), 715–725.

Parekh, Bhikhu. *Rethinking Multiculturalism: Cultural Diversity and Political Theory* (London: Macmillan, 2000).

Paris, Roland. 'Peace-Building and the Limitations of Liberal Internationalism'. *International Security* 22, no. 2 (1997), 54–89.

Parliamentary Assembly of the Council of Europe. *On an Additional Protocol on the Rights of National Minorities to the European Convention on Human Rights* (1993). Recommendation 1201. Available at: www.assembly.coe.int.

Parmelee, M. 'Introduction to the English Edition' in *Crime: Its Causes and Remedies*, Cesare Lombroso, trans. H. P. Horton (Boston, Massachusetts: Little, Brown, 1911).

Parsons, Talcott. *Societies: Evolutionary and Comparative Perspectives* (New York: Prentice Hall, 1966).

Peacock, James L., and Patricia M. Thornton (eds.). *Identity Matters: Ethnic and Sectarian Conflict* (New York: Berghahn Books, 2007).

Peel, John David Yeadon (ed.). *Herbert Spencer on Social Evolution – Selected Writings* (Chicago, Illinois: University of Chicago Press, 1972).

Pellet, Alain. 'The Opinions of the Badinter Arbitration Committee: A Second Breath for the Self-Determination of Peoples'. *European Journal of International Law* 3 (1992), 178–180.

Pentassuglia, Gaetano. *Defining 'Minority' in International Law: A Critical Appraisal*, 2nd rev edn (Rovaniemi: Lapland's University Press, 2000).

'Minority Rights, Human Rights: A Review of Basic Concepts, Entitlements and Implementation Procedures under International Law' in *Mechanisms for the Implementation of Minority Rights*, ed. M. Weller and A. H. E. Morawa (Strasbourg: Council of Europe Publishing, 2004), 9–28.

Plog, Max. 'Democratic Theory and Minority Rights: Internal and External Group Rights in a Global Democracy'. *International Journal on Minority and Group Rights* 10 (2003), 52–82.

Poliakov, Leon. *The Aryan Myth: A History of Racist and Nationalistic Ideas in Europe* (New York: Barnes and Noble, 1996).

'Gobineau and His Contemporaries' in *Racism*, ed. Martin Bulmer and John Solomos (Oxford: Oxford University Press, 1999), 52–56.

Preece, Jennifer J. 'Minority Rights in Europe: from Westphalia to Helsinki'. *Review of International Studies* 23, no. 1 (1997), 75–92.

'National Minorities and International System'. *Politics* 18, no. 1 (1998), 17–23.

Preuss, Lawrence. 'National Socialist Conceptions of International Law'. *American Political Science Review* 29, no. 4 (1935), 594–609.

Prochaska, David. *Making Algeria French: Colonialism in Bone, 1870–1920* (Cambridge: Cambridge University Press, 1990).

Radan, Peter. 'Post-secession International Borders: A Critical Analysis of the Opinions of the Badinter Arbotration Commission'. *Melbourne University Law Review* 24 (2000), 50–76.

Ranke, Leopold von. 'The Great Powers (1833)' in *The Nationalism Reader*, ed. Omar Dahbour and Micheline R. Ishay (Atlantic Highlands, New Jersey: Humanities Press, 1995), 156–159.

Ratner, Steven. 'Does International Law Matter in Preventing Ethnic Conflict?'. *International Law and Politics* 32 (2000), 591–698.

Raynolds, Susan. 'Regional Sentiments and Medieval Communities' in *Nationalism*, ed. John Hutchinson and Anthony D. Smith (Oxford: Oxford University Press, 1994), 137–140.

Raz, Joseph. 'Multiculturalism: A Liberal Perspective'. *Dissent* (Winter 1994), 67–79.

'Multiculturalism'. *Ratio Juris* 11, no. 3 (1998), 193–205.

Reimann, Mathias. 'National Socialist Jurisprudence and Academic Continuity: A Comment on Professor Kaufmann's Article'. *Cardozo Law Review* 9 (1987–1988), 1651–1662.

Renan, Ernest. 'What Is a Nation? (1882)' in *Modern Political Doctrines*, ed. Alfred Zimmern (Oxford: Oxford University Press, 1939), 186–205.

Rich, Ronald. 'Recognition of States: The Collapse of Yugoslavia and the Soviet Union'. *European Journal of International law* 4 (1993), 36–65.

Richards, Paul (ed.). *No Peace, No War: An Anthropology of Contemporary Armed Conflicts* (Athens, Ohio: Ohio University Press, 2004).

Röhl, John C. G. *From Bismarck to Hitler: Problems and Perspectives in History* (London: Longmans, 1970).

Romanucci-Ross, Lola, and George A. De Vos (eds). *Ethnic Identity: Creation, Conflict and Accommodation* (London: AltaMira Press, 1995).

Ross, Marc H. *Cultural Contestation in Ethnic Conflict* (Cambridge: Cambridge University Press, 2007).

Roth, Brad. 'Popular Sovereignty: The Elusive Norm'. *Proceedings of the American Society of International Law* (1997), 363–370.

Roucek, Joseph S. *The Working of the Minorities System under the League of Nations* (Prague: Orbis Publishing, 1929).

Rudolph, Joseph R. (ed.). *Encyclopaedia of Modern Ethnic Conflicts* (London: Greenwood Press, 2003).

Rupsinghe, Kumar. *Civil Wars, Civil Peace* (London: Pluto Press, 2000).

Ryan, Stephen. *Ethnic Conflict and International Relations* (London: Dartmouth Publishing Company, 1995).

Saha, Santosh C. (ed.). *Perspectives on Contemporary Ethnic Conflict: Primal Violence or the Politics of Conviction?* (Lanham, Maryland: Lexington Books, 2006).

Said, Edward W. *Orientalism* (London: Penguin Books, 1995 [1978]).

Samarasinghe, S. W. R. de A., and Reed Coughlan (eds). *Economic Dimensions of Ethnic Conflict* (London: Pinter, 1991).

Sansom, George B. *The Western World and Japan* (New York: Kenkyusha Press, 1951).

Schermerhorn, Richard, 'Ethnicity and Minority Groups' in *Ethnicity*, ed. John Hutchinson and Anthony D. Smith (Oxford: Oxford University Press, 1996), 17–18.

Schmitt, Carl. *The Nomos of the Earth in the International Law of the Jus Publicum Europaeum* (New York: Telos Press, 2003 [1950]).

Schnee, Heinrich. *German Colonization: Past and Future* (London: George Allen & Unwin, 1926).

Selassie, Alemante G. 'Ethnic Federalism: Its Promise and Pitfalls for Africa'. *Yale Journal of International Law* 28 (2003), 51–107.

Shils, Edward. 'Primordial, Personal, Sacred, and Civil Ties'. *British Journal of Sociology* 8 (1957), 130–145.

'Colour, the Universal Intellectual Community, and the Afro-Asian Intellectual'. *Daedalus* 96, no. 2 (Colour and Race) (1967), 279–295.

Sidgwick, Henry. *Philosophy – Its Scope and Relations. An Introductory Course Lectures* (London: Theommes, 1998 [1902]).

Simpson, Gerry. 'Two Liberalisms'. *European Journal of International Law* 12, no. 3 (2001), 537–571.

Great Powers and Outlaw States (Cambridge: Cambridge University Press, 2004).

Sinha, Surya Prakash. *Legal Polycentricity and International Law* (Durham, North Carolina: Carolina Academic Press, 1996).

Slaughter, Anne-Marie. 'Law Among Liberal States: Liberal Internationalism and the Act of State Doctrine'. *Columbia Law Review* 92 (1992), 1907–1996.

'Toward an Age of Liberal Nations'. *Harvard Journal of International Law* 33 (1992), 393–405.

'Pushing the Limits of the Liberal Peace: Ethnic Conflict and the "Ideal Polity"' in *International Law and Ethnic Conflict*, ed. David Wippman (Ithaca, New York: Cornell University Press, 1998), 128–144.

A New World Order (Princeton, New Jersey: Princeton University Press, 2004).

The Idea That Is America: Keeping Faith with Our Values in a Dangerous World (New York: Basic Books, 2007).

Smith, Anthony D. *Nationalism in the Twentieth Century* (Oxford: Martin Robertson, 1979).

The Ethnic Origins of Nations (Oxford: Basil Blackwell, 1986).

Nationalism and Modernism: A Critical Survey of Recent Theories of Nations and Nationalism (London: Routledge, 1998).

Smith, Woodruff D. *The German Colonial Empire* (Chapel Hill, North Carolina: University of North Carolina Press, 1978).

Smuts, Jan C. 'The League of Nations: A Practical Suggestion' in *The Drafting of the Covenant*, ed. David Hunter Miller, vols. I and II (New York: G. P. Putnam's Sons, 1928), 23–60.

Spencer, Herbert. *The Study of Sociology*, 7th edn (London: Kegan Paul, 1878).

Education: Intellectual, Moral, and Physical (London: Williams and Norgate, 1905).

Stavenhagen, Rodolfo. *Ethnic Conflict and the Nation-State* (New York: Palgrave Macmillan, 1996).

Steiner, Henry J. 'Ideals and Counter-Ideals in the Struggle over Autonomy Regimes for Minorities'. *Notre Dame Law Review* 66 (1991), 1539–1560.

Stewart, Frances (ed.). *Horizontal Inequalities and Conflict: Understanding Group Violence in Multiethnic Societies* (Basingstoke: Palgrave Macmillan, 2008).

Stokes, Gale, John Lampe, Dennison Rusinow, and Julie Mostov. 'Instant History: Understanding the Wars of Yugoslav Succession'. *Slavic Review* 55, no. 1 (1996), 136–160.

Suriano, Gregory R. (ed.). *Great American Speeches* (New York: Gramercy Books, 1993).

Tal, Uriel. 'Law and Theology: On the Status of German Jewry at the Outset of the Third Reich (1933/34) (1982)' in *Religion, Politics and Ideology in the Third Reich – Selected Essays of Uriel Tal* (London: Routledge, 2004), 130–170.

'"Political Faith" of Nazism Prior to the Holocaust (1978)' in *Religion, Politics and Ideology in the Third Reich – Selected Essays of Uriel Tal* (London: Routledge, 2004), 16–54.

Tamir, Yael. *Liberal Nationalism* (Princeton, New Jersey: Princeton University Press, 1995).

Taras, Ray C., and Rajat Ganguly. *Understanding Ethnic Conflict*, 2nd edn (New York: Longman, 2002).

Understanding Ethnic Conflict – International Dimension (New York: Longman, 2006).

Temperley, Harold William Vezeille (ed.). *A History of the Peace Conference of Paris*, vol. V (London: Henry Frowde and Hodder & Stoughton, 1921).

Tesón, Fernando. 'The Kantian Theory of International Law'. *Columbia Law Review* 92 (1992), 53–102.

'Ethnicity, Human Rights, and Self-Determination' in *International Law and Ethnic Conflict*, ed. David Wippman (Ithaca, New York: Cornell University Press, 1998), 86–111.

Thompson, Richard H. *Theories of Ethnicity – A Critical Appraisal* (London: Greenwood Press, 1989).

Thornberry, Patrick. *International Law and the Rights of Minorities* (Oxford: Clarendon Press, 1991).

Thornberry, Patrick, and Maria Amor Martin Estebanez. *Minority Rights in Europe* (Strasbourg: Council of Europe Publishing, 2004).

Todorova, Maria. *Imagining the Balkans* (New York: Oxford University Press, 1997).

Tonkin, Elizabeth, Maryon McDonald, and Malcolm Chapman. *History and Ethnicity* (London: Routledge, 1989).

Townsend, Mary Evelyn. *Origins of Modern German Colonialism, 1871–1885* (New York: Columbia University Press, 1921).

Tuck, Richard. *The Rights of War and Peace* (Oxford: Oxford University Press, 1999).

Turk, Danilo. 'Recognition of States: A Comment'. *European Journal of International law* 4 (1993), 66–71.

UNESCO General Conference. *UNESCO Declaration on Race and Racial Prejudice* (1978). UN Doc. E/CN 4/Sub. 2/1982/2/Add.1/annex V.

United Nations. *Fate of Minorities* (1948). General Assembly Res. 217c (III), 10 December 1948.

General Assembly Official Records (1948). 3rd Session, Part I, Resolutions, 77.

Study of the Legal Validity of the Undertakings Concerning Minorities (1950). UN Doc. E/CN4/367.

Declaration on the Granting of Independence to the Colonial Countries and Peoples (1960). General Assembly Res. 1514 (XV), 947th Plenary Meeting, 14 December 1960.

Principles which should Guide Members in Determining whether or not an Obligation Exists to Transmit the Information Called for under Article 73 e of the Charter (1960). General Assembly Res. 1541 (XV), 948th Plenary Meeting, 15 December 1960.

ECOSOC Official Records (1965). 41st Session, Supplement No. 8.

The International Convention on the Elimination of All Forms of Racial Discrimination (1965). General Assembly Res. 2106A, 20th session, UN GAOR Supplement No. 14. UN Doc. A/6014.48.

United Nations General Assembly Resolution 2106 (XX) (21 December 1965). Available at: www.unhchr.ch.

Declaration on Principles of International Law concerning Friendly Relations and Cooperation among States in accordance with the Charter of the United Nations (1970). General Assembly Res. 2625 (XXV), 25th Session, 24 October 1970.

International Convention on the Suppression and Punishment of the Crime of Apartheid (1973). General Assembly Res. 3068. UN Doc. A/RES/3068.

Sub-Commission on Human Rights Resolution 9A (XXXII) (1979). UN Doc. E/CN4/Sub.2/435.

Declaration on the Elimination of All Forms of Intolerance and of Discrimination Based on Religion or Belief (1981). UN General Assembly Records, 25 November 1981. A/RES/36/55.

The UN Declaration on the Rights of Persons Belonging to National or Ethnic, Religious and Linguistic Minorities (1992). UN General Assembly. UN Doc. A/RES/47/135.

The United Nations Human Rights Committee General Comment on Article 27 of the ICCPR (1994). 50th session, No. 23. UN Doc. CCPR/C/21/Rev. 1/Add.5.

The United Nations Committee on Elimination of Racial Discrimination General Recommendation, 'The Meaning and Scope of Special Measures in the International Convention on the Elimination of Racial Discrimination' (2009). 75th session, No. 32, UN Doc. CERF/C/GC/32.

United States Department of State. *US Department of State Bulletin* 8, no. 206 (5 June 1943), 479–482.

Vagts, Detlev F. 'International Law in the Third Reich'. *American Journal of International Law* 84 (1990), 661–704.

Van den Berghe, Pierre L. *The Ethnic Phenomenon* (New York: Elsevier, 1981).

Verstichel, Annelies. 'Recent Development in the UN Human Rights Committee's Approach to Minorities, with a Focus on Effective Participation'. *International Journal on Minority and Group Rights* 12 (2005), 25–41.

Vierdag, E. W. *The Concept of Discrimination in International Law – With Special Reference to Human Rights* (The Hague: Martinus Nijhoff, 1973).

Vitoria, Francisco de. *De Indis Reflection Prior*, trans. John P. Bates (Washington, DC: Oceana Press, 1917 [1532]).

De Indis et de Ivre Belli Reflectiones, ed. Ernest Nys, trans. John P. Bate (Washington, DC: Oceana Press, 1917 [1604]).

Von Joeden-Forgey, Elise. 'Nobody's People: Colonial Subjects, Race Power and the German State, 1884–1945'. Unpublished PhD dissertation, University of Pennsylvania (2004).

Waldron, Jeremy (ed.). *Liberal Rights: Collected Papers (1981–1991)* (Cambridge: Cambridge University Press, 1993).

Weber, Max. 'The Nation' in *From Max Weber: Essays in Sociology*, trans. and ed. H. H. Gerth and C. Wright-Mills (London: Routledge and Kegal Paul, 1948), 171–179.

Economy and Society, ed. Guenther Roth and Claus Wittich (New York: Bedminster Press, 1968 [1922]).

Westlake, John. *Chapters on the Principles of International Law* (Cambridge: Cambridge University Press, 1894).

Wheatley, Steven. 'Deliberative Democracy and Minorities'. *European Journal of International Law* 14, no. 3 (2003), 507–527.

Wheaton, Henry. *Elements of International Law*, 8th edn (Boston, Massachusetts: Little, Brown, 1866).

Whelan, Frederick. 'Democratic Theory and the Boundaries Problem' in *Liberal Democracy: NOMOS XXV*, ed. J. R. Pencock and J. Chapman (New York: New York University Press, 1983), 13–47.

Whyte, George R. *The Dreyfus Affair – A Chronological History* (Hampshire: Palgrave Macmillan, 2005).

Wiberg, Håkan, and Christian P. Scherrer (eds). *Ethnicity and Intra-State Conflict* (Aldershot: Ashgate, 1999).

Wilde, Ralph. 'From Danzig to East Timor and Beyond: The Role of International Territorial Administration'. *American Journal of International Law* 95, no. 3 (2001), 583–606.

'Representing International Territorial Administration: A Critique of Some Approaches'. *European Journal of International Law* 15, no. 1 (2004), 71–96.

International Territorial Administration – How Trusteeship and the Civilizing Mission Never Went Away (Oxford: Oxford University Press, 2008).

Wippman, David. 'International Law and Ethnic Conflict in Cyprus'. *Texas International Law Journal* 31 (1996), 141–180.

'Practical and Legal Constraints on Internal Power Sharing' in *International Law and Ethnic Conflict*, ed. David Wippman (Ithaca, New York: Cornell University Press, 1998), 211–241.

Wolff, Christian. *Jus Gentium Methodo Scientifica Pertractatum*, trans. Joseph H. Drake (New York: Oceana Press, 1964 [1749]).

Wolff, Stefan. *Ethnic Conflict: A Global Perspective* (Oxford: Oxford University Press, 2006).

X. 'Poland as a Free Nation'. *Current History* 10, part 2, no. 3 (September, 1919), 492–496.

Zimmerer, Jurgen. 'The Model Colony? Racial Segregation, Forced Labour and Total Control in German South West Africa' in *Genocide in German South-West Africa*, ed. Jurgen Zimmerer and Joachim Zeller, trans. E. J. Neather (Monmouth: Merlin Press, 2008 [2003]), 19–40.

'War, Concentration Camps and Genocide' in *Genocide in German South-West Africa*, ed. Jurgen Zimmerer and Joachim Zeller, trans. E. J. Neather (Monmouth: Merlin Press, 2008 [2003]), 41–63.

INDEX

Lightning Source UK Ltd.
Milton Keynes UK
UKHW01n0220120718
325599UK00008B/53/P

9 781107 096790